The Dynamics of Ethnic
Competition and Conflict

The Dynamics of Ethnic Competition and Conflict

Susan Olzak

Stanford University Press
Stanford, California

E
184
•A1
O455
1991

Stanford University Press
Stanford, California
Copyright © 1992 by the Board of Trustees of the
Leland Stanford Junior University
Printed in the United States of America

CIP data appear at the end of the book

For Mike

Preface

This book is an attempt to apply ecological theories of competition and niche overlap to explain instances of ethnic collective action that occurred in American society around the turn of the nineteenth century. It uses event-history methods of analysis to explore models of racial and ethnic confrontations, riots, violence, protest marches, and other forms of public and collective activity organized around ethnic and racial boundaries. My research strategy which I develop in the pages that follow involved a constant interchange with my research group of graduate students, undergraduates, and colleagues. I would like to take this opportunity to thank them.

This project greatly benefitted from collaboration with a particularly talented group of undergraduates who worked on my project while I was in the Sociology Department at Cornell University. Cornell's Undergraduate Independent Study program recruits highly motivated and exceptionally talented students into research shops. From 1985 to the present, I have been funded by the National Science Foundation's Research Experience for Undergraduates Program. As a result I have been able to hire the majority of these students after they completed one semester's training in Independent Study. These students meet weekly, prepare research memos, revise coding manuals, and assist in the preparation of research papers. Those who contributed their efforts include Judy Blumberg, Beth Bechky, Robin Rogers-Bloch, Amalia Driver, Adam Engst, Jennifer Frank, Erica Greenberg, Ross Greenberg, Crystal Jackson, Dan Lipson, Geri Mayer, Vivian Medina, Amy Levine, Lisa Mansfield, Jason McGill, Maria Melodia, Kevin Miller, George Pettinico, Arthur Piacenti, Karen Plump, Claudia Regen, Jon Schuster, Ulrike Szalay, Francine Simon, Luisa Trujillo, Clare

Tuma, Brian Wilhelm, Craig Wishman, Elizabeth Woodward, Melissa Youner. In addition to the undergraduate research assistants, I have had the pleasure of working with four highly skilled graduate students who not only contributed their coding, data management, and computer skills, but constantly questioned and challenged my theoretical ideas. Denise DiGregorio provided initial coding and research assistance during the first year of the project. Johan Olivier, and Elizabeth West were key research assistants on this project for four years, responsible for data collection, file-building, and supervision of the research team. Sarah Soule and Betsy McEneaney provided excellent suggestions and editorial comments during the final stages of preparation of this book.

My research was funded by a number of sources. They include: a research fund provided by the Dean of the Arts College at Cornell University, for 1984–85; National Science Foundation Grant SES–8420173, National Science Foundation; Supplementary Grant from the Research Experience For Undergraduates (REU) Program 1985–88; Cornell University, Junior Faculty Summer Research Fellowship, Summer 1987; the Max-Planck-Institut für Bildungsforschung, Berlin, BRD, 1987–88; Cornell University, Women's Development Fund Award, Summer, 1985; Cornell Production Supercomputer Facility, Center for Theory and Simulation in Science and Engineering, which is funded, in part, by the National Science Foundation, New York State, and IBM Corporation.

My colleagues at Cornell and elsewhere were extremely supportive and challenging over the last seven years. In particular, I would like to thank Ron Breiger, Steven Caldwell, John Freeman, Michael Hannan, Victor Nee, Rachel Rosenfeld, and Sidney Tarrow, for providing a stimulating research environment.

Finally, five chapters draw on materials that have been published separately. Earlier versions of Chapter 4 were published in Susan Olzak, "Analysis of Events in the Study of Collective Action," *Annual Review of Sociology* (1989) 15: 119–41. Chapter 6 is based on Susan Olzak, "Labor Unrest, Immigration, and Ethnic Conflict in Urban America, 1880–1914," *American Journal of Sociology* (1989) 94: 1303–33. Chapter 7 is based on Susan Olzak, "The Political Context of Competition: Lynching and Urban Racial Violence, 1882–1914," *Social Forces* (1990) 69: 395–421. Chapter 8 is based on Susan Olzak, "The Changing Job Queue: Causes of Shifts in Ethnic Job Segregation in American Cities, 1870–1880," *Social Forces* (1989) 68: 593–620. Finally, portions of Chapter 10 were published in Susan Olzak and Elizabeth West, "Ethnic Conflict and the Rise and Fall of Ethnic Newspapers," *American Sociological Review* (1991) 56: 458–474.

In the chapters that follow I outline and test arguments from competition theory that challenge several leading perspectives that have been prominent in the area of collective action and race relations. My hope is that others will continue to debate and challenge the findings from this work in the same manner.

S.O.

Contents

Tables

Figures

The Dynamics of Ethnic
Competition and Conflict

1

Introduction

Outbreaks of ethnic violence were frequent in America's past and have not abated. Yet it appears that not all ethnic and racial groups were equally likely to be victims of violence. Historical evidence on the late nineteenth and early twentieth century shows that African-Americans and Asian immigrants were more likely to be attacked, excluded, and discriminated against than were other (mostly white) immigrants.[1] Despite considerable agreement about this pattern, its underlying causes have been widely debated. Some researchers claim that because terrorism against African-Americans was institutionalized by slavery, violence against them became easier to condone than violence against other groups. Indeed, it is difficult to ignore the history of American slavery and its consequences for African-Americans when trying to explain existing racial differences of any kind.

But while arguments resting on institutionalized racism seem reasonable, they do not explain the fact that equally vicious attacks against Chinese, Japanese, and white immigrants also took place during this period.[2] This book offers one possible explanation of the breadth of conflict during this period. It proposes that processes of competition account for patterns of conflicts and protests involving diverse ethnic targets. It tests this explanation using observations on targets, location, and timing of ethnic collective action.

This book analyzes the causes of racial and ethnic confrontations, protests, riots, and attacks in the largest American cities around the turn of the twentieth century. It uses daily newspaper accounts from the late

---

[1]For detailed historical accounts of ethnic and racial violence in America, see Higham 1955, Chalmers 1965, Woodward 1974, Higgs 1977, Bennett 1988, and Shapiro 1989.

[2]See Saxton 1971, Loewen 1971, Boswell 1986, Ichioka 1988, Bennett 1988, Loewen 1988, and Nee and Nee 1986.

nineteenth century through the beginning of World War I to reconstruct event-histories of the unfolding of ethnic and racial riots, marches, and attacks. Such event-histories record the location, timing, and spread of events within cities and across the country during the period.

The key explanation of the occurrence and spread of ethnic conflict offered here is that factors that raise levels of competition among race and ethnic groups increase rates of ethnic collective action. It is important to note at the outset that this argument diverges from conventional theories of race relations, which hold that racial poverty and inequality generate racial and ethnic attacks and that integration and racial equality of opportunity in education and occupations reduce grievances and thereby diminish ethnic and racial conflict.[3]

Theories emphasizing ethnic segregation as a cause of ethnic unrest often specify that conflict is a function of extreme inequalities in opportunity or occupational attainment among ethnic and racial groups. In such arguments, extreme levels of ethnic segregation also imply disadvantage and inequality. For example, the cultural division of labor perspective holds that concentration of poverty among racial and ethnic minorities, extreme job segregation, and cultural differences cause ethnic collective action (Hechter 1975: 19–43). Such gaps in attainment purportedly fuel ethnic antagonism and give rise to higher levels of racial and ethnic unrest. A testable implication of the cultural division of labor perspective is that effacement of ethnic and racial differences diminishes conflict between groups. The converse should also hold. According to this perspective, segregation increases rates of conflict.

This book is motivated in part by the fact that recent research on ethnic collective action casts considerable doubt on these claims.[4] Concentration of poverty in minority populations does not appear to lead to protest against such conditions, and the poorest groups are not invariably the victims of ethnic attacks (Spilerman 1970, 1971, 1976). Moreover, it appears that integration in housing and occupations increases racial violence under some conditions (Wilson 1978).

How can we understand such patterns? One possibility is that theories that emphasize static levels of ethnic inequality fall short of an explanation because they have considered just the beginning of the process. That is, segregation may explain variations among groups in ethnic solidarity. But we know that ethnic solidarity does not invariably cause

---

[3]For examples, see Gordon 1964, Williams 1964, and Pettigrew 1969.

[4]For support of this claim see Banton 1983, Nielsen 1980, 1985, Ragin 1977, 1979, 1986, McAdam 1982, Olzak 1983, Ragin 1986, See and Wilson 1988, and Jenkins and Kposowa 1990.

ethnic collective action. This book emphasizes instead that reductions in ethnic/racial inequality and in levels of segregation can also foster ethnic conflict and protest. The central argument is that *ethnic conflicts and protests erupt when ethnic inequalities and racially ordered systems begin to break down.*

The empirical analysis which follows highlights a core claim from leading theories of ethnic conflict—that the degree of ethnic job segregation affects ethnic conflicts. In contrast to models emphasizing that *segregation* of ethnic and racial populations causes ethnic conflict, competition arguments hold that *desegregation* causes ethnic conflict. A core hypothesis from the competition perspective which is tested in this book is that *desegregation of labor markets intensifies ethnic competition, which in turn raises the rate of ethnic collective action.* To address this issue, the analysis uses information on ethnic conflicts from the late nineteenth and early twentieth century in urban America.

Causes of protest against ethnic attacks and discrimination are even less well understood than ethnic conflicts. What conditions lead victims to respond to widespread ethnic and racial attacks? There is scattered evidence from as early as 1900 that some ethnic groups protested against ethnic hostility, while other victims of ethnic attacks remained relatively quiescent (Higham 1955). At first glance, it is tempting to explain these different rates of protest by attributing them to differences in ethnic groups' resources. This view suggests that only groups with sufficient economic resources (and discretionary time) protest against hostility, while poorer groups must struggle just to survive. Yet case histories from the turn of the nineteenth century suggest that some of the poorest minorities engaged in protest activity.

Intriguing evidence from the South suggests that African-Americans mobilized local community organizations (especially African-American churches) to protest lynchings, beatings, and discriminatory actions as early as the 1870s and 1880s. Eastern European Jews also organized anti-discrimination movements around the turn of the nineteenth century, despite their relatively high levels of poverty and illiteracy (Lieberson 1980). Yet other groups—such as the Polish, Italians, and non-Jewish Germans—rarely organized protests against discrimination until recently. Certainly one plausible explanation might be that attacks on the latter groups were less frequent; as a result they may have fewer reasons to protest. Is this true? To date, few studies have analyzed this question. As a result, we lack broadly comparative information about the frequency of attacks and the responses to those attacks.

While attacks on ethnic groups may incite protests against these hostilities, other factors may also influence ethnic protests. One prominent view in sociology argued that persistent antagonism directed at African-, Jewish-, and Asian-Americans may have reinforced ethnic solidarity and bolstered ethnic institutions. In this view, ethnic enclaves and ethnic organizations act as a buffers against further discrimination. Some collective action theorists have hypothesized that groups that construct indigenous organizations will have higher rates of ethnic protests (Jenkins 1983). Considerable evidence from the civil rights movement of the 1960s supports this claim.[5] However, these ideas have not been applied to other ethnic groups and to other periods of history.

We also know little about the geography and the timing of ethnic conflicts. Why do levels of ethnic conflict and protest vary from place to place and from period to period? One underanalyzed claim of collective action theorists has been that diffusion affects the spread of events.[6] This view holds that processes of contagion (and exhaustion) drive cycles or waves of social protest. Racial unrest in one region may thus affect the temporal and geographical spread of events to others. Periods of racial turmoil that broke out in the Northeastern United States apparently affected subsequent rates of urban riots across the country during the 1960s (United States Advisory Commission on Civil Disorders 1968). Analysis of race riots of the 1960s finds that similar types of rioting, looting, and violence diffused across cities and neighborhoods (Spilerman 1971; Stark 1974). It would be interesting to learn if similar cycles of racial and ethnic violence also operated a hundred years earlier.

Which groups typically become targets of violence appears to vary by period. Peak periods of lynching of African-Americans in the rural South, of violence against Asians on the West Coast, and of nativist attacks on European immigrants in the urban Northeast do not appear to coincide. The incidence of lynching rose sharply after 1900 in the rural South and declined by the 1930s. Violence against Chinese and Japanese immigrants on America's West Coast appears to have risen for several brief periods before 1890, then it nearly disappeared until the anti-Japanese internments of World War II. And ethnic conflict involving European immigrants rose briefly during 1890–1910, then appeared to subside.[7] How can we account for the variation in timing of violence

---

[5]For convincing empirical evidence on these civil rights protests, see McAdam 1982, Morris 1984, and Jenkins and Eckert 1987.

[6]For examples, see Hamblin, Jacobsen, and Miller 1965, Spilerman 1971, 1976, Stark et al. 1974, Doreian 1981, and Tarrow 1983.

[7]McAdam (1982), Tolnay, Beck, and Massey (1989), Saxton (1971), and Ichioka (1988) provide evidence showing that ethnic violence against these targets followed a similar trajectory.

against ethnic targets? It seems reasonable to begin our investigation of racial and ethnic violence by exploring whether or not these cycles share similar causes.

Ethnic Group Solidarity and Ethnic Collective Action. This book treats cases of ethnic violence and protest as instances of collective action.[8] The study of any type of collective action almost invariably encounters a tricky issue: can group solidarity be distinguished from collective action? That is, does the occurrence of collective action by some aggregate imply a high level of solidarity within the aggregate? If collective action refers to any kind of goal-directed behavior by a group, as Olson (1965) uses the term, then the occurrence of collective action and a high level of group solidarity are indistinguishable. However, others use the term collective action to refer to spontaneous, public, and often disruptive activity by challenging groups outside the political system, in which case solidarity and collective action can be distinguished (Tarrow 1988b; Jenkins and Perrow 1977). We will follow the second strategy.

The question of whether solidarity and collective action can be distinguished analytically is not merely a dispute about definitions. This is an especially central issue for the study of *ethnic* collective action because *ethnic solidarity* has not always been clearly distinguished from the likelihood of ethnic collective action, either conceptually or empirically. If the two concepts are not distinguished, arguments that strength of group solidarity affects behavioral outcomes, such as riots and protests, become tautologies.

The distinction between these core concepts becomes even more crucial in the case of resource mobilization theory. This leading theoretical perspective seeks to explain the occurrence of collective action. It holds that an increase in organizational resources raises the probability of collective action. In this view, group solidarity is an important source of organizational strength and potential for mobilization.[9] Collective action and group solidarity must be distinguished conceptually and empirically for this proposition to have empirical import. Tilly (1973: 214) puts the matter as follows:

If I, a Greek, meet a new Greek and because he's a Greek I prepare to do him favors, we have some evidence that solidarity among Greeks is high. If this

---

[8] For definitions characterizing collective action as spontaneous behavior jointly undertaken on behalf of some formation, see Tilly 1978, Paige 1975, and Zald and McCarthy 1986.

[9] Proponents of resource mobilization theory and its variants include Gamson 1975, McCarthy and Zald 1977, Tilly 1978, Jenkins 1983, Morris 1984, and Tarrow 1988b.

sort of solidarity is high, the group in question probably has great potential capacity for collective action, all other things being equal. However, this sort of solidarity may be high in a group whose members are widely dispersed and have little contact with each other, so there is no reason to expect a close connection between collective action and solidarity ...

This book maintains Tilly's distinction.[10] *Ethnic collective action* is a public action of two or more persons that articulates a distinctly ethnic (or racial) claim, expresses a grievance, or attacks members of another ethnic group (or their property). Such actions include protests involving proactive claims of one group as in civil rights' activity. They also include conflicts, as when members of two or more ethnic populations confront one another. *Ethnic solidarity* is the conscious identification by persons in an ethnic population as members of an ethnic group and includes the maintenance of strong ethnic interaction networks and institutions that socialize new members and reinforce social ties. One advantage of distinguishing these concepts as we have here is that more realistic arguments about ethnic solidarity as a cause and/or a consequence of ethnic collective action can be explored.

Ethnic Boundaries and Collective Action. Before investigating questions about targets of ethnic hostilities, we must first consider why ethnicity invokes such extreme behavior as riots, lynchings, and attacks. One formerly dominant perspective held that ethnicity and race are fundamental, ascriptive, and immutable identities—that is, that ethnic boundaries are given. In this primordialist view, ethnic and racial distinctions reflect ancient cultural (and perhaps genetic) differences in the origins of peoples (Isaacs 1975). This view assumes that ethnic and racial strife is inevitable and invariant. Recent criticisms of this view suggest that it cannot account for the variation in rates of conflict experienced by the same populations over time, nor can it account for cases of ethnic identity shifts, where members "cross over" boundaries (see Barth 1969; Haaland 1969). Ethnic movements in industrialized regions in modern states, such as Great Britain, Canada, France, Spain, and the former U.S.S.R. present additional problems for those primordial conceptions that depict ethnicity as rooted in anti-modern traditions and regions. As a result of these criticisms, the primordial view of ethnicity has fallen into disfavor.

Contemporary perspectives on ethnicity view race and ethnicity as *reactive*, as emerging from inequalities in power, income, and other

---

[10]The strategy taken here differs considerably from those that assume that ethnic collective action is an indicator of high levels of ethnic solidarity. For examples of strategies that take this view, see Nielsen 1980 and Hechter 1987.

rewards.[11]   A major assumption is that racial and ethnic boundaries are socially and politically constructed and rest upon characteristics that cannot be objectively traced by examination of genetic inheritance. This perspective directs attention to ethnic boundaries rather than to the content of ethnicity as a defining feature. The content of ethnic or racial categories such as language, skin color, or cultural attributes, is assumed to be essentially arbitrary. An important by-product of the reactive and situational view is that it raises questions about why ethnic boundaries become salient in competition with other potential loyalties or boundaries. That is, it leads researchers to ask why ethnic boundaries are activated in given circumstances, rather than other boundaries, such as social class or occupational group.

The advantage of treating race and ethnicity as instances of a type of social boundary is that the probability that any action will based on ethnic boundaries becomes a variable to be explained rather than assumed. Ethnic mobilization is only one of many possible bases for organization and collective action. By opening up the possibility that ethnicity competes with other loyalties, new questions about the causes of ethnic collective actions arise. Treating ethnicity as situational leads one to ask when collective actions will become based upon ethnic rather than some other set of identities or roles.

Reactive theories of ethnic collective action can be divided into two broad categories. Each type is concerned with explaining how ethnic identity becomes a rallying point for collective action. The first perspective, which derives from Marxist principles, links class solidarity with the likelihood of collective action along ethnic lines.[12] It holds that ethnic collective action is most likely when ethnically distinct populations are most exploited economically and culturally.

The second perspective combines arguments from resource mobilization theory and competition theory. The key claim of competition theories is that changes in levels of ethnic and racial competition for valued resources—such as jobs, housing, and marital partners—ignite ethnic collective action. This claim is explored first by examining the consequences of large-scale historical changes that affected competition among newly competing race and ethnic populations in cities. We work first at the national level using data on immigration flows, economic contraction,

---

[11]See Gellner 1973, Hechter 1975, and Ragin 1979 for discussion of reactive perspectives of ethnicity and ethnic movements.

[12]For examples, see Hechter 1975, 1978 and Hechter, Friedman, and Appelbaum 1982. For empirical evidence examining this theory see Ragin 1977, Olzak 1982, Nielsen 1980, and the July 1979 Special Issue on Internal Colonialism, *Ethnic and Racial Studies*.

and growth of working-class organizations in the form of labor unions. Then we examine the claim at the community level, where we focus on local labor markets. This analysis concentrates on evaluating the claim that cities with lower levels of ethnic and racial job segregation experience higher levels of ethnic conflict and protest.

When evaluating competition arguments, it is useful to analyze ethnic and racial distinctions as products of ongoing social processes. Since ethnicity is an outcome of boundary creation and maintenance, there is no obstacle to treating race as a special case of an ethnic boundary, one that is believed to be correlated with inherited biotic characteristics.[13] Hereafter the term ethnicity refers to both racial and ethnic boundaries, unless otherwise qualified.

Conflict and Protest: Definitions and Examples. As noted above, ethnic collective action involves either the public expression of ethnic grievances or actions that exclude, attack, or harm some racial/ethnic population. It is therefore useful to distinguish two kinds of ethnic collective action which differ in their target or audience (Tarrow 1983). *Ethnic conflict* involves a confrontation between members of two or more ethnic groups. The target of a conflict is another ethnic population involved as participants in the confrontation, or involved symbolically, as in the case of desecration of a Jewish cemetery with swastikas. Some ethnic conflicts involved attacks by the white majority against another ethnic group. For instance, on June 2, 1882, in New Orleans,

A crowd of hoodlums from this city crossed over to the town on the other side of the Mississippi River, and, with the cooperation of some lawless characters there, set fire to and burned down the handsome frame building of the colored fire company and the colored Baptist Church ... In connection with this there was a negro hunt on the part of whites ... (*New York Times,* June 3, 1889, p. 2).

Other ethnic conflicts involved confrontations between two ethnic minorities. For example,

The ill feeling which has long existed between the Irish and Italian denizens of the tenements of Mulberry Street, between Canal and Hester Streets, culminated last evening in a street conflict which at one time assumed serious proportions ... (*New York Times,* March 23, 1884, p. 5).

---

[13] A convincing argument for treating the term ethnicity as inclusive is provided by van den Berghe (1983: 222): "By race, I do not mean a sub-species of Homo sapiens in the genetic sense, but a *socially* defined group which sees itself and is seen by others as being phenotypically different from such groups ... While I still think that the greater rigidity and invidiousness of racial, as distinct from cultural distinctions makes for qualitatively different situations, both race and ethnicity share the basic common element of being defined by descent, real or putative. Therefore, I now tend to see race as a special case of ethnicity ..."

A second kind of ethnic collective action is *ethnic protest*. Its defining features are that it has the general public or some office of government as its audience, and it seeks to present a grievance to this audience on behalf of its own ethnic group. A civil rights march is a modern prototype. In a few protests, more specific goals (or targets) are mentioned, such as the change of some law, policy, or regulation. Protests are distinguished from conflicts in that only one group is making a claim on its own behalf. An example of ethnic protest is a pro-French-Canadian gathering in Worcester, Massachusetts:

French Canadians of this city at a meeting today to protest against the statement of Frank Foster of Cambridge and Senator Vance, in regard to the employment of French Canadians, adopted resolutions ... [against statements of the two men to not hire French Canadians in Worcester] (*New York Times*, March 4, 1883, p. 1).

As should be clear from this discussion, protests and conflicts may be causally related. Civil rights protests by one group may evoke attacks by enemies, and attacks on one ethnic group may later spark civil protests on the victim's behalf. Our conceptual scheme allows us to deal with these complexities. Events having multiple stages of ethnic confrontations are separated into sequences of conflicts and protests. Events directed against African-Americans, Asians, European immigrants, or native-born whites are counted as ethnic conflicts. Protest events also may involve any racial and ethnic group (including those by the white majority, as in Ku Klux Klan activity occurring in a city).

The Scope of the Study

The period from 1877 through 1914 holds special interest for students of ethnic relations because during this time immigration surged, as Figure 1.1 shows. Overall nearly twenty-three million immigrants from highly diverse origins entered the United States. This period was also a turbulent one in American history, marked by economic depressions and rising industrialization. It was also punctuated by other kinds of collective actions, including union organizing, strikes and picketing, as well as the hiring of immigrants and African-American migrants as strike breakers. Such variation provides a good backdrop for testing models that take the choice of ethnic boundaries in collective actions as a central problem to be analyzed.

The starting point of the study period, 1877, marks the beginning of recovery from a series of economic depressions and recessions. It also coincides with a significant rise of European and Asian immigration (United States Report on Immigration 1901). It also marks the start of President Rutherford Hayes' administration, which at least some

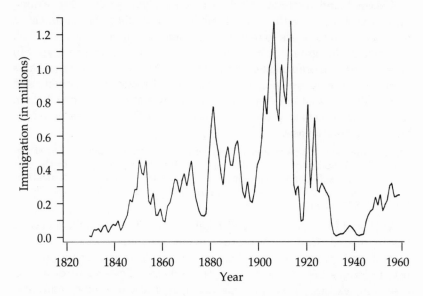

FIG. 1.1 Historical Variations in Immigration

historians claim signalled the end of Reconstruction in the South and a significant shift in race relations in America (Bruce 1959; Woodward 1974; Schlesinger 1986).

The ending point, the close of 1914, marks the beginning of World War I in Europe. This constitutes a natural ending point for two reasons. First, immigration flows dropped significantly after that year and remained relatively low for half a century (United States Bureau of the Census 1975: 105). Second, beginning in 1915 in the United States, most conflicts instigated by native-born whites were directed against German-Americans suspected of being disloyal, according to our analysis of the *New York Times Index*. During 1915–19 ethnic conflict apparently acquired a distinctly international focus (Higham 1955). Because the concern here is with internal processes, the period after 1914 is much less interesting.

Since most immigrants located in urban settings during this period and cities were arenas in which ethnic labor-market competition took place, this study concentrates on events in major cities.[14] The analy-

---

[14] An exception is Chapter 7 which compares the causes of lynching, a mainly rural phenomenon, with those of urban ethnic conflict.

sis concerns the largest 77 cities in 1880, on which the Census Bureau provided demographic information over much if not all of the period of interest. (Appendix B provides a detailed account of the research design, and Table B.1 provides a list of cities.)

We gathered information on events in the 77 cities from multiple sources, including *New York Times Index*, historical case studies of relevant cities, and microfilms of the daily *New York Times*. Daily reports from the *New York Times* were used as the primary source of data on ethnic conflicts and protests in the 77 cities, in a two-stage process. We identified "candidate events" from the *New York Times Index* and then coded characteristics of events from microfilms of daily accounts from this same newspaper. (Appendix B provides details on coding procedures.)[15]

We combined data on the occurrence of ethnic conflicts (and lynchings) and protests with information on economic, social, and political change. Some key explanatory variables are measured at the national level. These include immigration, economic contraction and expansion, the strength of Populist candidates in national elections, the price of cotton (in analyses that focus on the South), incidence of strikes and lockouts, and dynamics of the population of national labor unions. Others are measured at the city level. These include racial/ethnic composition of the population, size of population, levels of literacy of subpopulations, and occupational segregation of various ethnic/racial populations.

Objectives of the Book

This book explores the general argument that competition sparks ethnic collective action. The various analyses presented have several objectives. The first objective is to sharpen understanding of the relationship between economic participation of ethnic and racial populations and collective actions involving ethnic conflicts and protests. Much of the argument concentrates on resolving a paradox suggested by prior research on race relations (to be reviewed in Chapter 2): while rates of collective action rise with economic contraction, the expansion of resources under some conditions also causes these rates to increase. These contradictory tendencies present a puzzle—but one that can be resolved within a competition theory framework. Economic contraction shrinks the pool

---

[15]Comparing this method with the more traditional method of counting events using only the Index (discussed in Chapter 4) reveals that nearly half of the candidate events from the Index did not meet the criterion that events be both collective and ethnic. The two largest categories of problematic events from the Index are speeches by politicians and editorials on immigration or race issues, which are not collective events under our coding rules (discussed in Chapter 4 and in Appendix B).

of available resources and thereby intensifies competition. This in turn causes ethnic conflicts. But prosperity can elevate competition as well. Rates of ethnic collective action rise if the standard of living rises for ethnic or racial groups at the bottom of the occupational hierarchy. As fortunes for the disadvantaged rise, they come to compete with those just above them, igniting ethnic conflict and protest on the part of those on the next rung.

One useful indicator of competition is change in the occupational segregation of an ethnic population. According to the perspective developed in this book, changes in the isolation or concentration of ethnic populations in occupations affect rates of ethnic collective action. The analysis in subsequent chapters uses data on ethnic collective events and census data on labor force participation, poverty rates, immigration and migration flows, and life histories of ethnic language newspapers to address this issue.

A second objective is to clarify the effects of changing levels of *ethnic inequality* on the rate of ethnic collective action. Past research has relied mainly on static theories of ethnic dissimilarities in occupational prestige, income, mobility, residential segregation, and other factors related to achievement.[16] The research reported here takes a different tack. Chapters 8 and 9 examine the *dynamics* of movement into and out of disadvantaged occupations as major causes of conflict. They use techniques specifically designed to estimate the effects of changing levels of economic inequality on the rates of ethnic collective action.

A third objective concerns the development and evaluation of instruments for collecting data on ethnic collective action. As noted above, previous studies of ethnic conflict in American cities have been limited to using the *New York Times* Index as a major source of information on events involving racial confrontations.[17] The method used here involves gathering information on events from microfilms of daily editions of the *New York Times.* Although many critics are skeptical about the value of newspaper accounts as sole sources of data on collective actions, few studies have analyzed sources of bias.[18] Appendix B discusses the results of our efforts to do so.

A fourth objective of this project is to exploit the advantages of

---

[16]Lieberson (1980) and Farley (1984) provide two impressive examples of this tradition.

[17]See United States National Advisory Commission on Civil Disorders 1968, McAdam 1982, Burstein 1985, and Jenkins and Eckert 1986 for examples of research on racial protests and riots using the *New York Times Index* as a source of information on events.

[18]For exceptions, see Danzger 1975, and Snyder and Kelly 1977.

event-history methods for studying collective actions. These methods allow analysis of the effects of time-varying characteristics, such as economic depression (and recovery), ethnic segregation (and dispersion), and economic mobility of ethnic and racial groups into and out of enclaves within American cities on rates of ethnic conflict and protest. The event-history approach enables one to analyze sequences of spontaneous and often unanticipated collective action. Chapter 4 in particular compares event analysis to other commonly used methods of analyzing collective action.

The analysis reported in this volume uses event-history methods to estimate the impact of competition among ethnic groups reacting and adapting to changes in the resource environment. It analyzes the processes at three levels: (1) the *national level*, the effects of immigration and indicators of economic well-being, in Chapters 5, 6, and 7; (2) the *city-level* analysis of the effects occupational concentration of ethnic and racial groups in Chapters 8 and 9; and (3) analysis of the growth (and decline) of one type of *ethnic group organization*, ethnic newspapers, in Chapter 10.

A fifth objective is to explore the causal links between conflicts and protests. The analyses reported here address questions such as: Do racial attacks cause subsequent rates of civil rights' protest to rise? Do events involving some ethnic populations also imply that conflict rates involving others are also high? Perhaps conflict against some group generates later ethnic protests against these acts of hostility. The analysis undertaken here compares multi-stage models across time periods to analyze any causal links across types of events. Such comparisons are highlighted in Chapters 6 and 7.

This book represents a shift in emphasis away from considering static conditions. It focuses instead on processes of change that ignite racial and ethnic strife. The argument developed here emphasizes that changes in inequality foster ethnic conflicts and protests. For these reasons, efforts to explain racial and ethnic conflicts need to move beyond consideration of static conditions of inequality and political repression as primary causal factors. Current theories of race relations cannot explain patterns of ethnic violence that have varied over time and across targets. Explaining such patterns demands theories that directly take the dynamics of changing conditions into account. The core claim of this book is that ethnic conflicts and protests erupt when ethnic inequalities and racially ordered systems begin to break down.

This book adds new evidence to the debate about the relationship of inequality and the occurrence of collective action. The approach offered here breaks with tradition and emphasizes the crucial role of *chang-*

ing levels of resources that become available to the disadvantaged. To the extent that we uncover processes of competition that spark ethnic conflict we will have moved away from the static models that equate poverty, race, and hostility. If competition arguments are supported by the evidence which follows, then we can begin to consider how similar mechanisms involve changing conditions that affect other forms of collective action as well.

2

Strategies for Analyzing Ethnic Conflict and Protest

Conventional wisdom held until recently that modernization would gradually destroy ethnic loyalties and replace them with loyalties based on class or occupation (Lipset and Rokkan 1967; Rokkan 1970). Such claims have been spectacularly disconfirmed, as ethnic mobilizations in such modern states as Belgium, Canada, France, and Great Britain attest.[1] As yet no one perspective on ethnic movements has emerged to take the place of the classical view.

This book argues that the competition theory advanced here provides a unifying framework for analyzing diverse instances of ethnic collective action. This chapter relates early human ecology theories to recent empirical research on collective action and ethnicity. It shows that contemporary theoretical strategies for analyzing ethnic relations originated with ecological theories of competition and conflict. Ecological theories emphasize that analysis of processes of migration, immigration, competition, and adaptation is key to understanding racial and ethnic relations. The central claim is that competition between ethnic or racial groups tends to produce conflict between them. That is, socio-economic changes that intensify competition between ethnic groups indirectly increase the rate of conflict. More recent ecological theories of ethnic competition and conflict build on the assumption that large-scale changes in the structures of the economy and polity (that is, modernization) shift levels of competition among groups and therefore affect rates of ethnic/racial conflict.

---

[1]Smith (1981), Olzak and Nagel (1986), Nielsen (1980, 1985), and Ragin (1977) provide evidence on this point.

Modernization and Ethnicity

Social scientists during the 1940s and 1950s investigated ethnic movements in a variety of national settings outside the United States. They related levels of ethnic conflict with levels of industrialization, nationalism, and modernization cross-nationally using developmental theories (Deutsch 1966). Although these developmental theories did not explicitly rely on competitive mechanisms, they did hold that ethnic movements represented regional mobilizations in opposition to (often ethnically different) nation-builders (Eisenstadt and Rokkan 1973). Such regional cleavages were viewed as impediments to modernization. In this view ethnic movements represented *traditional* loyalties based in peripheral regions that were in competition with the modern state center, as the phrase center vs. periphery suggests (Rokkan 1970).

The dramatic rise of ethnic politics and conflicts in developed as well as developing countries underscored the need for new explanations of the persistence of ethnicity in the modern world.[2] This need was filled by a flurry of empirical studies of ethnic and racial movements in Nigeria, Belgium, Canada, Italy, France, Great Britain, Ethiopia, Pakistan, Bangladesh, and Scotland.[3] But these studies too have limitations. Because case studies necessarily focus on historical specifics, they cannot tell whether the various eruptions reflect the same underlying processes. With its heavy reliance on case studies, the study of ethnic movements has not produced a cumulative and theoretical research tradition.

Contemporary theory and research has produced two empirical generalizations from studies of ethnicity that reveal the perplexing nature of ethnicity in the modern world. First, *modernization decreases ethnic heterogeneity.*[4] An extensive literature in political science and sociology notes that where economic development, state formation, and nation-building coincide with declines in the importance of (small-scale) ethnic dialects, subregional identifications, and tribal political divisions, a concomitant rise in "modern" loyalties and politics based on class occurs. Second, *modernization and development spark ethnic movements.* Cases that fit this claim include the mobilization of the industrialized region

---

[2]Many good critiques of functionalist theories of ethnicity exist, such as Hechter 1975, Ragin 1977, 1979, and 1987, Hannan 1979, Allardt 1979, Nagel and Olzak 1982, Olzak 1983, and Nielsen 1985.

[3]For examples, see Smith 1981, Gellner 1983, and Horowitz 1985.

[4]Modernization is a notoriously difficult concept to define and measure. Factors that have been empirically associated with modernization include industrialization, urbanization, and bureaucratization of market and political organization (Tilly, Tilly, and Tilly 1975; Meyer and Hannan 1979).

of the Basque region of Spain, or the resurgence of Scottish Nationalist activity in the wake of Scottish oil development, and the rise in industrialization of Québec province in Canada which coincided with Québecois separatism.[5]

Is it contradictory to claim that modernization both destroys and reaffirms ethnic boundaries and conflicts? Not necessarily. Both claims make sense once the effect of modernization on the *scale of organization* is taken into account. While modernization may erode the bases for smaller-scale ethnic identities, such as dialects or village and tribal identities, it simultaneously favors identification and mobilization along large scale regional or national ethnic party lines.

Most analysts of ethnicity now take the view that contemporary ethnic movements are fundamentally *products* of modernization (Bonacich 1972; Ragin 1977, 1979; Hechter 1975, 1987; Smith 1981; Banton 1983; and Yinger 1985). At least two perspectives have offered general theoretical arguments that modernization favors mobilization of large-scale rather than small-scale organizations. Competition theorists have advanced the idea that economic and political modernization encourages collective action based on regional or national constituencies. This is because modernization *erodes* small-scale loyalties, such as kinship, dialect, or village identities. This erosion opens up the possibility for organization on the basis of large-scale identities (Hannan 1979; Nielsen 1985). Hannan (1979) argued that modernization simultaneously erodes smaller-scale ethnic organizations while it favors large-scale ethnic movements. It does so because "The smallest scale identities are impediments to organization on the basis of widely shared identities. As long as the smallest scale identities remain strong and salient to collective action, the likelihood of effective and sustained action on the basis of widely shared ethnic identities is low. However, any process that lowers the salience of small-scale identities will weaken this impediment to large-scale collective action." (Hannan 1979: 255–56).

Similarly, Tilly (1986) argues that modernization has fundamentally altered the form and size of collective actions. He shows that, since the eighteenth century, the *scale* of collective violence in France shifted in the direction of large-scale protests and movements.[6] In examining

---

[5]For examples of studies supporting both of these generalizations, see Eisenstadt and Rokkan 1973, Glazer and Moynihan 1975, Banton 1983, Horowitz 1985, and Olzak and Nagel 1986.

[6]Tilly's studies of contentious actions in eighteenth and nineteenth century Great Britain provide more evidence on this point. His analysis of events finds that broad categories of types of collective action increased over this period, and that such actions

the historical emergence of national-level politics and political social movements, Tilly and other resource mobilization theorists have argued that nation-building in particular reinforces or even facilitates mobilization of large-scale identities and political movements. Thus, modernization transforms politics into national contests between large-scale organizations that command broadly-based memberships and resources. Does this same principle also apply to *ethnic* collective action? Some have suggested that it does (Hannan 1979; Nagel and Olzak 1982; and Nielsen 1985).

Modernization also penetrates markets for labor, turning local markets into industry-wide markets.[7] One consequence is that competition intensifies among groups. That is, modernization affects ethnic movements by stimulating ethnic competition within increasingly homogeneous markets, particularly labor markets, as education, training, and other rationalized measures of productivity replace particularistic and personal networks as bases for obtaining jobs. As Nielsen (1985: 142) puts it:

Modernization entails the extension of a rational labor market in which individuals are allocated to occupations on the basis of universalistic criteria. Therefore, the likelihood of competition between members of different ethnic groups for the same occupations increases ... Competition between members of different ethnic groups makes the utilities of individuals more sensitive to events that may give a competitive edge to all individual members of an ethnic group as opposed to others.

It is important to recognize that activation of ethnic boundaries does *not* inevitably follow modernization. Ethnicity competes with other large-scale bases of organization, notably class mobilization, for the loyalty, time, and resources of potential members. Whether ethnic or class boundaries predominate in any given setting (or time period) depends upon a constellation of factors. These include previous political party cleavages, variation in stages of political development, colonial and imperial legacies, the parliamentary or other political structures, representative chambers, and a variety of other political and state characteris-

---

increasingly targeted the Parliament (Tilly 1990). Other studies have documented that a similar mobilization phenomenon also took place in Italy and Germany (Tilly, Tilly, and Tilly 1975).

[7]Note that this implies that under conditions of free markets, labor, goods, and services cross national boundaries, creating what some theorists refer to as an increasingly interdependent world economy (Meyer and Hannan 1979; Delacroix and Ragin 1981; and Bornschier and Chase-Dunn 1985). While the implications for the world system for ethnic subnational movements have not been worked out fully, Nagel and Olzak (1982) present propositions linking these trends.

tics which determine the size and contents of political power in states.[8] They also include the distribution of different ethnic populations into productive roles such as legacies of a division of labor based on ethnic segregation, as exists under various caste systems or *Apartheid*. In this view, ethnicity is expected to be more potent where the legacies of ethnic political parties or economic caste systems have prevailed.

Strategies for Analyzing Ethnic Conflict

At least four theoretical perspectives have influenced the study of ethnic conflict. While all share the assumption that modernization processes hold the key to understanding ethnic hostilities, they differ considerably with respect to the processes they emphasize. Two are variants of functionalist theories of development: early human ecology and the assimilationist models of ethnic relations. The other two—cultural division of labor and split labor market perspectives—emphasize that economic inequalities provide the basis and motivation for ethnic antagonism and social movements.

Human Ecology Perspectives. Human ecologists, notably Robert Park and Amos Hawley, first made the claim that modes of adaptation of immigrant and migrant populations shaped the responses they encountered. Drawing on classical biological theories, they focused on processes of niche exploitation and competition. As immigrants and migrants seek to exploit niches in the social structure, they adapt and change in order to take into account the constraints of their new environments, according to this perspective. In one well-known application, Park and Burgess (1921) proposed that cities experience a set of life cycle stages of race relations. The initial stages consist of invasion, competition, and conflict. Park and Burgess held that ethnic conflict results from rising competition initiated by the invasion of ethnic populations (or racial groups). But ethnic and racial conflict eventually subsides as inequality in income and occupational segregation dissipate. For Park and Burgess (1921), assimilation indicates a final (or equilibrium) stage, in which accommodation is characterized by declining conflict and competition.

Other ecologists thought that segregation and dispersion were the primary correlates of ethnic discrimination. Hawley (1945) highlighted the role of residential segregation and he proposed that ethnic discrimination and conflict would decline with residential dispersion:

Separation in space is probably an indispensable condition of subordinate status applied to a group as a whole ... Given the hypothesis of a necessary

---

[8] For exploration of these themes, see Rokkan 1970, Gellner 1983, and Horowitz 1985.

dependence of subordinate group status upon spatial segregation, it follows that a breakdown of the isolation and a scattering of the group is the essential first step in obviating the position of inferiority ... Redistribution of a minority group in the same territorial pattern as that of the majority group results in a dissipation of subordinate status and an assimilation of the subjugated group into the social structure. (Hawley 1945: 669, 674)

Though there were differences among them, these early theorists drew an analogy between adaptation of cohorts of immigrants and biotic invasion and succession. They reasoned that struggles among ethnic groups decline when racial opportunities improve and inequalities among ethnic groups lessen.

Assimilation Perspectives. Assimilation perspectives hold that cultural differences between groups, especially in language and customs, impede the success and social acceptance of newcomers. Some theorists in the assimilation tradition thought that diminishing ethnic inequality (with respect to income, occupation, education, or some other resource) erodes the basis for ethnic and racial strife (Gordon 1964; Williams 1964). That is, immigration (or migration) initially increases ethnic/racial conflict, as awareness of differences between groups peaks. But when immigrants acquire the language of the host country, and other processes of assimilation and acculturation occur, conflict is replaced by accommodation and an eventual decline in antagonism. In some versions of assimilation theory, the reduction of conflict occurs only when inequalities of opportunity are effaced (Gordon 1964).

Such claims have been investigated largely in American settings, where the ideology of a "melting pot" has been examined and questioned. One problem in evaluating this perspective is that assimilation has (at least) two different meanings in social science. Assimilation has been alternatively viewed as a theoretical perspective on ethnic relations as well as a prescription for decreasing the deprivation experienced by ethnic and racial minority populations. As a result, evidence on various "unmeltable ethnics" has been used to discredit the theoretical claims about ethnic conflict and discrimination.

Some analysts using this tradition, such as Blalock (1957, 1967), Gordon (1964), and Williams (1964), have emphasized that competition and conflict among groups prevent assimilation. But an opposite causal relationship is equally plausible: Partial assimilation of formerly deprived groups increases competition among groups, as once-deprived groups come to compete with more successful natives. In the short run then, assimilation may raise rates of racial and ethnic conflict.

Others have approached the issue of assimilation from a social-psychological perspective.[9] They have emphasized the causes of individual and group variations in prejudice and discrimination. Blalock (1967), for instance, noted that African-Americans in particular were more likely to become targets of ethnic and racial hostility when they represented a "power-threat" to the status quo, as opposed to a competitive economic threat. While this theory seems plausible, empirical evidence for it has been mixed (see Corzine, Creech, and Huff-Corzine 1983; Corzine, Huff-Corzine, and Creech 1988; Tolnay, Beck, and Massey 1989; and Beck and Tolnay 1990).

Internal Colonialism and the Cultural Division of Labor. Recent research has rejected the assumption that assimilation is inevitable or even desirable. Instead, some sociologists have developed broad theories to account for the reawakening of ethnic movements in the modern world. One of the most impressive of these is the combined internal colonialism and cultural division of labor theory. An internal colony refers to a situation in which a rich, culturally dominant core region dominates and exploits an ethnically different periphery.

In an influential statement of this perspective, Michael Hechter (1975) analyzed the persistence of cultural voting patterns in the Celtic Fringe in Great Britain. He found that cultural factors, including Non-conformist religion and use of the Welsh language, accounted for voting patterns in economically disadvantaged counties but not in wealthier or more English counties.[10] His explanation applies models of inequality between states to regional inequality and to ethnic regionalism in partic-ular. The key argument is that a combination of uneven industrialization and cultural differences among regions causes ethnic grievances to be-come the basis of political conflict. The sources of ethnic solidarity cited include uneven regional development that reinforces or creates inequal-ity, dependence on external or international investment, and an occu-pational structure that is highly segregated along ethnic lines. Hechter argues that strong ethnic solidarity provokes ethnic conflicts among re-gions within nations and between ethnically distinct peripheries and the core.

Yet regional disparities alone cannot account for the spread of ethnic conflicts. According to Hechter (1984), there are numerous examples of huge regional disparities in natural resources, industrial development,

---

[9]There is a large and impressive empirical literature on social psychological bases of prejudice and discrimination. For reviews of research, see Hovland and Sears 1940, Pettigrew 1958, 1969; and Hepworth and West 1988.

[10]Ragin (1977, 1979, 1986) presents evidence that runs counter to the internal colonialism arguments using essentially the same data as Hechter.

and wealth that have not generated ethnic movements. To the internal colonialism imagery, Hechter adds the concept of a cultural division of labor. A cultural division of labor exists when jobs are allocated on the basis of cultural and ethnic boundaries. The relegation of minority group members to occupations with low wages and poor conditions reinforces ethnic solidarity, so that organizations, networks, and political parties based upon ethnicity develop. So the persistence of regional inequality, ethnic segregation, and ethnic solidarity fosters ethnic conflict within nations. Specifically, Hechter (1975: 43) claims:

1. The greater the economic inequalities between collectivities, the greater the probability that the less advantaged collectivity will be status solidary, and hence, will resist political integration.

2. The greater the frequency of intra-collectivity communication, the greater the status solidarity of the peripheral collectivity.

3. The greater the intergroup differences of culture, particularly in so far as identifiability is concerned, the greater the probability that the culturally distinct peripheral collectivity will be status solidary. Identifiable cultural differences include: language (accent), distinctive religious practices, and life-style.

With the general argument that underdevelopment and cultural subordination lead to ethnic resurgence, Hechter was able to explain variation in ethnic movements in peripheral regions of the United Kingdom. His theory specified the conditions leading to ethnic persistence. Because these conditions could be met by a wide variety of contexts, this work set the agenda for future research on ethnicity and ethnic movements in the decade that followed.[11]

Despite the impressive theoretical advance, much subsequent research on ethnic relations presents contradictory evidence for Hechter's theory. According to one version of this argument, segregation of ethnic populations into low wage jobs produces economic grievances that become channeled into ethnic movements (Hechter 1984). Support for this view has been mixed. While Hechter's (1975) analysis of ethnic voting in the Celtic Fringe showed support for the ethnic segregation hypothesis, Ragin's (1977, 1979) subsequent reanalyses refuted these claims and showed support for competition theory arguments. So too did Nielsen's (1980) empirical work on Belgium and Olzak's (1982) analysis of ethnic separatism in Québec.[12]

---

[11]For empirical studies using this internal colonialism strategy, see Leifer 1981, Hechter and Levi 1979, and the Special Issue on Internal Colonialism, July 1979 in *Ethnic and Racial Studies.*

[12]In his recent and innovative work applying rational choice theory to the problem of group solidarity, Hechter (1987: 5) argues that the cultural division of labor theory (and more generally, structural theories) fall short because they cannot explain the variation in *timing* of ethnic subnational movements. Despite this shortcoming, he

Split Labor Markets and Middleman Minorities. In contrast to the cultural division of labor theory, Bonacich (1973) contended that deprivation of ethnic or racial populations cannot explain some forms of ethnic hostility. Ethnic conflict is often directed at highly successful ethnic minorities, those that exploit a "middleman" niche. Middlemen typically work as traders, money lenders, brokers, rent collectors, and in other job categories that intervene between producers and consumers (or employees and employers). So success in exploiting such niches also threatens job monopolies enjoyed by dominant groups, which causes ethnic conflict from above. Middleman minorities may also experience attacks from groups below them, as subordinate groups feel exploited and resentful of middleman minority success. In this case, the resulting three-group competition intensifies attacks against the middlemen minority population.

A related argument holds that ethnic conflict peaks under conditions of a *split labor market* (Bonacich 1972). A split labor market is one in which two or more racially distinct populations who are in the same labor market command different wages for the same work. According to Bonacich (1972: 549),

The central hypothesis is that ethnic antagonism first germinates in a labor market split along ethnic lines. To be split, a labor market must contain at least two groups of workers whose price of labor differs for the same work, or would differ if they did the same work. The concept 'price of labor' refers to labor's total cost to the employer, including not only wages, but the cost of recruitment, transportation, room and board, education, health care (if the employer must bear these), and the cost of labor unrest. The degree of worker 'freedom' does not interfere with this calculus ...

Bonacich argued that violence against African-Americans during the early twentieth century was encouraged by the fact that economic self-interest drove employers to maintain low labor costs. If employers were successful, they could replace higher wage (white) workers with cheaper African-American labor, thereby undercutting union organization. White workers sometimes responded to this threat with racial violence (Foner 1982). That is, racial antagonism intensified when and where labor markets were split along racial lines. Analysis of urban violence in the North during strikes from 1900 to 1930 and in mining communities in California from 1852 to 1882 has provided support for this view (Bonacich 1976; Boswell 1986). This book expands on these themes by investigating whether split-labor-market processes might explain attacks on other ethnic minorities as well.

---

maintains that the general argument about economic deprivation and group solidarity is basically correct (see also Hechter, Friedman, and Appelbaum 1982, Hechter 1984).

Fundamental Processes of Competition Theory

This book applies competition theory arguments that have implications for models of ethnic conflict and violence. Specifically, this section considers how competition theory treats three issues. First, it examines the advantages of considering ethnic boundaries as a type of social organization. Second, it expands the discussion introduced earlier of competition processes involved in niche overlap and its consequences. Third, this section sharpens the distinction between competition and conflict in order to test competition arguments.

The Stability of Ethnic Boundaries. Barth (1969) proposed that the *stability* of ethnic relations depends on the level of competition among ethnic groups reacting and adapting to changes in the resource environment. More generally, competition shapes collective action organized around ethnic boundaries. The emphasis is on boundaries rather than on description of the cultural content within boundaries or behaviors shared by some ethnic group. Thus Barth (1969: 15) defines ethnic boundaries as *organizing principles*:

> The critical focus of investigation from this point of view becomes the ethnic *boundary* that defines the group, not the cultural stuff it encloses ... The organizational feature which, I would argue, must be general for all inter-ethnic relations is a systematic set of rules governing inter-ethnic social encounters ... If people agree about these prescriptions, their agreement on codes and values need not extend beyond that which is relevant to the social situations in which they interact.

The competitive theory of ethnic relations offered here does not deny the reality of cultural differences. Obviously, skin color, language, and country of origin matter. It seeks only to free the concepts of race and ethnicity from the usual assumption that ethnic and racial categories are primordial, immutable, and prior to ethnic conflict, as the previous chapter noted. So, in reaction to earlier theories that emphasized cultural differences, the perspective taken here suggests that cultural features may also result from collective action as well. That is, mobilizing groups may seek to emphasize one or more distinctive markers, in an effort to recruit members to their cause. The most common examples of this reverse causal process involve the revival of regional languages in ethnically identified regions. Examples include the teaching of Welsh, Corsican, Basque, and Scottish languages, in their presumed regional origins, in recent years.[13] Such markers, over time, may become institutionalized and believed to be primordial features of ethnic or racial identity. Such presumptions clearly deserve scrutiny.

---

[13]For evidence, see Horowitz 1985.

Ethnicity is a social boundary that partitions a population with distinctions about membership (by the group and/or by others) that are based on one or more of the following criteria: (a) characteristics presumed to be based upon shared genealogy, (b) cultural traits, including language, religion, dress, custom, or assumed shared history, and (c) nationality or regional origin.[14] By definition, *race* is a specific instance of ethnicity, defined by membership based upon what are *assumed to be* inherited phenotypical characteristics (as was discussed in Chapter 1).

Barth (1969: 17) adds to these characteristics the assumption that ethnic identity is "*imperative*, in that it cannot be disregarded and temporarily set aside by other definitions of the situation." While ethnicity appears dominant in the types of preindustrial settings analyzed by Barth, its imperative character is open to question in modern settings. Because of this fact, I treat this issue as a question which asks under what condition ethnicity is likely to become predominant.

Niche Overlap. Despite the convincing claims of early human ecologists that there is a link between competition and conflict, the mechanisms by which competition becomes transformed into active conflict remained unclear until the influential paper of Barth (1956) and his edited book, *Ethnic Groups and Boundaries* (Barth 1969). His view builds on the proposition that racial and ethnic violence surges under conditions of *niche overlap*. In order to understand this argument, we must first define the components of the theory.

Competition has been defined as a type of rivalry or contest, particularly in economic struggles for markets, customers, or clients (Banton 1983). An important aspect of competition perspectives is the view that competition is a process rather than a static characteristic. But examining a process is a difficult task. We need some benchmarks before deciding whether groups or individuals are acting in concert or in competition.

Ecological theory offers one approach. Human ecologists have defined competition more narrowly than other sociologists. They hold that competition exists between two populations when the presence of one

---

[14]Many have observed that ethnic identity often appears to be based on distinctions that do not hold up to empirical scrutiny (Banton 1983; Horowitz 1985). Sometimes these involve myths that are political strategies of ethnic social movements (B. Nagel 1986; J. Nagel 1986; Padilla 1986). Others involve assumptions about the invariance of the genetic transmission of traits. This is especially true for those definitions of race which assume racial characteristics (including some highly pejorative ones) are inherited. For provocative discussions of this issue, see van den Berghe 1978, Banton 1983, and Horowitz 1985.

reduces the opportunities for the other (Hawley 1950).[15] By this definition, it becomes a straightforward task to draw out the implications for
some competing human populations, such as ethnic groups.

Competition theorists maintain that the likelihood of racial and ethnic conflict is minimized when groups occupy nonoverlapping habitats.
Within habitats, groups have a set of potential roles for exploiting that
habitat. Ecologists also refer to this potential set of conditions under which a group can maintain itself as a group's niche. Most human
ecologists further distinguish between a population's fundamental and
realized niche. A population's fundamental niche is the environment
within which it can survive in the absence of competitors. Its *realized
niche* is "the part of the fundamental niche which the group actually
occupies or exploits in the presence of other groups, the state, and other
social groups" (Lauwagie 1979: 313). The realized niche is the set of
repertoires and strategies a group actually uses to maintain itself within
some environment (B. Nagel 1986; see also Hutchinson 1957 and Hannan 1979). The relevant conditions for maintaining a fundamental niche
for human beings include not only strategies for obtaining economic resources (such as food, shelter, and housing), but also constraints on
the ability to exploit these resources—for example, laws that segregate
racial or ethnic populations. Persistence of an ethnic group in some social system means that the ethnic boundary persists and continues to
shape interaction. An ethnic boundary can disappear either because the
members of an ethnic population fail to survive as individuals, or they
emigrate, or because they shift ethnic identity.

The relevance of this distinction can be seen in Barth's (1957) discussion of how competition caused changes in the realized niches exploited
by two groups in Swat, North Pakistan. According to Barth, originally,
a population engaged in mixed agriculture and herding lived alongside
a population of herders in the same region. Due to their military superiority, the mixed agricultural and herders came to dominate the region,
pushing the herders up into the highlands where the environment was
unfit for agriculture. In other words, although the two groups originally
shared the same fundamental niche, over time, the herder's realized niche

---

[15]Blalock (1967: 73) offered a similar definition in his theory of minority-group
conflict. He defined ethnic competition as "involving the idea that two or more individuals are striving for the same scarce objectives, so that the success of one implies
a reduced probability that others will also attain their goal." Kindred definitions of
competition among competing forms of organizations has been more formally drawn
recently by Hannan and Freeman (1989: 97–106), which draws heavily on Gause's
(1934) discussion of competition among species and Levins' (1968) generalization of
these competition principles.

became restricted as competition between the two ethnic groups was reduced. This is an instance of *competitive exclusion*. The implication is that the *potential* for competition nearly always exists, but that the more powerful group will always prevail. Niche overlap increases the level of competition; however, lack of overlap in the realized niches does not imply that competition is (or has been) absent.[16]

The key argument derived from general ecology is that competition potentially occurs under conditions of *fundamental niche overlap*.[17] Niche overlap occurs when two or more groups come to exploit the same realized niche. According to Barth (1969: 20), niche overlap has direct consequences for the stability of ethnic relations: "Stable inter-ethnic relations presuppose such a structuring of interaction: a set of prescriptions governing situations of contact ... [but] when two or more interspersed groups are in fact in at least partial competition within the same niche ... one would expect one such group to displace the other, or an accommodation involving an increasing complementarity and interdependence to develop."

The relationship of ethnic populations and the resource environment (or niches) they exploit is a core problem in these theories. To the extent that populations maintain separate niches, stable ethnic relations can result. But when ethnic populations attempt to exploit the *same* niche, they compete. This book draws on Barth's insight that displacement and exclusion result from competition. It suggests that the onset of niche overlap causes competition among groups to rise, which in turn encourages attempts to exclude the competitors. Such attempts often entail violent conflict.

But we can also see that ethnic conflict is not the only consequence of niche overlap. Accommodation of one group to a more powerful group is one possible result of competition (as Barth noted). In particular, in systems with highly skewed power relations, the habitat may be partitioned into ethnic divisions so that overlap in realized niches is quite low. *Apartheid* is an obvious example. In other words, a type of accommodation may be achieved through subjugation and repression—when resources are partitioned so that inferior resources are relegated to the

---

[16]Seen from this perspective, a cultural division of labor could be the outcome of an ethnic competitive process. That is, dominance and exclusion of one group over another may be the result of successful competitive exclusion. As far as I am aware, proponents of cultural division of labor perspective have not considered this possibility.

[17]This argument is drawn from Gause's (1934) *principle of competitive exclusion*. This principle holds that two species which attempt to exploit that same set of finite resources cannot coexist: one will exclude the other.

powerless. When the dynamics of such a highly asymmetric power balance are considered, we can further see that the system may not be stable in the long run.

What then causes ethnic instability in systems such as *Apartheid*? One possibility is that conflict erupts when institutionalized segregation begins to break down (Olivier 1989). As Weber (1924) noted long ago, highly skewed power systems lack legitimacy, making long-term stability precarious. In other words, these competitive models imply that relationship between competition and conflict is a dynamic one. Lack of observed competition may mean that competitive exclusion was once a successful strategy. The point here is that neither conflict nor accommodation result inevitably from competition.[18] What the theory tells us is that niche overlap *releases* competition forces. This in turn initiates exclusionary measures which may or may not prevail.

So when competitive forces among ethnics are released, ethnic boundaries become highly salient during periods of intense competition over resources. What kinds of social processes activate ethnic boundaries? A central hypothesis derived from the ecological theory of Barth and others is that *ethnic competition intensifies ethnic boundaries when two or more ethnic populations try to acquire the same valued resources, such as jobs, housing, or marriage partners.*[19] That is, by this argument we expect that social changes that alter the relationship between ethnic boundaries and their niches so that two or more ethnic populations compete for the same jobs, housing, or within the same political contests, increase the salience of ethnic boundaries. In this way we can begin to understand that *ethnic* boundaries are activated in contrast to other possible boundaries in any given interaction setting.

The ecological perspective suggests that competition processes spark ethnic conflict. They do so when ethnic groups attempt to occupy the same resource environment and compete for the same limited set of resources. By viewing changes in ethnic relations in light of these ecolog-

---

[18]We can extend the concept of competitive exclusion to include other forms of ethnic exclusion as well. The passage of laws restricting some ethnic and racial groups was used successfully against competition from Asian workers during the late nineteenth century (Saxton 1971; Nee and Nee 1986). In the 1880s, anti-Chinese violence, which began in earnest during the 1850s, did not continue unabated. Rather, it led to the Anti-Asian Exclusion Act of 1882 and to the eventual end to Asian immigration (Garis 1927; Saxton 1971; Bennett 1988).

[19]Recently this proposition has been applied to organizational ecology. McPherson (1983) and Hannan and Freeman (1989) have applied the concept of niche overlap in useful ways. These authors apply the concept of niche overlap to the process of competitive exclusion, in which competing organizations aim at reducing the competitive threat.

ical processes, we can analyze factors that increase and decrease levels of competition and conflict. But while Barth's pathbreaking work suggested that niche overlap and competitive exclusion of ethnic groups were the key to understanding unstable ethnic relations, he considered only nonindustrial societies. It has not been clear how to apply these ecological themes to more complicated ethnic and racial systems, where the operationalization of niche and resource exploitation is less straightforward.

This book explicitly extends the process of niche overlap and competitive exclusion to consider if analogous processes also hold for ethnic job segregation and conflict. Specifically, the argument is that ethnic integration of labor markets intensifies ethnic competition. Under certain conditions, the majority group tries to exclude ethnic competitors, leading to ethnic conflict and protest. If this ecological argument holds, *desegregation of jobs causes rates of ethnic protest and conflict to rise.*

Competition and Conflict. A important insight from human ecologists concerns theoretical distinctions between competition and conflict. Does conflict differ from competition, or does one always imply the other? Park's answer to this question, patterned after that of his teacher Georg Simmel, help set the agenda for more recent research. Writing with Ernest Burgess (Park and Burgess 1921: 574–75), he argued for the distinction as follows:

Both [competition and conflict] are forms of interaction, but competition is a struggle between individuals, or groups of individuals, who are not necessarily in contact and communication; while conflict is a contest in which contact is an indispensable condition ... Conflict is always conscious, indeed it evokes the deepest emotions and strongest passions and enlists the general concentration of attention and effort. Both competition and conflict are forms of struggle. Competition, however, is continuous and impersonal, conflict is intermittent and personal ... In general, then, one may say that competition becomes conscious and personal in conflict. In the process of transition, competitors are transformed into rivals and enemies.

This distinction is crucial to modern applications of competition theory because it allows consideration of the processes that causally link competition and conflict. Without this distinction the two concepts become blurred or even tautological.

Research Implications of Competition Theory Strategies

If competition does not lead to conflict in every instance, then we need to consider under what conditions and in what settings competition does and does not generate conflict. We can also examine how conflict subsides. If competition among groups diminishes or is prevented, will the hostilities generated dissipate? These questions have become the focus of the current generation of competition theorists and researchers in race relations.[20] The arguments made below emphasize the effects of (1) economic competition and (2) political competition. In particular, I argue that increasing labor market competition between ethnic populations raises the likelihood of ethnic collective action. Likewise, political challenges to existing ethnic power structures increase rates of ethnic and racial conflict and protest.

To be convincing, competition theories require evidence that racial and ethnic groups actually compete for valued resources. In the context of the research reported in this book, this means investigating whether racial and ethnic groups actually competed for jobs and political control during this period. Because the data on occupational distribution and political party membership by race and ethnicity are scarce for the period under observation, this question is difficult to answer with certainty. However, it is not necessary that workers from different racial/ethnic groups always compete *directly* for the same jobs for ethnic antagonism to flare. Nor is it necessary to find cases of political parties organized solely around one ethnic issue. *Potential* competition can spark such antagonism before direct (head-to-head) competition has occurred. In the case of labor market competition, workers in the late nineteenth century quickly discovered that employers could and often did substitute low-wage workers in order to maintain profits and subdue trade unions (or both). This book develops the implications of such processes of indirect and potential competition by considering the effect of immigration and migration of populations who are racially or ethnically different who might have been viewed as potential competitors by native whites.

What evidence do we have in support of this claim? There is substantial evidence that processes of potential job competition mobilized action on the part of members of some trade unions. The anti-immigrant and antiblack discrimination practiced by at least some trade unions over much of their histories provides support for this view. And, according to some labor leaders such as American Federation of Labor leader Samuel Gompers, or the Knights of Labor organizer, T. V. Powderly, the rising number of unskilled immigrants and African-Americans in the industrializing North constituted just such a threat to white and native workers (Powderly 1884; Gompers 1925). Sometimes such trade union opposition helped mobilize political movements to restrict immigration as well (Garis 1927). It is in this sense that *niche overlap* between newly com-

---

[20]For examples, see Ragin 1977, 1987, Nielsen 1980, 1985, Olzak 1982, Olzak and Nagel 1986, Boswell 1986, and James 1988.

peting racial/ethnic groups characterized American labor markets and political contests. Thus when low-wage groups move into a country or region, competition for jobs, housing, and political resources rises, at least initially.[21]

Conclusion

We began with the claim of the human ecologists Park, Burgess, Hawley, and others that ethnic and racial competition caused the outbreak of conflict among these groups. We reviewed several leading strategies for studying race and ethnic conflict. The most important of these share the fundamental assumption that modernization forces have encouraged mobilization along ethnic lines.

Modernization increases the benefits attached to ethnic solidarity because (a) small-scale loyalties among populations become eroded and less potent and (b) *ethnic* and large-scale cleavages are encouraged when they mobilize significant segments of the population. In other words, when modernization is successful in breaking down traditional and small scale organizations, ethnicity can surge in its wake.

Other strategies for analyzing ethnic movements diverge in a number of important ways. Though early human ecologists emphasized the importance of social change and especially adaptation and change in newcomer populations, they held the view that a life-cycle process of race relations begins with conflict and ends with accommodation. Other strategies—including cultural division of labor and split labor market theories—have emphasized the role of ethnic inequalities in producing collective action based upon both class and ethnic grievances. Such theories have met with only scattered empirical success, but they have influenced current competition theories that emphasize the importance of economic factors as key determinants of ethnic conflict.

Recently, theories of ethnic relations have applied ecological models of niche overlap to explain sources of ethnic conflict. These theories claim that the potential for conflict arises when two or more groups come to exploit a similar set of political and economic resources. The theory draws our attention to those factors which intensify competition within similar settings. We turn now to processes which cause conflicts and protests involving race and ethnic groups.

---

[21]Mink (1986) presents a similar argument and evidence on the labor movement's opposition to incoming immigrants, particular the activity of organized labor against the Chinese and other Asians in California during this period. For further evidence of anti-Asian hostility using competition arguments, see also Saxton 1971, Nee and Nee 1986.

3

Competition Processes:
Arguments and Propositions

We turn now to the specifics of ethnic competition. This chapter considers four processes: immigration and migration, economic contraction, increases in ethnic-group resources, and political challenges to ethnic dominance. Although each is discussed separately, it is important to note that they also interact in important ways. For instance, economic prosperity has historically acted as a pull on migration and immigration patterns, while economic contraction decreases these trends. Furthermore, it is likely that high levels of two or more processes have nonadditive effects, so that economic contraction in combination with immigration intensifies competition even more. These and other complexities are considered in the empirical chapters which follow.

Migration and Immigration. Migration and immigration tend to flow from regions with lower economic opportunities toward those with greater opportunities (Easterlin et al. 1982). As a result, large-scale immigration increases the supply of workers willing to work at lower than the prevailing wage. Economists have argued that the influx of ethnic and racial populations willing to work at low wages may initially drive wages down. The resulting downturn in wages only serves to confirm workers' worst fears about the impact of immigrant and migrant newcomers. Under such conditions it is not surprising that these newcomers are the victims of discrimination, violence, and exclusionary movements.

Around the turn of the twentieth century in America, a growing supply of low-wage labor combined with economic depression or panic to intensify competition among immigrants, African-Americans, and native whites (Foner 1982; Mink 1986; Olzak 1987). Ethnic competition was magnified because immigrants who were concentrated in low-wage, un-skilled occupations could undercut wages earned by earlier arriving im-migrants and natives. And immigrants (and African-Americans) could be distinguished from native whites ethnically, by language, dress, cus-tom, if not always by skin color. Immigration therefore heightened con-sciousness of ethnic and racial boundaries.

Were immigrants and African-American migrants disproportionately found in low-wage jobs? One way to explore this question is to ask whether European immigrants and African-American migrants were also concentrated in unskilled and laboring occupations. Because wage infor-mation is scarce and notoriously unreliable for this period (see Wright 1986 and Higgs 1977), occupational distributions provide stronger evi-dence than do wage differences. The historical evidence is clearcut. Not only were these groups willing to work at lower than prevailing wages, they were also recruited to sites of labor unrest and union organizing by employers seeking to break strikes. As a result, wages of nonunionized immigrants and African-Americans remained low and did not directly benefit from union victories which raised wages of other workers (United States Report on Immigration 1901; Commons 1918; Archdeacon 1983; Bonacich 1976; Bennett 1988).

What mechanisms cause hostility to be generated against those seg-regated at the bottom of the occupational hierarchy? According to Bonacich, the conditions of a labor market where wages are split along ethnic lines incite ethnic antagonism as a by-product of native whites' attempting to hold onto their jobs, as was discussed in the previous chapter. Proponents of split labor market theory also claim that, under industrial capitalism, employers engaged in struggles with workers to pay different wages to race and ethnic groups so they could "divide and conquer" workers effectively (Boswell 1986; Bonacich 1972).

Labor historians and sociologists have also claimed that the use of African-American (and sometimes white immigrant) strikebreakers undercut union mobilization and union organizational success (Foner 1964; Gordon, Edwards, and Reich 1982; Fink 1983). Many have ques-tioned the empirical evidence supporting this claim on the grounds that African-Americans were included in some union activities and were not always viewed as the enemy of labor. But, whether or not they were actually employed as scabs, African-American and ethnically different populations became symbols of potential threats to the standard of liv-ing of native whites (Higham 1955; Bonacich 1976; Bennett 1988). Com-petition theory holds that when this threat rises, majority groups will react with exclusionary measures.

Competition theorists regard this type of reaction as an instance of *competitive exclusion* (Barth 1969). Threats to prevailing wage levels from immigrants were often met with collective behavior designed to remove or terrorize immigrant populations. Notable examples of exclusion movements include the anti-Asian movement that surfaced during the 1880s in California and the nativist movements organized against European immigration throughout the late nineteenth and early twentieth century (Bennett 1988).[1] The magnitude of the response presumably depends on the characteristics of migration flows that affect perceptions of severity of the threat. Relevant characteristics might be the relative size of the incoming group, their visibility, and their freedom to return to their place of origin.

The size of an ethnic or racial group has also been cited as having an independent causal effect on residential and job segregation of African-Americans compared to European immigrants in American cities (Lieberson 1980). For instance Lieberson (1980) found that large groups were more likely to be *less* segregated at the bottom of the hierarchy than small ones, even if distributions of human capital and productivity are equivalent (see also Bodnar, Simon, and Weber 1982). Even more revealing is the fact that shifts in patterns of residential segregation took place around the turn of the century in America. Recent analysis of residential segregation supports this claim. For instance, it appears that a significant reversal in fortunes characterizes segregation patterns of African-Americans when compared with South Central and Eastern Europeans from 1900 to 1920. Lieberson (1980) finds that in 1900, some groups of new immigrants from South, Central, and Eastern Europe were actually more residentially isolated in northern cities than were African-Americans from 1890 through 1910. However, between 1910 and 1920 this relationship was reversed, meaning that African-Americans in the North became more isolated from whites.[2]

How can we explain these trends? One explanation suggested by Lieberson is that both the relative sizes of ethnic populations and racial discrimination contributed to this re-segregation of African-Americans. Lieberson (1980: 291) explains this reversal as partially due to shifts

---

[1] Competitive exclusion processes may be relevant to recent American history as well. For analysis which suggests that ethnic competition was instrumental in producing confrontations between African-Americans and Latinos in Los Angeles during the 1980s, see Oliver and Johnson, 1984: 79. They identify the major cause of ethnic conflict to be job competition, "in which Latinos, usually undocumented aliens, are seen as taking away low-status, menial jobs from blacks ..."

[2] Lieberson's analysis is limited to analysis of the impact of the proportion of African-Americans on the residential segregation of whites and African-Americans in the 17 northern cities for which spatial data exists by race and ethnicity.

in population composition, resulting from African-American migration to northern industrial centers by 1920 and partially due to increasing preferences on the part of whites to maintain isolation from African-Americans:

... increasing black isolation occurred simply because whites in each city were attempting to maintain the degree of isolation from blacks that existed before the new flows from the South started. Because the growing black population in each city made the maintenance of such isolation from blacks that existed more difficult, the net consequence was greater segregation of blacks.

Size of minority population was also found to be a predictor of the occurrence of race riots in American cities during the 1960s (Spilerman 1970a, 1971, and 1976). One interpretation of these results is that the effect of influx of a population that differs in language, nationality and/or skin color depends on its numbers relative to the majority population. The larger the size of the incoming group, the greater the impact.

Continuous migration of members from the same ethnically distinct population into a region may further intensify the negative reactions of native populations, as Wilson (1987: 178) points out:

Many present-day problems in the ghetto are partly the result of the heavy black urban migration that occurred throughout most of the first half of this century. As Lieberson has appropriately pointed out, because substantial black migration to the metropolises continued several decades after the early Asian and new European migration ceased, urban blacks, their ranks continually replenished with poor migrants, found it much more difficult to follow the path of both the Asian immigrants and the new Europeans in overcoming the effects of discrimination.

These various arguments lead to the prediction that *large immigration and migration flows increase levels of ethnic competition, at least initially, which in turn increases the rate of ethnic collective actions.*

Rapid *increases* in immigration, indicated by sharp jumps from a previous year, produce shocks in labor markets, over and above the effect of constant high levels of immigration. They do so because big waves of immigration affect perceptions of threats to jobs and wage levels. The impact of a sudden arrival of large numbers of a distinctly different population can be expected to place burdens on existing housing, labor, and other markets, sharpening perceptions of in- and out-group relations (Park 1949). Such an effect has been documented in case studies of the arrival of large numbers of Italians and Eastern Europeans in Philadelphia during the 1880s and 1890s (Bodnar et al. 1982), and for South and Central Europeans in general in northern cities in the late nineteenth century (Lieberson 1980). I hypothesize that *growth in immigration (from year to year) increases rates of ethnic collective action net*

of the effect of the level of immigration. This means that I expect that
the effect of immigration peaks when there are sharp annual increases
from year to year. For example, this hypothesis suggests that there
would be an effect of changes in immigration when there was an especially big shift in numbers of immigrants, as happened in 1910, when the
number of incoming immigrants was more than 200,000 persons higher
than in 1909. This hypothesis is expected to hold even when the fact
that annual immigration reached over 1 million persons in the majority
of years between 1905 and 1914 is taken into account in the same model.

So far we have argued that competition arising from immigration
results in hostility against those ethnic groups who compete against natives and earlier immigrants who are in the *same* labor market (Bonacich
1972; Boswell 1986). In most cases, we would expect the most recent
arrivals to be the target of ethnic violence. But apparently this was
not always the case (Bennett 1988). In some cases, when multiple ethnic groups were present, those groups with least capacity to retaliate
became targets of hostility. This pattern might have been especially
common when one ethnic or racial group had low political power with
which to counter hostility. This seems to have been the case with unskilled African-American workers during periods of high immigration
(Bonacich 1976). This argument suggests that the target of attacks may
not always be the same group raising the levels of competition. So we
add that rising levels of competition are more likely lead to attacks on
least powerful workers in the labor market.

Economic Contraction. Labor market competition intensifies when
there are signs that the economy is weak. The most potent sign is
likely to be a decline in employment opportunities. In particular, occurrence of economic recessions, depressions, and waves of business failures
shrink the number of jobs, which in turn intensifies competition over
fewer and fewer jobs. Economic contraction may also force those with
middle-level jobs and wages to search for unskilled jobs, thus pitting
older, upwardly mobile cohorts (perhaps from earlier waves of immigration) against ethnic and racial newcomers to the city (Wilson 1978).
*Factors that indicate a downturn in the economy are therefore expected
to produce ethnic collective action in response to shrinking job markets.*

Other analysts of ethnic collective action have made a different claim.
They argue that the effects of economic hardship are greater when combined with ethnic job segregation. For instance, as noted in the previous
chapters, the cultural division of labor perspective holds that high levels of ethnic job segregation and economic exploitation intensify ethnic
solidarity, increasing the likelihood of ethnic collective action.

Competition theories, including split labor market formulations, specify this relationship by emphasizing that it may not be job segregation and economic hardship per se that activates ethnic antagonism. Rather, economic hardship sometimes increases competition among ethnic groups, and the ensuing ethnic conflicts may be directed against the source of competition.

Both competition and split labor market formulations imply that the combination of a rising supply of ethnic/racial labor willing to work at lower than prevailing wages *and* economic contraction intensifies ethnic competition. That is, these formulations imply an interaction effect between a declining set of job opportunities and immigration in affecting the rate of ethnic collective action. Thus competition theories contrast with economic hardship formulations in arguing that economic decline does not inevitably aggravate ethnic relations. Rather, I argue that *economic contraction in combination with high immigration flows raises levels of ethnic competition, which in turn increases rates of ethnic collective action, at least initially.*

Thus, the argument holds that two processes elevate ethnic tensions. In the first, economic contraction causes the number of jobs open to immigrants and other less-skilled workers to shrink, raising the level of competition. In the second process, immigration expands the size of the population within the less-skilled niche, fostering competition for jobs, housing and other resources. Competition is further intensified when both conditions hold. In anticipation of the empirical analysis that follows, these arguments can be specified as a straightforward interaction effect of economic contraction and levels (and changes) of immigration.

Local Competition: Labor Markets and the Dynamics of Job Segregation. Thus far the argument has considered only the effects of national factors, namely immigration and economic cycles, on competition and thus on ethnic conflict and protest. Racial and ethnic conflicts and protests are likely to be as sensitive—if not more sensitive—to competition at the *local* level. For example, nation-wide depressions had very different consequences for the coal industries in the Northeast than for the industrializing cities of the Midwest (Corbin 1981).

So it seems reasonable to examine how competition for jobs and other resources affects the rates of ethnic confrontation at the local level. A good place to begin is with variations in occupational opportunities in cities during this period (Lieberson 1980; Bodnar et al. 1982; Thernstrom 1973). Recent work on ethnic and racial job segregation suggests that discrimination and lack of skills initially forced African-Americans and unskilled South Central and Eastern Europeans to take jobs that were disproportionately low-status and low paid.[3] Lieberson (1980) has documented, however, that considerable mobility took place as well. Some (mostly white) groups moved out of highly segregated occupations around the turn of the century.

A high level of occupational segregation of immigrants in a city indicates that a type of cultural division of labor exists (Hechter 1975, 1978). That is, a cultural division of labor is maintained to the extent that ethnic or racial populations are segregated into distinct occupations that are also differentially rewarded (discussed in Chapter 2). Cultural division of labor theories of group solidarity generally suggest that high levels of occupational (and residential) segregation contribute to high degrees of group solidarity and loyalty. In this view, ethnic solidarity causes collective action based on ethnic (rather than some other) identities.

Thus, cultural division of labor theories link ethnic solidarity with the propensity to engage in collective action (Hechter 1975: 43). Competition theorists agree only with the first part of this proposition, that niche specialization reinforces ethnic identity and solidarity (Barth 1969; Nielsen 1985). But evidence from the race riots in the 1960s and from the civil rights movement in the United States suggests that something more is needed for collective action to take place. The evidence suggests that while segregation reinforced boundaries, it did not by itself spark collective action. Moreover, it appears that during periods of intense deprivation, African Americans mobilized far less than they did during periods of economic decline (Woodward 1974; Wilson 1978). Put somewhat differently, in order to transform an exploited minority into a mobilized group, some change in the level of resources must take place. In contrast, then, to models that posit that class and ethnic deprivation fosters ethnic collective action, these competition theories suggests just the opposite: *low levels of ethnic job segregation for immigrants and others who are disadvantaged indicate higher levels of competition for jobs at the local level.*

Ethnic Enclaves and Collective Action. Research on ethnic enclaves suggests that concentration of an ethnic population in a local job market affects their ability to create ethnic organizations, including ethnic enterprises (Bonacich and Modell 1981; Aldrich and Waldinger 1990). Following Tilly (1978), we ask whether such community characteris-

---

[3]For excellent social histories from this period see Higham 1955, Saxton 1971, Walkowitz 1978, Hershberg 1981, Fink 1983, Bodnar et al. 1982, Ross 1985, and Gutman and Bell 1987.

tics might also affect mobilization and collective action. Here I draw a parallel between resource mobilization theories emphasizing the role of organizational resources and research on ethnic enclave communities as a type of resource (Sanders and Nee 1987). Ethnic enclaves might be considered as one empirical indicator of an ethnic population's organizational strength and potential for collective action. Above we argued that factors which increase ethnic competition raise ethnic consciousness and the salience of ethnic boundaries. According to resource mobilization theories, a rise in the salience of ethnic boundaries can be analyzed as a type of resource, a set of ready-made loyalties that groups and organizations can draw upon. So here we shift our causal analysis to see if ethnic collective action affects the formation of ethnic organizations.

The examining of ethnic organizations has been central to the study of ethnic enclaves and communities in social science.[4] The concept of ethnic enclave has proved difficult to define and even more difficult to measure. I follow Portes (1981: 291) who defines an *ethnic enclave* as "... consisting of immigrant groups which concentrate in a distinct spacial location and organize a variety of enterprises serving their own ethnic market and/or the general population. Their basic characteristic is that a significant proportion of the immigrant work force works in enterprises owned by other immigrants."

Others have emphasized the network quality of enclave communities. Such networks are marked by a high density of ties of marriage, exchange, and information. Information networks appear to have been dependent on the presence of ethnic newspapers (Park 1922; Olzak and West 1991). Other variations on the concept of enclave stress the coincidence of ethnicity and occupation (for example, Slavic mine workers constituting a large proportion of all mine workers in a city) or high concentration of ethnics within an industry (Light 1972). Drawing on these network imageries, Wilson and Martin (1982: 135, 138) have defined ethnic enclaves as "self-enclosed inner city minority communities" that have businesses that are "vertically and horizontally integrated."

The literature on ethnic enterprises and ethnic enclaves has several implications for our arguments about the salience of ethnic boundaries in multiethnic communities. An ethnic enclave lies at one end of a continuum representing the extent to which social organization of ethnic groups is marked by dense social interaction networks.[5] But whether

---

[4]For reviews of the literature on ethnic enterprises, see Waldinger et al. 1990, and Aldrich and Waldinger 1990.

[5]Although it is outside the scope of this research, a lively debate exists about the

or not ethnic enclaves become financially successful, they do tend to reinforce identification with cultural symbols in an ethnic community, such as language, customs, religion, and other practices. In the United States, the strength of ethnic identification depends upon continuing immigration, which acts as a replacement mechanism, even if assimilation rates are high (Portes and Bach 1984). As long as ethnic enclaves continue to replace members (through ongoing recruitment, immigration, or high rates of population expansion in the enclave), ethnic identity remains salient in a variety of interaction settings. So this research on enclaves suggest a hypothesis, that *immigration encourages the founding of ethnic organizations and enhances their persistence.*

Is there a relationship between the strength of an ethnic enclave and hostility toward that enclave? The answer is not immediately obvious. Solidary enclaves do not experience uniformly high rates of discrimination and hostility, nor do they automatically form organizations to protest for ethnic civil rights. For example, highly insular groups such as the Amish or Mennonites have received relatively little hostility, while violence directed against Chinese sojourners and Eastern European immigrants has been relatively common (Loewen 1988). Why would this be the case?

One answer is found in "middleman minority" formulations (Blalock 1967; Bonacich 1973). Middleman minorities are distinguished from other immigrant enclaves by their sojourner status and by their concentration in finance, commerce, and other jobs that mediate between producers and consumers (or employers and employees), such as labor contractors, rent collectors, and brokers. As was discussed in the previous chapter, Bonacich (1973) claims that such middleman minorities are commonly victims of prejudice, discrimination, and violent repression. When they are successful, they run the risk of competition with those groups above them in the status hierarchy. Such potential competition generates hostility and repression from elites. At the same time, those occupying the lower status positions also view success of middlemen minorities with resentment and hostility. Bonacich argues (1973: 592) that such conditions cause violence against successful middleman enclaves to escalate:

The difficulty of breaking entrenched middleman monopolies, the difficulty of

---

impact of enclave participation for individual members. The development of ethnic enterprises that have clients outside the ethnic community appears to be crucial in determining whether an ethnic enclave community enhances the economic success of their members. For reviews and debates about the impact of ethnic enclave economies on individual life chances see Light 1972, Wilson and Portes 1980, Wilson and Martin 1982, Portes and Bach 1985, Sanders and Nee 1987, and Portes and Jensen 1987.

controlling the growth and extension of their economic power, pushes host countries to even more extreme reactions. One finds increasingly harsh measures, piled on one another, until, when all else fails, 'final solutions' are enacted.

This book explores these ideas by examining whether ethnic conflict affects the growth and decline of ethnic organizations. One strategy for analyzing the persistence of ethnic boundaries is to investigate the organizational life cycle of growth, expansion, and decline within ethnic boundaries. Competition theory predicts that rates of ethnic collective action rise during the expansion stage. This stage encourages ethnic collective action because two processes interact. First, ethnic identity is strong and remains a crucial determinant of an individual's role in productive activities, residence, and other networks. Second, economic expansion beyond enclave boundaries increases levels of competition with other ethnic populations (at the firm, group, or individual level). Enclaves performing at peak levels expand, unless they encounter successful repression. Expansion creates the conditions leading to their decline and perhaps eventual dissolution (depending on replacement rates). In anticipation of our empirical analysis in Chapter 10, we test hypotheses about expansion and growth using data on ethnic newspapers to measure organizational growth and decline in ethnic communities.

Resource mobilization theory, rational choice theories of group solidarity, and research on social movements underscore the importance of specifying theoretically how incentives, resources, and organization combine with changing levels of niche overlap to produce ethnic collective action. As Tilly (1978) has argued, the occurrence (and nonoccurrence) of a collective event is a transitory phenomenon, involving movement between stages (or states) of mobilization and nonactivity. It is clear that mobilization for ethnic collective action does not automatically occur with the addition of each new nationality to a population. Mobilization depends upon (1) the *incentives* (and the changes in costs and benefits) attached to mobilization along ethnic lines, compared to mobilization along some other lines, or nonactivity (Hechter, Friedman, and Appelbaum 1982; Opp 1988), (2) the *resources* amassed by ethnic populations, including the distribution of income relative to other and majority-population groups, membership size, information networks, and (3) degree of *organization,* including levels of hierarchy, leadership, and success of former mobilizations.[6]

---

[6]Attempts to test rational choice theories with empirical data on participation in social movements have met with varying levels of success, in part because of measurement problems in assessing measurement of selective incentives, monitoring capacity, and other key theoretical variables (see the discussion in Hechter

Mobilization theories suggest that theoretical links among organizational potential of a population and enclave status might be useful in measuring solidarity. That is, both resource mobilization and rational choice theories emphasize the importance of measuring solidarity and collective action independently, as we discussed in Chapter 2. If ethnic enclaves represent a type of ethnic resource available for leaders and movements, then resource mobilization arguments suggest a proposition linking these ideas: *Ethnic communities which experience more ethnic collective action will be more likely to form ethnic organizations than communities with less collective action based on ethnic and racial boundaries.*

Increases in Ethnic-Group Resources. Related causes of increased ethnic competition in labor markets are factors that increase the resources available to an ethnic population. Examples of increases are upward shifts in educational attainment, reduction in barriers to participation in the political system (e.g., the extension of voting rights), or legal changes forcing a redistribution of opportunities. Increases in resources for disadvantaged ethnics tend to be viewed as a threat by advantaged populations. More advantaged groups view each advancement of groups below them as a threat to their position.[7] This argument implies a relationship between upward mobility for a disadvantaged minority and the likelihood of ethnic collective action.

One way in which disadvantaged groups gain resources is by moving out of segregated occupations with low wages. Ethnic competition thus increases following desegregation in labor markets (Portes 1984). An earlier literature, which referred to this process as ethnic assimilation (Gordon 1964), predicted that desegregation should reduce overall rates of ethnic conflict (Park 1950). I make the opposite prediction, at least for the initial stages of desegregation of ethnic labor markets: *rising advantage and rewards for disadvantaged ethnic populations increase levels*

1987). For empirical studies and simulation of payoff matrices in collective action, see Oliver 1984, Oliver, Marwell, and Texiera 1985, Oliver and Marwell 1988, and Opp 1988.

[7]This argument is consistent with classic relative deprivation theory. Yet classic relative deprivation arguments tend to emphasis that static conditions of inequality (in combination with future expectations) cause collective action. They also rely on individual-level arguments about perceptions of well-being. As Tilly noted some time ago, such individual-level data are nonexistent when studying most cases of collective action, and so are inferred most often *following* the occurrence of a revolution or revolt. Fortunately, competition arguments do not rest on evidence about individual attitudes or expectations. Instead, the structural argument offered here emphasizes the fact that it is *changes* in the opportunity structure that activate collective action.

of ethnic competition initially, leading to higher rates of ethnic collective action.

We have noted that competition intensifies when (1) economic contraction shrinks the available amount of resources to be divided, and (2) economic prosperity causes upward mobility among the very disadvantaged. Does this mean that the theory encompasses all instances of economic fluctuation, leaving only conditions of stability or unchanging equilibrium as a cause of ethnic and racial peace? A critic might reasonably complain that the theory loses meaning if it holds that both prosperity and depression cause conflict to rise.

Fortunately the contradiction is only apparent. Recall that the theory holds that rising competition is due to *niche overlap*. Economic contraction increases competitive relations among groups to the extent that barriers among groups decline. In this case, economic contraction represents an unfavorable change in economic well-being for those sharing a resource environment. But prosperity may encourage competition as well, as when a formerly disadvantaged ethnic group invades the niche of another group. In this case, competition arises as the result of differential rates of upward mobility. Thus prosperity which expands at the same rate for all groups in the system as a whole would have little or no effect on niche overlap and competition.

Political Competition and Racial Conflict. Some critics have claimed that competition theories have focused too narrowly on material interests and economic struggles (James 1988). They argue that changes in political contexts and structuring of political opportunities affect timing of challenges and success of challengers and contending groups. In the case of the historical period under consideration, some historians and social scientists hold that the political context of race conflict differed by region and period. For instance, political and economic forces in the South underwent turmoil during the late nineteenth and early twentieth centuries, characterized by both progressive and reactionary social movements. Initially, the progressive movement (especially the Farmers' Alliance) mobilized considerable biracial support throughout the rural South (Hahn 1983). Challenges to local and state monopolies enjoyed by the all-white Democratic party became more common. During the mid-1880s in the South (and later in the West), the progressive movement matured and found fleeting success as a national third party, the People's Party (Schwartz 1976).

These examples suggest that the monopoly of all-white Democratic rule in the South may have cast a particular racial shadow over any and all political challenges. More generally, they suggest that the political context of racial competition ought to be taken into account at the same time that economic contests are considered (James 1988). By this logic, we would expect that *periods of political challenges by third parties and other social movement organizations raise rates of collective action.*

Another facet of the political opportunity structure not often empirically analyzed involves the relationship between collective action and changes in laws and policies regarding race.[8] For instance, the passage of anti-immigrant laws from 1882 through 1924 is an example of highly successful political activity taken against immigrants and African-American migrants during this period. Initial mobilizations began on the West Coast against Chinese and Japanese in San Francisco and elsewhere (Saxton 1971; Nee and Nee 1986). Such movements culminated in the Asian Exclusion Act of 1882. The success of this effort was evidently taken as a model for subsequent exclusionary immigration laws and policies (Bennett 1988; Ichioka 1988).

Were these legal actions influenced by collective street actions? Some historians claim that they were undoubtedly related. Initially, conflicts against newcomers were spontaneous and public, as earlier immigrants harassed and attacked African-Americans, Chinese, and recent European immigrants in cities where they were concentrated (Bruce 1959; Jackson 1967; Saxton 1971; Nee and Nee 1986; and Olzak 1987). Later, native whites organized sophisticated political movements, often with a national scope, such as the Workingman's Association and the Immigration Restriction League (Garis 1927; Higham 1955; and Archdeacon 1983). These national social movements initially sought federal laws to end immigration from China. In 1924, a more general anti-immigration movement culminated in the passage of the National Origins Act, which restricted immigration by a system of national quotas (Keely 1979; Cafferty et al. 1983).

Certainly ethnic movements and governments were not the only political actors during the late nineteenth and early twentieth centuries. While some anti-immigrant movements formed new political organizations, others coopted existing ones.[9] A variety of organizations and

---

[8]Burstein's (1985) analysis of the relationship between public protest and the passage of civil rights laws is a notable exception.

[9]Many of these organizations formed a distinctly national social movement. According to Bennett, many anti-immigrant organizations of the 1880s were reconstituted from nativist groups founded decades earlier: "Henry Baldwin ... formed the National League for the Protection of American Institutions, and he organized conferences for 'executive officers of the patriotic societies of the United States ... The records of these meetings suggest the range of groups assembling under the old banners of the anti-alien crusade. To Morton House came representatives of the Order of the United American Sons of America, the Order of the United Americans, the

groups exhibiting exclusionary tactics based on ethnic or race boundaries competed with American nativist and racist political organizations
during this period. Such organizations should also be considered part of
the political environment. For instance, national labor unions played a
central role in anti-immigration activity, as many bitter labor conflicts
attest (Yellen 1936). Because these issues are complicated, the causal
relationships among the various factors require close attention in the
analysis which follows. For example, while expansion of the labor force
encouraged immigration, prosperity and expansion also encouraged the
founding of national labor unions during this period (Hannan and Freeman 1987). While some cases in the historical record show how that
national labor unions recruited and received strong support from various ethnic populations, as can be seen in the German names of some
unions (Fink 1977), other unions participated vigorously in lobbying and
campaigns designed to restrict further immigration (Garis 1927). Labor
union histories make clear that increasing immigration was sometimes
met with swift and vocal resistance by national unions, most notably
those in the American Federation of Labor. For some white and native-
born workers and for white immigrants arriving prior to 1880, national
unions were seen as organizations designed to protect their economic
self-interest (Commons 1918; Gompers 1925). Exercising this protection often meant that union policies also discriminated against distinct
racial or ethnic immigrants because it was usually African-Americans
and immigrants who were willing to work for lower than the prevailing
wages (Gompers 1925; Foner 1982). For these reasons we expect that
growth of labor organizations raise rates of ethnic collective action.

Contagion and Exhaustion

Theories of collective action have long suggested that collective action
of all kinds follows a dynamic process of growth and decline. A variety
of arguments about the diffusion of events suggest that a wide variety of
collective actions cause imitative behaviors so that events spread rapidly
across locations (Lieberson and Silverman 1965; Spilerman 1971; Hamblin, Jacobsen, and Miller 1973). Beginning with Durkheim's analysis
of social disorganization in the late nineteenth century, sociologists have
been intrigued with the idea that social movements come in recurrent

---

United American Mechanics, The Patriotic Order of Sons of America ... the Red,
White and Blue Organization ('Red to Protect Protestantism, White to Protect the
Purity of the Ballot Box, Blue Against the Domination of Dictation by Foreign Citizens') ... Big or small, old or new, most of them called for concerted action to 'crush
the foreign elements' that had invaded the country." (Bennett 1988: 170).

waves. Recent analyses of protest and social movements have investigated "cycles" or waves of conflict (Tarrow 1988a).

As early as 1900, there is convincing evidence that details of various race riots spread rapidly across regions in the United States. Newspapers were evidently a key source of such contagion, intensifying fears and tensions of police authorities as well as ordinary residents. In her study of the 1908 race riot in Springfield, Illinois, Roberta Senechal (1990: 191) discusses how the process of contagion affected racial tensions:

As a northern writer warned, 'the conditions in Springfield are not peculiar to that city. Almost every community in the country is face to face with the same possibilities. A mob may form in an hour.' (*Chicago Record-Herald*, August 30, 1908). For a brief time there was speculation that Springfield's riot had sparked a 'contagion' of violent antiblack incidents. Newspapers reported numerous smaller, but potentially volatile, outbreaks of interracial violence in a number of northern communities late in the summer of 1908 ... soon city authorities in places like St. Louis and Chicago called up police reserves to prevent 'sympathetic race riots', as they termed them.

There were also widespread suspicions that contagion affected the eruption of race riots during the 1960s (United States National Advisory Commission on Civil Disorders 1968). A wide variety of sociological studies examined the occurrence, participation, and spread of race riots across (mostly urban) America during the 1960s (McPhail and Wohlstein 1983; Olzak 1983). This research informed theoretical debates about causes of civil unrest. The findings challenged the conventional wisdom that economic hardship, poverty, and relative and absolute deprivation increase the probability of race riot. Instead, the proportion of nonwhites in a community appeared to be the most important predictor of riots (Lieberson and Silverman 1965; Spilerman 1970, 1971, and 1976).

In examining the spread of riots, rebellions, and other disturbances, information on the timing and sequences of events became particularly important. For instance, Paige (1971), Spilerman (1970, 1971), and McPhail and Wohlstein (1983) suggest that riots in particular spread rapidly across communication networks. Some have also suggested that geographical contagion of unrest may also be important in the contagion or diffusion of riot disturbances (Spilerman 1970, 1976).[10] On the basis of these studies, it appears that investigation of the intersection of social geography and diffusion holds promise for examining how proximity affects contagion in a wide variety of cases (Markoff 1985).

---

[10]Doreian (1981) provides an example of spatial contagion involving rebellions. He found that spatial autocorrelation affected estimates of factors causing local variations in participation in the Huk rebellion in the Philippines.

A process of diffusion might induce links between the rates of occurrence of different types of racial violence. Yet, few studies have compared rates of various *forms* of conflict or *regional variations* in violence against the same ethnic/racial target. Such comparisons can speak to the generalizability of sociological theories across time and place. For instance, we know that lynching declined after the 1930s but that collective actions in the forms of riots and other intimidation did not (Kelly and Isaac 1984; McAdam 1982). Does this mean that they are different forms of collective action? Or does it mean that some other process, which also varied over time, caused lynching to decline and urban violence to rise? One possibility, considered here, is that urban and rural, and southern and northern violence against African-Americans are instances of the same process.

There also appears to be a ceiling on contagion processes. After some (large) number of events have occurred, the process declines. Why this decline occurs is not well understood, although some have suggested that exhaustion, increase in social control and repression of events, or political cooptation of participants (and their leaders) may be responsible (Obershall 1978; Kelly and Isaac 1984). The research reported in this book develops a new approach to conceptualizing and analyzing processes of contagion in collective action. It regards contagion as a source of time dependence in rates of occurrence of events and estimates parametric models of such time dependence. We expect that time dependence affects rates of ethnic conflicts and protests such that *rates of ethnic collective action decline with the passage of time since the previous event.*

Conclusion

Race and ethnic conflict erupts when the level of ethnic and racial competition in a social system intensifies. I identified four processes as instrumental in raising levels of ethnic and racial competition: migration and immigration, economic contraction, segregation and dispersion from niches, and increasing prosperity for the disadvantaged ethnics. To these mostly economic factors we have also added two other factors which emphasize the dynamic nature of ethnic conflict: the occurrence of political struggles and challenges, and diffusion of events over time and across regions. We turn first to analyses of these processes at the national level.

4

Analysis of Events in the
Study of Collective Action

Sociologists interested in the causes of social movements and their success or failure have long considered natural histories of movements and revolutions, profiles of activists, and catalogues of grievances. Recently, spurred mainly by Charles Tilly's pathbreaking research, they have begun to focus on the rate of occurrence of collective events. In order to motivate the methods used in this book, this chapter reviews and evaluates methods for using information on events—especially their timing and sequences—to analyze social movements and collective action.[1]

Event analysis has an extremely broad scope. Studies of conflicts have included race riots (Spilerman 1970), strikes and industrial protests (Aminzade 1984), political violence (Tilly, Tilly, and Tilly 1975), peasant rebellions (Paige 1975), revolutionary activity (Markoff 1986), lynchings (Inverarity 1976), and coups d'état (Hannan and Carroll 1981). Studies of protest have considered African-American civil rights' protests (McAdam 1982), marches against nuclear power plants (Walsh and Warland 1983), Québecois separatist demonstrations (Olzak 1982), union organizing of farm workers (Jenkins and Perrow 1977), protests by American Indians (Nagel 1988), and social protests in Italy (Tarrow 1988b).

Event analysis treats the occurrence of collective actions and evidence that a social movement exists as variable and open to empirical examination. This stance anticipates the possibility that events might occur after a revolution had ended or before a social movement sup-

---

[1] Jenkins (1983), Marwell and Oliver (1984), Zald and McCarthy (1987), Tarrow (1988a), and McAdam, McCarthy and Zald (1988) provide recent substantive reviews of theory and research on collective action.

posedly begins. This strategy stands in contrast to traditional ones that analyze social movements only within conventional temporal boundaries defined by the history of some movement or revolution.

Event analysis allows diverse forms of collective action to be measured and compared because observations are collected in commensurate dimensions. Thus information about revolutions consisting of thousands of acts of violence and about one-time confrontations are enumerated and described in terms of number of participants, duration of unrest, magnitude of violence, and other characteristics. This feature of the strategy is important because it permits cases of unsuccessful and/or short-lived movements to be compared with instances of successful and long-lived ones. It also allows stages that emerge during collective actions to be analyzed as a sequence of different kinds of events rather than as one continuous action. In short, the strategy of studying events uses more information about the dynamics of change in social movements than strategies that treat movements as unitary phenomena.

The Development of Event Analysis

Event analysis took shape during the 1960s in research on variation among countries in collective violence and on causes of race riots. Subsequent advances in methods for analyzing historical and time-ordered data on events have increased the power of event analysis and encouraged research on classic questions about the influence of timing and organizational dynamics on rates of collective action.

Brief History of Event Analysis. Cross-national research on collective violence in the 1960s related annual counts of events to economic, political, and other structural variables to learn whether peak periods of economic hardship were peak periods of unrest. These studies developed formalized rules for coding information on collective events using records from archives, newspapers, historical documents, and police or magistrate records (Taylor and Jodice 1983). They also produced data banks that allowed researchers to compare effects of structural and political variables on classes of events among nations and over historical periods (Rule and Tilly 1965; Feierabend and Feierabend 1966). During this period, research moved beyond description and categorization of stages in conflicts to analyze causes of unrest. This shift had two important consequences. First, use of event counts opened up the possibility that diverse social science methods could be used to analyze questions about social movements. Second, the substantive findings informed theoretical debates about social upheavals. In particular, theories of social protest that highlighted mechanisms of relative deprivation and social disorganization unraveled once they were subjected to empirical scrutiny (Snyder and Tilly 1972; Rule and Tilly 1972; Tilly, Tilly, and Tilly 1975; Tilly 1981; Weede 1987).

A concurrent line of research related demographic and socioeconomic characteristics of communities to counts of race riots. This research also informed theoretical debates about civil unrest. The findings challenged the assumption that communities experiencing greatest economic hardship, poverty, and relative and absolute deprivation were most likely to experience race riots (Lieberson and Silverman 1965; Wanderer 1969; Eisinger 1973; Spilerman 1976; McPhail and Wohlstein 1983).

Motivations for Event Analysis. Choice of a method for analyzing data on collective action depends upon a researcher's purpose. If the goals involve testing generalizable theories with replicable evidence as in this book, then event analysis has several potential advantages. First, as noted above, event analysis can use statistical techniques and models that have been useful in other subfields of sociology and other sciences. Hypotheses can be tested and models can be compared on their relative merits (Spilerman 1971; Paige 1975). Although case studies provide rich detail and historical background, they rarely provide systematic evidence appropriate for testing hypotheses.

For example, in studies investigating the causes of events,[2] social scientists commonly study only places that have collective events. For instance, Wanderer's (1969) analysis of riot severity used data only for cities that had race riots, thereby ignoring characteristics of cities that did not have a riot and sidestepping the question of why riots occurred. Sampling on the dependent variable, as in these examples, confounds causal interpretation because (by definition) some observations have been excluded from analysis based upon their levels on the dependent variable (success or not, participation or not). Any attempt to infer causal relationships will be crippled by sample selection bias (Heckman 1979; Berk 1983).

Sample selection bias has often been confused with the issue of representativeness of samples. They are not the same. For example, data on events occurring in Utah may be questioned on the grounds that the sample is not a random one and because Utah is not representative of other geographical regions. If the goal is to estimate some mean number of events in the country as a whole, then using this sample will cause problems. If the goal is to estimate the effects of some covariates on the rate of activity, the estimates from such a sample may be unbiased. This is because nonrepresentativeness hampers one's ability to estimate

---

[2]See Skocpol 1979 for an example. Further debates over this issue can be found in Skocpol and Somers 1980, and Tilly 1981, 1984.

population means and variances but does not necessarily affect estimates of structural parameters, for example, effects of covariates on the rates. Sample selection bias, on the other hand, means that a sample has been chosen based upon some value of the dependent variable, and effects of covariates on the rates will be biased unless appropriate corrections are applied (Heckman 1979).

Thus an important motivation for event analysis is to avoid sample selection bias. Research designs in event analysis, like the one used in this book, avoid sample selection bias by including cities with and without racial conflicts (Spilerman 1970). Event history allows the researcher to examine an entire historical period that is not defined by the occurrence (or nonoccurrence) of events. This is in contrast to analysts who study revolutions, strikes, or some other social movement activity, where the occurrence of some event determines the temporal boundaries of the study.

Furthermore, case studies of social movements normally do not exploit information on timing and sequences of events. The form of event analysis used in this book, event-history analysis, does analyze such information. This is particularly important in studying processes of geographical and temporal contagion in the spread of riots, rebellions, and other disturbances.

Restricting research to a priori temporal units of revolution, civil war, or social movements may miss much variation in activity over time and over regions. For instance, Tilly, Tilly, and Tilly (1975) show that the number of collective disturbances in France has three peaks during 1830–1930: disruptions of the revolution of 1830, strikes around 1900 and social unrest during the 1930s. What surprised even the authors was that the three peaks contained comparable numbers of violent events. Apparently other "revolutions" of equal significance occurred in addition to that of 1830.

Event analysis also allows empirical investigation of changes in forms of collective action. For example, Tilly's (1986) analysis of French contentious gatherings reveals that the scope of collective actions was transformed over a hundred years from local to national. This approach also allows forms of conflict to be analyzed separately by target and violence, facilitating examination of similarities and differences in effects of covariates on types of events. In other words, claims that causes of various types of collective action differ can be examined empirically rather than assumed. In the chapters that follow, we pay close attention to shifts in the forms of ethnic/racial protests over time.

Another source of the increasing popularity of event analysis is its flexibility in using different levels of spatial aggregation (see Doreian

1981). Events have been studied as products of groups, neighborhoods, electoral districts, export sectors, and nation-states. Consider the case of American race riots during the 1960s. Stark et al. (1974) focused on geographical spread during one year of race rioting over census tracts of one city, Los Angeles. Spilerman (1970) analyzed data on the annual occurrence of riots in numerous cities in order to learn whether characteristics of cities affect the probability of a riot. Still others analyzed yearly counts of riots for the United States as a whole in order to learn whether they fluctuated with variation in the national political and economic environment (Kelly and Isaac 1984).

The occurrence of strikes, riots, attacks, or revolutionary activities are usually taken as evidence that the system is not in equilibrium, that relationships among actors and institutions are fundamentally shifting. One implication of this assumption is that methods that assume static equilibrium or even moving equilibrium states of some unit of analysis are inappropriate when applied to collective action.[3] For instance, in Chapter 3, arguments by Spilerman and others were reviewed that whether or not a city experienced race riots changes its calculus of racial unrest (and affects other causal factors as well) in fundamental ways. It is useful to test this idea directly, with "process" models that can take such disequilibrium hypotheses into account. Why not take these shifts directly into account? As Tuma and Hannan (1984: Chapter 1) point out, though most social theorists now reject assumptions of equilibrium when analyzing social change, methods of analysis that assume static properties or invariant sets of causal relationships are still commonplace. Fortunately, event-history methods have been developed and applied recently to use information on the timing and occurrence of events, allowing us to consider the kinds of abrupt changes implied by the processes of collective action.

Another reason for preferring event analysis is somewhat related to this disequilibrium problem. Event analysis facilitates empirical investigation of "cycles" or waves of protest because it takes the sequence of events directly into account. Beginning with Durkheim's analyses of social disorganization, the idea that social movements come in recurrent patterns has intrigued social scientists (Tarrow 1988a). For example, if, in a particular city or region, the experience of having had a riot, or coup, or revolution significantly alters the likelihood of future unrest, then static models are inherently deficient in capturing the history of the process. Others have claimed that long periods without conflict

---

[3]For an expanded and more technical version of this argument, see Tuma and Hannan 1984: Chapters 1 and 10.

equally affect the likelihood of future stability. Both sides of contagion are worth investigating here. Although waves, cycles, and episodes serve as a core concepts in theories of collective behavior (Turner and Killian 1957), few researchers have directly analyzed such patterns, beyond simple time-series graphs which show peaks and declines in action. Hamblin, Jacobsen, and Miller (1973) suggested that mathematical models of contagion could be applied to analysis of diffusion of collective events. Only Spilerman (1971) and Olzak (1987) have estimated stochastic processes of contagion of events of collective action.

Definitions in Event Analysis

Conceptual Definitions. Events analyzed in this tradition are commonly defined as nonroutine, collective, and public acts that involve claims on behalf of a larger collective (Paige 1975; Tilly 1978). Thus a minimal definition of collective action is that it (1) involves more than one person and (2) makes claims of agency (or corporate) status. Tilly's (1978) list of claims includes petitioning, memorializing, and opposition or support of an enemy of the government. Tilly (1978: 275) defines agency status as involving acts that "make a visible claim which, if realized, would affect the interests of some specific person(s) or group(s) outside their own number."

Should social movements and events be defined independently? If so, what should be the distinguishing criteria? According to the minimal definition, social movements and collective actions are separable. social movements are "a group of people identified by their attachment to some particular set of beliefs" (Tilly 1978: 9). Conceptual definitions of collective actions normally do not require the presence of shared beliefs among actors. However, some researchers stipulate that collective actions involve groups with pre-existing solidarity (for example, Paige 1975: 90).[4] Others implicitly assume that solidarity is necessary for the types of collective actions they have analyzed, but leave open the issue of whether solidarity is necessary in other instances.

Some researchers also stipulate that collective action be noninstitutional (Paige 1975), while others take this position implicitly by limiting analysis to actions instigated by challenging groups that are "countercultural" or that have little formal power (Kriesi 1988). Perhaps because it implies a process, institutionalization has proved to be difficult to operationalize. Groups that have already gained acceptance in the political arena are thus often excluded from analysis of social movements

---

[4]Paige's (1975: 87, 390) motivation for including solidarity was to therefore exclude collective behaviors such as "panics, mass movements of refugees, crazes ..."

and collective action. Lowi (1971) provided a rationale for this practice, claiming that social movement organizations that succeed in establishing routinized and stable ties with a government agency have been transformed into interest groups. In this view, strikes by most labor unions are now actions of interest groups, not social movements (Snyder 1975). Using Lowi's criterion, actions of some "countermovements," could be excluded, despite the fact that research on them has illuminated ways that members of groups with access to power sometimes form significant social movements. Examples include studies of the pro-nuclear power movement (Useem and Zald 1982), the anti-abortion movement (McCarthy 1987), and coups d'état by dissatisfied army units (Feierabend and Feierabend 1966).

Tilly takes a different tack. He defines collective action to (potentially) include actions of all contenders, including both "members," who are those who have "routine, low-cost access to resources controlled by the government," and "challengers," who are other contenders (Tilly 1978: 52).

If, as Tilly suggests, both members of the polity and outsiders can conduct social movements, then we should analyze transformations of outsiders into members of the polity as events in the life histories of social movements. Such analysis requires attention to the boundaries that separate insiders from outsiders. But there is disagreement about whether institutionalization of social movements belongs in the study of collective action. Some researchers argue for excluding institutional behavior because it concerns elite activity rather than spontaneous grassroots mobilization (Jenkins and Perrow 1977; McAdam 1982). Others think that it is unreasonable to truncate observations on social movement organizations at the point when they gain access to the political arena. Such exclusion assumes that institutionalization is a one-way process and ignores the fact that some established groups become delegitimated and excluded from the polity. Excluding institutional action from studies of collective action by definition makes it impossible to address a fundamental sociological process: how charismatic movements become routinized and institutionalized over time.

If we add institutional activities to the list of potential collective actions, we face the prospect that the concept encompasses virtually all social behavior including everyday actions such as business conferences, professional meetings, and church assemblies. Tilly's (1978) emphasis on excluding routine activity has been a key solution to reduce the scope. There are often good reasons to exclude anniversary marches or annual celebrations since their timing is pre-determined and not spontaneous. Researchers also usually exclude routine congressional activities, court sessions, political party conventions, and regular government activity from the concept of collective action (Burstein 1985). According to Tilly's guideline, routine church activities would not be coded as events, but nonroutine actions of church members participating in civil rights marches under the leadership of a minister might be.

The minimalist definition of collective events has advantages over definitions that include dimensions such as size, noninstitutional, violence, and political orientation as defining features of collective action. Relaxing the requirement that collective action involves self-conscious identity, solidarity, or shared sentiment allows researchers to examine whether solidarity affects rates of collective action. In contrast, enumerating only events that reflect solidarity vitiates the possibility of studying the effects of variations in solidarity. It renders tautological the key claim of resource-mobilization theory, that solidarity affects collective action.

For these various reasons the research reported in this book uses a minimalist definitions of events, so that the effects of solidarity, institutionalization, and other dimensions can be examined empirically.

Operational Definitions. At what size does an event becomes collective? The answer varies widely among studies and type of event. Most researchers choose a minimum in the range of 10 to 20; Tilly (1978) proposed a minimum of 50. I have used a minimum of two participants for several reasons. First, events mobilizing fewer than 10 persons constituted nearly 8% of all events reported in the daily *New York Times* accounts. City population and scale of social movement organizations were smaller in 1880 than today, suggesting why gatherings that made ethnic claims involving even three or four persons in the *New York Times* were reported, often on page 1. To examine this hypothesis, we investigated a wide variety of alternative sources of ethnic events, including historical case studies, local newspapers, and labor newspapers to see if the *New York Times* systematically ignored events of fewer than 50 persons. To our surprise, we found the *New York Times* to show no such bias, and we conclude that it is more complete than any alternative sources of collective actions over this period.

Nevertheless, nearly all sources of data often lack information on exact numbers. My research group learned that daily accounts of ethnic protests in the *New York Times* provide reliable counts of participants for only about half of the events. Fortunately, newspaper reports nearly always contain key phrases such as "small group of hooligans" and "large crowd" that indicate approximate size categories.

Decisions about temporal boundaries of events are especially complicated. When does one event stop and a new one begin when events are closely spaced in time? Following Paige (1975) and Tilly (1978), I judge a new event to have begun if activity resumes after a pause of at least 24 hours in a locale. Otherwise, activity of more or less continuous actions by the same group is considered as one event. This rule has proved particularly useful in untangling a report from the occurrence of an event. Such problems plague those who have used only the index as a sole source of data, where multiple events are often summarized in one article under one event's (or one city's) listing. Approximately 10% of our events were embedded in articles about similar events in different cities, or similar events in the same city presumably leading up to one main event.

Is the event the appropriate unit? Marwell and Oliver (1984) argue that "collective campaigns" are more useful units for the study of collective action than are events. Certainly the concept of campaign can be useful, as in the case of the civil rights movement in which marches carried across state boundaries. However, the concept of campaign also faces serious problems. When does an event become a campaign? This would be a problem for an abortive campaign, or an isolated event that began as a campaign but failed. And finally, when does a campaign end? Just as smaller geographical units are more easily aggregated to larger entities than vice-versa (Markoff and Shapiro 1973), a strategy of analysis (rather than measurement) that specifies how to link events that make up a campaign may be more useful than one that begins with observations on campaigns. Moreover, collapsing brief episodes of many events into one campaign makes the occurrence of many small events indistinguishable from one uninterrupted protest. Such a coding strategy makes it difficult to discover cycles of protests.

Ethnic/racial violence features prominently in the theories reviewed in the previous chapter. Exactly what constitutes a violent event? And whose violence provides the benchmark—protestors, police, or outsiders, or all three? Tilly (1978: 248) defines a violent event as "an instance of mutual and collective coercion within an autonomous political system which seizes or physically damages persons or objects" (Tilly 1978: 248). Because this book analyzes ethnic collective action in general, the extent of violence in my data is considered as a variable rather than as a defining feature of the events. The data suggest that actual deployment of violence during this period was far less common than its presence as a threat to others. In particular, shootings, bombings, and killings were rare, while glass, bricks, fire, and physical violence was commonly used to threaten victims.[5] So I treat events as violent if weapons or attacks are used merely to threaten property or persons.

Data and Measurement

Sources and Methods of Data Collection. Collection of information on timing of events, participants, targets, and violence relies increasingly on (1) official archival records, such as police records and municipal records of arrests and/or deaths from civil unrest (Tilly, Tilly, and Tilly 1975), (2) annual newspaper indexes (Spilerman 1970; McAdam 1982; Burstein 1985; Jenkins and Eckert 1986), (3) daily newspaper accounts (Paige 1975), (4) published listings of events originally compiled from various newspaper sources, for example, the widely used data on strikes in the United States (Griffin 1939; United States Bureau of the Census 1975), lynchings (NAACP 1919; United States Bureau of the Census 1975), and political turmoil (Taylor and Jodice 1983), and (5) organizational histories in newsletters or other secondary historical accounts (Griffin 1939; Hannan and Freeman 1988; McCarthy et al. 1988).

Much research on collective action, like that reported in this book, has come to rely primarily on newspaper reports in part because such sources can be followed forward in time and because at least some researchers have found that newspapers provide the most complete account of events for the widest sample of geographical or temporal units (Tilly, Tilly, and Tilly 1975: 16). Research on the United States has treated the *New York Times* (hereafter *NYT*) as a source for the entire country and much of the debate has focused on the *NYT*.

Reliance on newspapers as a primary source of data has its critics. The most common criticism leveled at this approach is the suspicion that the data contain some systematic biases (Johnson, Sears, and McConahay 1971; Chermesh 1982; Franzosi 1987). For example, Danzger (1975) finds that the location of UPI and AP wire offices affected coverage of riots in the *NYT*. Kielbowicz and Schere (1986) claim that more violent, larger, or longer events are more likely to be covered in newspapers and that coverage affects subsequent events. Unfortunately there is rarely a way to evaluate these claims directly since few alternative sources contain as much information. However, Snyder and Kelly's (1977) analysis comparing coverage in local and national newspapers shed light on these issues. They compared accounts of riots in daily *NYT* accounts

---

[5]In analysis of a later period of ethnic and racial conflict we have hypothesized that deployment of weapons in collective actions escalates to the extent that ethnic and racial groups challenge state authority (especially local police) (Olzak and West 1989).

with those from local newspapers in 43 U.S. cities, 1965–69. They found that the location of offices of major wire services was not related to the likelihood that an event in a local newspaper would be reported in the *NYT*, but that conflict intensity, measured in terms of size, violence and duration of an event did. So Snyder and Kelly (1977) recommended that some threshold of the number of participants in events should be used, or that events of similar intensity should be analyzed separately when using data from the *NYT*. For problems related to geographical bias that arise when for instance, only the *NYT* is used, Franzosi (1987) suggests that some alternative source—preferably a local newspaper—be used as a comparison. However, the *NYT* remains the most complete source of data on events, according to analyses that compared coverage in the *NYT* with the Los Angeles Times and other West Coast newspapers for data on collective actions that occurred only on the West Coast (Jenkins and Perrow 1977).

An important difference among studies that code newspaper data concerns reliance on a newspaper's annual index or daily accounts. Most studies of race riots and civil rights activity used only an annual index, usually from the *NYT* (Spilerman 1970; McAdam 1982; Burstein 1985; Jenkins and Eckert 1986). This approach has several drawbacks. Even a quick perusal of the *NYT Index* shows that an event can be easily confused with a "report." For example, in practice it is hard to distinguish the *NYT* index entry of "Miami riots" from these alternative "events": (a) editorial comments on one or more riots, (b) subsequent stages of the same riot, (c) political speeches on a previous riot, or (d) follow-up reports such as arrests, court trials, demonstrations following arrests (Olzak and West 1987). Moreover, the actual timing of an event usually cannot be inferred from the Index, which is a crucial defect when using event-history analysis. Finally, reading and coding a full account of a set of similar events is necessary for learning how or even if events are linked.

It is useful to consider the trade-offs between the costs of additional coding of microfilms and the ease of coding the annual indexes. What is the price paid for consulting only the *New York Times Index*? My research group found that about one-half of all events would be either miscoded, or missed completely, if the index were the sole source. In almost no cases are the number of participants or the duration of events recorded in the index. Sometimes the title is misleading and needs further clarification.[6] An example of how easily events could be missed comes from the *New York Times Index* in 1891 which refers to an

---

[6]A more humorous example occurred in our coding of ethnic events during the

article about New Orleans dated March 15, 1891 titled "Chief Hennessy Avenged." Without consulting the daily microfilms, no additional information about this event exists. Using our two-stage method, we first uncovered a series of candidate events, beginning with the murder of the police chief by supposedly Italian assailants in March of 1891. Only after consulting the daily accounts for several weeks around the murder did we learn that an article title "Chief Hennessy Avenged" described an ethnic lynching by a mob of 50 persons, in which violent anti-Italian rioting continued for at least six hours, ending with the storming of the city jail and the lynching of 11 Italian prisoners (March 15, 1891, *New York Times*, p. 1, columns 5–7). Without searching through the daily accounts, this lynching would have been omitted from our data.

Based on these findings, my research uses an index only as a guide to the daily accounts, suggesting candidate events and periods of unrest. Master lists from an index are sorted by date, location, and event-type, to eliminate redundancies.[7]

Varieties of Event Analysis: Research Designs

Four research designs have dominated studies of counts in collective events: (1) *cross-sectional designs* record occurrences of events in one period for multiple units, as in Paige's (1975) study of peasant rebellions in agricultural export sectors; (2) *time-series designs* record occurrences of events by period for a single unit, as in Snyder and Tilly's (1972) analysis of collective violence in France from 1830 to 1930; (3) *panel designs* (or time-series/cross-section designs) record occurrences for multiple units in two or more periods, as Spilerman's (1976) analysis of race riots among cities and over time; and (4) *event-history designs* record the exact timing and sequence of events, as in McCarthy et al.'s (1988) study of founding rates of anti-drunk driving organizations.

A central research question in event analysis is how much to aggregate data on events over time and place. Table 4.1 classifies the four designs according to degree of aggregation by time and place. Cross-sectional designs aggregate completely over time and single time-series designs aggregate completely over geographical units. In the context of event analysis, this means it records the total number of events in a study period for each locality. Time-series designs record the total num-

---

recent period of American history in which a *New York Times* listing of "race conflict" was found to be an argument between two men over the outcome of a horse race.

[7]This is a problem since the *NYT Index* lists events under multiple headings but several riots can occur on one day in a city. Using the index makes it impossible to distinguish whether two reports having the same date, location, and event type refer to the same or different events.

TABLE 4.1

Classification of Approaches Used in Event Analysis

Data Structure	Non-process Orientation	Process Orientation
Cross section: complete temporal aggregation	Classical regression (Paige 1975) Logit regression[a] (Markoff 1985, McAdam 1986)	Poisson modeling (Spilerman 1970, Goldstone 1980)
Single time series: complete spatial aggregation	Time-series regression (Snyder 1975, Jenkins & Eckert 1986)	Time-series regression with lagged dep var (Hibbs 1976, Kelly & Issac 1984) Poisson regression (Hannan & Freeman 1989)
Time series/cross section: partial aggregation	Two-wave panel with lagged dep var used as a control (Muller 1985, Weede 1987)	Panel analysis used to estimate dynamic process (Spilerman 1976, Olzak 1982)
Event History: exact timing		Single point process (Olzak 1987) Models of transition rates: multiple units (Hannan & Carroll 1981, McCarthy et al. 1988 Liebman et al. 1988)

[a]Logit regression can also be considered as process oriented. See text.

ber of events over all localities for each period (which means that there is some temporal aggregation). Panel designs involve less aggregation on either dimension because they record event counts for each unit for each period. Event-history designs retain exact information on timing of events and locale. Readers should note that the classification into four categories is a heuristic device; both aggregation dimensions are really continual. Events can be aggregated in time to construct a single count for each locale (for example, Paige 1975), or aggregated to yearly counts for multiple locales (for example, Muller 1985), or not aggregated at all, retaining the actual dates of events (Olzak 1987). The same general point holds for spatial aggregation, although at least some aggregation into geographical units is usually necessary if independent variables are included in the analysis.

Analyses of data on collective events vary along a second dimension:

choice of an underlying probability model. For event counts, the main choices have been between (1) classical regression models which assume a normal distribution and (2) discrete-state stochastic process models. Most research on events uses the former. However, data on event counts have two characteristics that make the assumption of normality suspect. Event counts are non-negative and discrete. Estimation techniques that assume a normal distribution have been used more as a convenience than because they were appropriate. Now that software for estimating discrete-state stochastic process models are widely available, reliance on techniques based on normal distribution theory is likely to diminish.

Most previous research on the occurrence of collective events has used models that assume that the outcome is a continuous variable with a normal distribution. As noted above, counts of events, such as riots and revolutions, often have quite discontinuous distributions. Moreover, counts are by definition non-negative, and this restriction is inconsistent with the assumption of a normal distribution. Indeed, taking account of this constraint is important in analysis of counts of collective events because observed counts of zero are common. While counted data never strictly satisfy the assumptions of non-negativity and continuity, this does not make much practical difference when counts are large, as in the case of number of strikes per year in the United States.

Numerous studies of collective action use classical normal distribution theory methods to estimate the effects of community characteristics on variations in numbers of events at the community level. In cross-sectional applications this involves relating constant community characteristics to frequencies of events, aggregated over time to produce a total count for each community. This approach has been used in studies of strikes (Britt and Galle 1974; Lincoln 1978), lynchings (Inverarity 1976; Tolnay, Beck, and Massey 1989), peasant rebellions (Chirot and Ragin 1975), organizational success (Steedly and Foley 1979), and urban protests (Eisinger 1973). Some investigators, such as Markoff (1986), have collapsed information on event counts into binary distinctions between "no event" and "one or more events" and used logit analysis. There are serious drawbacks to applying cross-sectional designs to data on events that occur over time. Specifically, this approach ignores the possibility that the timing of events affected the flow of subsequent events.

Time-series analysis has also been common in research on collective events in diverse settings and historical periods: French collective violence, 1830–1960 (Rule and Tilly 1972; Snyder and Tilly 1972; Lodhi and Tilly 1973; and Tilly 1986), lynchings of African-Americans (McAdam 1982), American urban racial violence, 1948–79 (Kelly and

Isaac 1984), civil rights movement activity, 1950–80 (McAdam 1982; Jenkins and Eckert 1986), and analysis of all forms of domestic violence in the United States, 1890–1970 (Rasler 1986). This design highlights the effects of historical change. When there are theoretical or historical reasons to believe that effects differ among periods, analysts can estimate shifts in the parameters at pre-determined times. However, this approach too loses important information by aggregating over units and by aggregating over time within periods (to create period counts of events).

Use of both cross-sectional and longitudinal variation, or panel analysis, in events represents a third approach (see Table 4.1). When information on events is available for two or more time periods on multiple behavioral units, several estimation procedures can exploit more of the information than can be done with either cross-sectional or time-series analysis alone. These more general approaches are particularly advantageous when analyzing rare events. Nonetheless, this approach still involves temporal aggregation (to periods) and does not employ appropriate probability models for (small) counts.

Discrete-state stochastic models, such as the Poisson model and various other models discussed in subsequent chapters, are especially appropriate for data on the occurrence of riots, protests, or revolutions. The assumptions of normal distribution theory are frequently violated with such data because counts in particular localities or periods are nonnegative and are generally small (or even zero). Discrete-state models use data more efficiently because such methods take the non-negativity constraint into account.

Poisson models have been used to analyze cross-sectional data on the propensity of cities to riot (Lieberson and Silverman 1965; Spilerman 1970). Poisson regression has also been used to estimate models of the occurrence of yearly counts of events in a single time series (Hannan and Freeman 1989).

This book relies on continuous-time, discrete-state stochastic process models analyzed using the methods of event-history analysis. This approach involves application and generalization of methods originally designed for studying events in biostatistics and industrial engineering. Recently event-history analysis has been used to study rates of occurrence of collective actions, such as riots and protests, as well as the establishment and disbanding of social movement organizations. This class of methods uses information on the timing and sequencing of events to estimate models of transition rates. Two general forms of event-history analysis are relevant to the study of collective action and social movements. The first involves study of recurrent events, such as riots, where the typical duration of an event is small relative to the waiting time between events. In this case the attention focuses on the rate of occurrence, that is the transition from an event count of N to $N+1$ (Coleman, 1981; Amburgey and Carroll 1984; Amburgey 1986; Hannan and Freeman 1987). The second considers transitions between enduring states, such as different forms of political regimes (Hannan and Carroll 1981). The second approach can be used for studying transitions among phases in the histories of demonstrations, revolutions, and social movements (Tuma and Hannan 1984).

Event-history analysis is particularly useful for analyzing cycles or waves of protest and violence. As noted above, while the concept of cycles of social movement activity is not new, it has rarely been investigated empirically. Use of event-history analysis facilitates study of diffusion of events. Second, questions about whether contagion is restricted to particular forms or stages in collective protest can be investigated with event-history analysis as well. For example, questions about whether civil rights protests spark subsequent racial conflicts, or vice-versa, can be investigated with analysis that estimates the transition rates among multiple states (Tuma and Hannan 1984). As in panel analysis, event-history analysis can use information on the timing of events in a series of localities to estimate models that take both unit-specific characteristics and the timing of events. In contrast to the single point process models described above, examples of this combined cross-sectional and longitudinal design commonly analyzes events in a number of cities, Standard Metropolitan Statistical Areas or some other subunit over a number of observation points. This approach combines the advantages of using both cross sectional and temporal variation with the appropriateness of stochastic models that analyze events as outcomes of processes that unfold over time.

5

Immigration, Economic Contraction, and Ethnic Events

Nearly twenty-three million immigrants entered America between 1877 and 1914, a period of rapid industrialization, economic crises, unionization and labor strife (United States Bureau of the Census 1975: 105–6). A variety of studies on the residential and occupational mobility of various ethnic and nationality groups have investigated how immigrants fared economically (see Thernstrom 1973; Lieberson 1980; Lieberson and Carter 1982). Still others have compared white ethnics with African-Americans and other racial minorities. A wide variety of studies use both historical evidence and recent data on occupational attainment as measures of ethnic differences in income, mobility, residential dispersion, and adaptation to occupational opportunities (Saxton 1971; Wilson 1978; Farley 1984; Portes and Bach 1984; Massey and Denton 1989; Nee and Nee 1986). These studies of ethnic stratification and attainment generally examine differences in patterns of opportunities for and paths taken by various immigrant groups, in an attempt to explain current income differences and gaps in achievement. We reverse the causal relationship here in order to ask if such attainment processes affect the likelihood of ethnic collective action. Specifically, what is the impact of broad social changes—level and change of immigration, economic depressions, wage fluctuations—on the rate of ethnic conflict and protest?

In answer to this question we look first at the impact of changes in *national-level* characteristics over these thirty-eight years on fluctuations in rates of ethnic collective action. This emphasis reflects an emerging perspective in collective action which investigates the impacts of macro-level processes on rates of conflict, violence, and protest (Tilly 1986,

1978; Tilly, Tilly, and Tilly, 1975; Tarrow 1983). As noted above, I am interested in both conflict directed against immigrants and racial groups and social protests against discrimination. Because we also suspect that contagion affects rates of collective action, we also examine whether rates of collective action involving immigrants or racial groups diffuse, whether an event in one locality affects the rate in the system as a whole, and whether events of a particular type affect the rate of occurrence of other types of events.

The goal is to examine how rates of ethnic collective action depend on macro-level processes pertaining to immigration flows and economic contraction and recovery. So we test arguments from Chapter 3 that these national-level changes affect levels of competition among ethnic groups and thus affect rates of ethnic collective action. The analysis addresses the following questions bearing on the theory proposed in the previous chapters:

1. *Did immigration affect rates of ethnic collective action over this period of American history?* As explained in Chapter 3, competition theories (including split labor market theory) suggest that increases in the supply of low wage labor due to immigration stimulates ethnic collective action designed to contain the threat to wage standards, housing, job opportunities, and other resources. Moreover, large increases in the flow of immigrants (rather than constant but high immigration flows) ought to intensify the levels of ethnic competition.

2. *How did economic hardship affect rates of ethnic collective action?* General theories of collective action hold that economic fluctuation has two potentially contradictory effects. First, theories of collective action commonly hold that contraction of economic resources, as in depressions or periods of high rates of business failures, raises rates of ethnic collective action. Social-psychological theories as well as traditional disorganization theories share the view that economic contraction causes discontent and turmoil.[1] Recent "breakdown" arguments also bear on this issue, suggesting that declining wages, depressions, and other indications of economic hardship create rising rates of all kinds protest activity (Useem 1985).

Research on collective action often distinguishes relative deprivation from absolute hardship (Gurr 1970; Useem 1980). In some cases the two types of deprivation have been operationalized independently in order to account for protest that paradoxically arises during periods of well-being

---

[1]For arguments applied to racial conflict, see Blalock 1967, Reed 1972, and Woodward 1974.

(Snyder and Tilly 1972).[2] Tilly and his collaborators have long disputed the generality of the claim that either relative or absolute economic hardship raises rates of collective action. Instead, they propose that favorable economic conditions enable groups to mobilize and act. That is, resource mobilization theories claim that rates of ethnic collective action rise for disadvantaged groups whose standard of living has improved.

Up until now, analysis of resource mobilization arguments has been limited to racial protest movements in recent American history. Recently, research on black insurgency and civil rights protest suggests that organizations, membership, and other resources directly affect the ability of groups to protest past discrimination.[3] Competition theories extend these ideas and inform us as to why resource accumulation might influence ethnic conflict as well. Because ethnic groups advancing in the opportunity ladder come to compete with others just above them, a rise in fortunes for the white immigrant and racial populations may also incite ethnic conflict on the part of those on the next higher rung (Olzak 1986).

So competition theory joins the two effects of economic change within the same perspective. First, to the extent that overall economic contraction intensifies ethnic competition, then it expects rates of conflict also to increase. Second, if rising levels of resources raise the standard of living for disadvantaged ethnic or racial groups relative to advantaged ones, antagonism among new competitors also intensifies.

Following this logic, analysis in this chapter distinguishes between overall economic contraction and contraction of economic well-being affecting manual laborers.[4] Competition theory arguments hold that

---

[2]National-level analyses presented here follow the lead of Tilly and others who argue that such theories are largely untestable in the absence of social-psychological indications of the gap between expected and actual well-being (which is, of course, unavailable for this distant era). We do, however, distinguish overall economic decline, measured by depressions, from decreased well-being for those in the lowest occupations, the common laborers. Note, however, that the theoretical approach taken here contests a key claim of relative deprivation theory. Competition arguments imply that rates of ethnic collective action rise when the gap in relative well-being among ethnic groups narrows.

[3]For evidence, see McAdam 1982 and Morris 1984.

[4]Ideally, examination of this question would include detailed analysis of wage rates in jobs broken down by race and immigrant status. Unfortunately, differences in wages earned by race and ethnic groups in the same occupational categories does not exist at the city level over this period. Based on historical arguments and evidence from this period, however, well-being for newer immigrants and racial minorities can be approximated with longitudinal data on wage rates for manual laborers. The historical evidence suggests that because manual laborers are far more likely to include new immigrants, African-Americans, and Chinese among their ranks, this measure indicates that fluctuations in well-being affect these groups disproportionately. For

overall economic contraction raises rates of conflict but that periods of prosperity for those in the immigrant niche may do so too. To see if these arguments hold, it is important to distinguish these two relevant indicators of economic well-being.

3. *Did diffusion processes affect rates of ethnic conflict and protest?* As the previous chapters pointed out, previous research on race riots and protest uprisings during the 1960s in the United States indicated that there were waves of contagion of race riots that occurred in regular cycles or patterns. Does diffusion also apply to ethnic collective action of other kinds? Did events cluster in waves over this period, as they appeared to do during the 1960s?

4. *Did the causes of ethnic conflict and ethnic protest differ?* It is clear that collective actions involve at least two kinds of interactions: one involving confrontations in conflict with another ethnic group based upon both (or more) groups' ethnic or national identity; the other a more pro-active, civil rights actions in which one group marches, demonstrates, or protests for their own behalf. An interesting and largely unexplored research question asks if these two forms of protest are related systematically. Were there periods of general unrest, in which immigration and economic disasters fostered collective actions of all kinds involving immigrants, or were the causes of conflict substantially different from proactive collective actions? Cultural division of labor and economic hardship theories generally claim that economic downturns cause rates of collective action of all kinds to rise based upon the fundamental assumption that class cleavages become more salient during economic contractions. In contrast, competition theories suggest that conflict and protest may be instigated by different processes that affect the levels of competition experienced. That is, economic hardship is more likely to affect levels of inter-ethnic conflict, while protest should be more sensitive to economic gains differentially enjoyed by lower-status minorities and newcomers.

Diffusion may also affect conflict and protest differently. For example, we suspect that diffusion is likely to affect inter-ethnic conflict more than protest at the national level, as news of ethnic violence is more likely to be carried by Associated Press wires and other national news services than are local protest events. These protests have a more bounded and parochial nature during this period (Olzak 1986); they involve city ordinances regarding housing or segregation in schools, regional laws on voting, and other grievances common to pro-active events. Yet there is some

further evidence on this point, see Saxton 1971, Wilson 1978, Bodnar et al. 1982, Lieberson 1980, Archdeacon 1983, and Gutman and Bell 1987, among many others.

impressive evidence from analyses of the recent civil rights movement in the United States which suggests that protest techniques, strategies, symbols and even leadership routines transfer across movement groups in systematic ways (McAdam 1982; Morris 1985). If these comparisons of diffusion effects show evidence that ethnic events in one city had implications and serious consequences for other parts of the country, then we will have some additional support for analyzing national-level collective action data using newspaper (as well as other archival) reports on revolutions, protests, spontaneous conflicts, and other gatherings.

5. *Did the causes of events involving different ethnic/racial populations differ?* Some have argued that violence is more systematically directed against African-Americans than any other group in the United States. While this seems plausible, there are many documented cases of hostility and violence that were directed against Asians during the turn of the century, as well as attacks on Jews and others, that appear to challenge this claim. To find out if the causes of all types of ethnic and racial violence share similar underlying features, we need to compare causes of ethnic attacks across a variety of targets.

Design of the Analysis

Below we consider events in all 77 cities taken as a whole over the entire period of study, 1877–1914 (see Table B.1 in Appendix B). It considers the occurrence of events in any one of the cities. This means that the dependent variable in this analysis is the duration between events in this set of cities. The appendix provides full details on the design and measurement of the dependent variable.

As noted above, we analyze the rate of occurrence of events of ethnic collective action in the set of large cities taken as a unit. An important assumption being made here is that urban America constituted an identifiable, bounded system of information and social action in which reactions to and adaptations to immigrant and migrant newcomers were played out during the late nineteenth and early twentieth centuries. Finding identifiable patterns at the national level depends in part on the validity of this assumption. For example, earlier research on race riots during the 1960s in the United States often debated whether national-level rates of riots could be analyzed meaningfully, or whether city-level or even community-level characteristics (such as the proportion of blacks in cities) were more appropriate for analyzing diffusion and causal processes instigating racial tensions (see Lieberson and Silverman 1965; Spilerman 1970, 1976; Oliver and Johnson 1984). Nagel and Olzak (1982) have described how arguments from competition theories might be applied to neighborhood, city, country, and even world-system levels of analysis. The stand taken here is that several levels of analysis involving collective action (for instance, national-level and city-level) should be used in empirically investigations to learn whether these processes hold at one or more levels of analysis.

While the ties among cities were undoubtedly weaker a hundred years ago than now, there is considerable evidence that rates of collective action were sensitive to extra-local events during the period of interest. There are reasons to believe that newspaper reports of conflicts in one city were often carried by newspapers in other cities. Apparently such reports sometimes affected behavior as well. For instance, Tuttle (1970: 92) reports that the editor of the black newspaper, the *Chicago Defender*, received numerous letters of outrage from southern whites in response to its editorials and articles comparing the favorable racial conditions in that city to those in the South. In 1919 the *Defender* also spread the news of the Chicago race riot that year to African-Americans in the South and West, causing several southern cities to outlaw its circulation. Tuttle reports (1970: 92) that in one of these cities, Jackson, Mississippi, whites adopted a ban and stated that the *Defender* was designed to "create race antagonism." Rudwick (1964: 224) claims that both the *Chicago Defender* and the *Detroit Times* contributed to rumors that prolonged the East St. Louis riot of 1917.

The choice to conduct analysis at the national level assumes that country-level trends systematically affected ethnic conflict in the same way in very different cities and regions. We test this assumption directly. Since the hypothesis that national-level trends affect rates is a controversial one, we think that conducting analysis first at the national level is a good place to begin. If competition processes affect national level rates, then our arguments hold promise for analysis at local levels, where competition is likely to be more potent. But another consideration in choice of level of analysis is pragmatic. Reliable measures of key explanatory variables used in this chapter (immigration, real wage rates, incidence of economic depressions) as well as those added in the next chapter (strike frequencies and number and foundings of unions) are available only at the national level during this period. It makes sense to begin systematic analysis of these issues with the available data. Findings at the national level then provide motivation for attempts at reconstructing data at the city level (see Chapter 9). So this research begins by exploring the idea that local areas were affected by national trends as well as by events in other cities.

Dependent Variable. This analysis uses data on the *timing* of ethnic events in any of the largest (in 1880) 77 cities in the United States (see

Table B.1 in Appendix B). An ethnic event is judged to have occurred if two or more persons are involved in a public event that makes ethnic or racial claims or articulates an ethnic grievance. Regularly scheduled events and institutionalized events such as congressional hearings are excluded, as are random crimes between individuals from different nationalities or race groups (Olzak and DiGregorio 1985).

Daily reports from the *New York Times* were used as the primary source of data, in a two-stage process. We identified "candidate events" from the *NYT Index* and then coded characteristics of events from microfilms of daily accounts. Comparing this method with the more traditional method of counting events using only the *NYT Index* (discussed in Chapter 4) reveals that nearly half of the candidate events from the *Index* did not meet the criterion that events be both collective and ethnic. The two largest categories of problematic events from the *Index* are speeches by politicians and editorials on immigration or race issues, which are not *collective* events under our coding rules.

Data were collected on protests and conflicts. Ethnic protests are collective actions that articulate claims for civil rights or grievances on behalf of (usually) one ethnic group. Ethnic conflicts are confrontations between members of two or more racial/ethnic populations. An event was coded as violent if the conflict involved threats to deploy weapons, or the actual use of weapons such as sticks, bottles, stones, guns, and firebombs.

Figures 5.1 and 5.2 show how events of ethnic collective action were distributed over time. Figure 5.1 is a conventional plot of incidence per year for the set of 77 cities taken together. The early 1880s and early 1900s were peak periods of ethnic collective action. They were dominated by anti-Chinese and antiblack actions respectively. Figure 5.1 also shows that the number of events also varies significantly over these 38 years, suggesting that explanations that imply simple time trends will not fit these data. Figure 5.2 displays the data in a form closer to that used in the analyses that follow. This figure shows the cumulative count over time, using the exact timing of events to the day (coded as decimal years). Flat portions of such a plot show periods of inactivity, and steep rises show periods of intense activity.

Independent Variables. The analysis relates occurrences of ethnic collective actions to covariates that describe national conditions over the period of study: proportional change in immigration, real wages of common laborers, and a dummy variable that indicates years of economic depression and panics. The immigration statistics come from the *Historical Statistics of the United States: Colonial Times to 1970* (United States Bureau of the Census 1975). Changes in immigration are calcu-

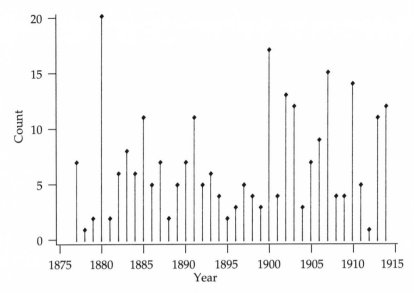

FIG. 5.1 Ethnic Collective Action by Year

lated as a relative changes from the previous year. Proportional change in immigration is defined as the change in level of immigration between year t and $t + 1$ divided by the level in year t.

Level of economic prosperity for the disadvantaged is measured using an index of the real wage rate for common laborers (from David and Solar 1977). This index estimates the standard of living of unskilled laborers, standardized to equal 1 in 1860. This wage rate can be considered to be a crude measure of immigrants' well-being, since common laborers were disproportionately foreign-born and nonwhite in American cities during this period. The foreign-born comprised nearly 60% of the common laborers in cities in 1880, while they are only 20% of the labor force in these same cities in 1880 (United States Census 1880). African-Americans too were concentrated in such jobs in cities. According to Spero and Harris (1931: 85), "There were 825,321 Negroes employed in manufacturing industries in 1920. Only 16.6 per cent of them were skilled workers; 67.9 per cent of them were laborers; and 15.5 per cent were semi-skilled."

As noted above, the effects of several measures of more general economic contraction were also explored. Here we concentrate on the most straightforward ones: economic depression and business failure rate. The index of economic depression and business panics is taken from Thorp

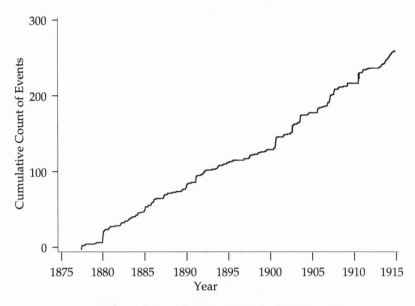

FIG. 5.2   Cumulative Count of Ethnic Collective Events

and Mitchell (1926). This is a dummy variable that equals one if the spell occurs in a year of economic depression and equaling zero otherwise. The business failure rate is from *Historical Statistics of the United States: Colonial Times to 1970* (United States Bureau of the Census 1975) and is the number of business failures per 1000 existing businesses in a year.

In previous analyses of these data, I have explored several specifications of diffusion. These involve combinations of time dependence in rates and effects of the number of recent events on the rate. The analyses reported in this chapter include a monotonic effect of the number of events in the month prior to the beginning of the spell. This relationship is specified as log-linear.[5] That is, the log of the rate of occurrence is

---

[5]To examine whether this log-linear specification is the best one, we compared results with other competing models. In another approach diffusion is specified as a log-linear spline function. The first piece is a dummy variable set to 1 if no event took place in the past month, and equals 0 otherwise. The second piece is an event count for the previous month, ranging from 1 to 11 events in these data. While it usually does not differ significantly from zero, the coefficient of the dummy variable indicating no event occurred 30 days prior to the beginning of a spell is negative. The estimated effect implies that the rate is about 5% lower when no event occurred in the previous month. But the effect of the non-negative number of events is positive and significant. However, in most cases, use of the spline function does not improve the fit significantly over the model with a single parameter indexing the effect of recent events.

assumed to depend linearly on the number of events of ethnic collective action that took place during the month that preceded the initiation of the spell (not including the event that initiates the spell). This specification allows the rate of occurrence to be particularly high when a large number of events have occurred during the previous month, that is when a wave of ethnic collective actions is taking place. The choice of a month's time is not arbitrary. McAdam's (1982: 173) analysis of civil rights events during the 1950s and 1960s in the United States shows that waves of events tended to occur in 30-day cycles.

Duration Dependence. We recast processes of contagion in terms of duration dependence in the rate of occurrence. The existence of cycles implies that the rate varies with the time that has elapsed since the previous event. Thus we explore whether long periods of quiescence in ethnic activity generate low levels of ethnic conflict.

Does the rate of occurrence vary as the time since the previous event varies? One way to explore this question is to consider plots of the integrated hazard by duration. If the rate does not vary with duration, then the plot of an integrated hazard (or the minus-log survivor function) against duration will be approximately linear (Tuma and Hannan 1984: Chapter 3). Figure 5.3 provides such a plot for the data on ethnic collective actions using Aalen's (1978) estimator. In order to emphasize the period over which the rate changes rapidly, the range of duration in this plot is 0 to .25 years (the maximum observed duration is 1.35 years). The solid line is the integrated hazard; the dashed lines are 95% confidence intervals. Notice that the relationship is decidedly nonlinear; and the confidence intervals are sufficiently narrow that a linear relationship can be ruled out with considerable confidence. The integrated hazard rises sharply at short durations but then flattens out. This pattern suggests that the rate is high at short duration and declines with duration. In other words, this empirical pattern is consistent with the view that ethnic collective actions unfold in cycles because it means that the rate of occurrence is low when considerable time has elapsed since the most recent event.

The next question is whether the pattern of duration dependence can be summarized well by a tractable parametric model. Explorations of cumulative hazard functions and of the fit of various parametric models suggest that the well-known Weibull model does a good job. According to the Weibull model, the rate changes monotonically with time. Let T_n denote the random variable that tells the time of the nth event in the set of cities. The waiting time from the $(n-1)$th event to the nth event

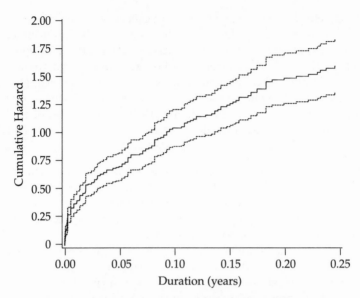

FIG. 5.3   Cumulative Hazard Versus Duration

is $U_n = T_n - T_{n-1}$. The Weibull model can be defined as

$$r(u_n \mid t_{n-1}) = \rho u^{\rho-1},$$

where $r(u \mid t_{n-1})$ is the rate of ethnic collective action at waiting time u_n (given that the previous event occurred at t_{n-1}). If the events are generated by a Weibull model, then there is a linear relationship between the log of the cumulative hazard (the log-minus-log survivor function) and log-duration (Cox and Oakes 1984: 25). This seems to be the case in the plot in Figure 5.4. Therefore we use a Weibull model of duration dependence in the analyses that follow.

In order to incorporate the effects of measured covariates, we use what is called an *accelerated* Weibull model. The model has the form:

$$r(u \mid t_{n-1}) = \exp\left[\beta' \mathbf{x}(t_{n-1})\right] u^{\rho-1}. \tag{5.1}$$

The vector β contains parameters that tell the effects of covariates on the rates, and $\mathbf{x}(t_{n-1})$ denotes a vector of covariates expected to affect the rate. Under the hypothesis that the rate declines with the waiting time, the Weibull parameter, ρ, lies between zero and one.

A convenient way to estimate accelerated Weibull models is by estimating regression models for the log of the waiting time between events:

$$Y(u_n) \equiv \log(u_n) = \beta^{*\prime} \mathbf{x}(t_{n-1}) + \sigma W, \qquad \beta^* = -\sigma\beta, \tag{5.2}$$

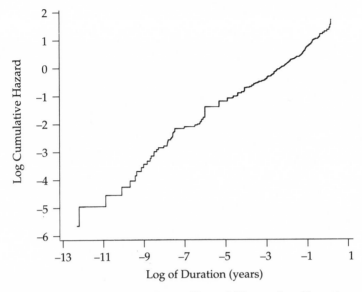

FIG. 5.4 Log of Cumulative Hazard Versus Log-Duration

where W has an extreme value distribution, and σ is the so-called *scale parameter* (Kalbfleisch and Prentice 1980). The relationship between the scale parameter and the Weibull parameter is $\sigma = 1/\rho$.

Note in (5.2) that the coefficients of the covariates in the regression model are the negative of the corresponding coefficients in equation (6.1) multiplied by the scale factor. The tables below and in subsequent chapters report maximum likelihood (ML) estimates of the scale parameter and the negative of the regression coefficients in (5.2), that is $-\widehat{\sigma\beta}$, using PROC LIFEREG (SAS Institute 1985). If propositions regarding contagion are correct, then σ exceeds 1. This means that ρ is less than 1, and the time dependence is negative: the rate falls with the passage of time since the previous event.

An important research decision concerns the definition of spells. Should we define durations between conflicts only? Or between any type of ethnic collective event? Prior research found that the occurrence of *either* a conflict or a protest affected the rate of subsequent conflict (Olzak 1986, 1987). To take this fact into account, spells are defined as the waiting times between events, either conflicts or protests. This period experienced 156 conflicts and 106 protests. So the total number of spells used in the analysis is 263. The spells include a left-censored spell beginning on January 1, 1877 and ending at the time of the first observed event, 262 uncensored durations between events, and a last right-censored spell from the final event in 1914 to the end of that calendar year. Analyses of particular types of events, for instance conflicts or events involving a particular target, treat durations that end in an event other than the one of interest as being censored on the right. Thus, in analyses of the rate of conflict, durations that end in a protest are treated as censored on the right. The maximum likelihood estimator used in analyzing regressions of durations in the form of (5.2) accommodates information on censoring in a natural way (Kalbfleisch and Prentice 1980).

Results

Table 5.1 reports the size and type of ethnic collective actions for the set of 77 cities.[6] As expected, black-white confrontations and civil rights protests by blacks were by far the most numerous, accounting for over half of all actions. This table also shows that a fairly wide range of events were picked up by the *NYT* during this period. Events involving civil rights protests and confrontations between white natives and African-Americans, Chinese, Hispanics, Eastern and Western Europeans were found, as well as inter-ethnic conflicts involving two or more of the latter populations (Olzak 1987). Our initial concern was that the *NYT*'s accounts would be insensitive to events involving only a few persons; Table 5.1 shows that such events constitute nearly 8% of the sample.[7]

Conflicts and Protests. Table 5.2 reports estimates of the effects of immigration and economic hardship on the national-level rate of ethnic collective action. The table reports estimates over the overall rate (in columns 1 and 2) and of the rate of ethnic conflicts (in columns 3 and 4) and ethnic protests (in columns 5 and 6).[8] Each model includes dura-

---

[6]Size was coded from newspaper reports in nearly 50% of the events. Where missing, keywords estimating the size of the collective action provided guidelines for the qualitative categories listed in Table 5.1 (see Appendix B).

[7]Other critics suspected that a proximity bias might exist, that the *NYT* would be likely to ignore events outside of the New York City metropolitan area. This imagery was captured well in the famous *New Yorker* cartoon of a map of the United States, which shows that just to the West of New York City, a vast uninterrupted wasteland extends across the nation and ends at the Pacific Ocean. While we initially suspected this New York bias was present in the *New York Times* accounts, subsequent analysis found that (adjusting for a per capita rate) New York's number of events is below average, while Fall River, Massachusetts and Seattle, Washington show high per capita rates of ethnic collective action.

[8]In the analysis of one kind of event, events of the other kinds are treated as censoring a spell, in the classic competing risks approach (Tuma and Hannan 1984: Chapter 3).

TABLE 5.1

Sizes of Black/White, Chinese/White, and Other Ethnic Events
in 77 American Cities, 1877–1914

	Size					
Type	'Small' (2–9)	'Medium' (10–99)	'Large' (100-49)	'Very Large' (500-1000)	'Thousands' (1000+)	Total
Black/White	8 (5.6%)	44 (30.8%)	41 (28.6%)	23 (16%)	27 (19%)	143 (100%)
Chinese/White	3 (7.3%)	11 (26.8%)	9 (22%)	14 (34.1%)	4 (9.8%)	41 (100%)
Other Groups	9 (11.5%)	23 (29.5%)	27 (34.6%)	9 (11.5%)	10 (12.8%)	78 (100%
Total Events	20 (7.6%)	78 (29.8%)	77 (29.4%)	46 (17.6%)	41 (15.6%)	262 (100%)

tion dependence of a Weibull form and a log-linear effect of the number of events in the previous month. The odd-numbered columns report estimates of effects of proportional change in immigration, real wages for laborers, annual change in business failure rate, and a dummy variable for a depression year. The even-numbered columns report estimates of models that add the theoretically important interaction effect of change in immigration and the real wage.

The first step in interpreting the results involves making a decision about whether to include an interaction of proportional change in immigration and the real wage of common laborers. Since even-numbered columns contain this interaction and odd-numbered columns do not, we can form likelihood ratio tests of the null hypotheses of no interaction using the log-likelihoods reported in each column. Such tests reveal that the null hypothesis of no interaction can be rejected in the case of all forms of ethnic collective action (column 2 versus 1) and the rate of ethnic protest (column 6 versus 5).[9] The interaction is insignificant in the case of the rate of ethnic conflict. We discuss the implications of this difference below.

Given the result of the tests for interactions, we focus on different

---

[9] A likelihood ratio test statistic comparing models with and without the interaction term yields χ^2 of 5.08 when comparing the likelihood in the second column against that in the first. The interaction effect is also significant for protests, where the same comparisons of the log-likelihood in the sixth column against the one in the fifth column yields a χ^2 of 10.74. Also take notice of the fact that the test for the addition of the interaction effect is not significant for conflict events. But tests do suggest that the effects of immigration and wage levels depend on each other for protests analyzed separately.

TABLE 5.2

Effects of Immigration and Economic Conditions on the Rate of Ethnic Collective Action in 77 American Cities, 1877–1914

(Asymptotic Standard Errors in Parentheses)

	All Events		Conflicts		Protests	
	(1)	(2)	(3)	(4)	(5)	(6)
Intercept	1.00 (.877)	1.79* (.921)	-.232 (1.27)	.440 (1.36)	-.723 (1.20)	.664 (1.22)
Proportional change in immigration	.934*** (.318)	-1.86 (1.34)	1.66*** (.417)	.834 (1.71)	-.247 (.523)	-7.55*** (2.77)
Real wage of common laborers	.778 (.634)	.115 (.688)	1.09 (.914)	.874 (1.01)	.617 (.870)	-.491 (.920)
Real wage*proportional change in immigration		2.65** (1.23)		.791 (1.60)		6.50*** (2.28)
Change in business failure rate	.012** (.005)	.010** (.005)	.018*** (.006)	.019*** (.006)	-.002 (.008)	-.006 (.008)
Depression year	.028 (.257)	.117 (.254)	-.602* (.366)	-.563 (.370)	.852** (.382)	.885** (.365)
Number of events in previous month	.189*** (.050)	.178*** (.050)	.122* (.068)	.119* (.068)	.292*** (.075)	.266*** (.073)
Scale parameter	1.83*** (.090)	1.81*** (.089)	1.93*** (.123)	1.92*** (.123)	1.66*** (.128)	1.62*** (.125)
Number of spells	263	263	263	263	263	263
Uncensored spells	262	262	156	156	106	106
Log likelihood	-574.52	-571.98	-428.11	-427.99	-308.71	-303.34

* $p < .10$, ** $p < .05$, *** $p < .01$.

models for the different outcomes. In the case of the rate of ethnic conflict, we focus on the estimates from a model that does not contain an interaction effect (column 3). For the other two rates, we interpret the estimates of models that do contain the interaction effect (columns 2 and 6). Note also that that a likelihood ratio test for separating conflicts and protests from the pooled models in columns 1 and 2 was significant, which means that the conflict and protest models should be analyzed separately.

Recall that a key proposition from competition theory involved the effect of changes in immigration on rates of conflict. We thus focus first on the effect of proportional change in immigration in models of conflict without the interaction term (column 3). When the results for immigration on the rate of conflicts and protests are combined, as seen in column 1, the effect is positive. However, when conflicts are separated from protests (columns 3 and 5, respectively), proportional change in immigration has opposite effects. Proportional change in immigration has a significant positive impact on the rate of ethnic conflict (column 3).[10] That is, as immigration surged, the rate of ethnic conflict rose, as competition arguments suggest.

How large is the implied effect? In order to answer this question, we must adjust the estimated effect by dividing by the scale parameter.[11] In the case of ethnic conflict, the estimated effect of proportional change in immigration is 1.66 and the estimated scale parameter is 1.93. Taking the ratio 1.66/1.93 gives .860 for the estimated effect on the rate. Now consider the multiplier of the rate (given by the other terms in the model) at different levels of proportional change in immigration. For instance, consider the first and third quartiles of this variable over the years studied. The first quartile is −1.56 and the third quartile is .328. The multiplier for the first quartile level of change in immigration is therefore equal to $\exp(.860 \times -1.56) = .26$; the multiplier for the third quartile level equals $\exp(.860 \times .328) = 1.32$. So the predicted rate of ethnic conflict is five times (1.32/.26) higher when proportional change in immigration was at the third quartile level than when it was at its first quartile level. So fluctuations in immigration had a powerful effect on the rate of ethnic conflict.

Now consider the interaction effects of proportional change in immi-

---

[10]No effect of level of immigration was uncovered for this 38-year period, despite the fact that immigration levels did have significant effects for a different subset (1877–89) of years (see Olzak 1987). For this full 38-year period, only the proportional change in immigration had a significant independent effect on the rate and so is included in these models.

[11]Recall that the entries in this and other parallel tables are estimates of $-\widehat{\sigma\beta}$.

gration and real wages in columns 4, and 6. A key claim of competition theory advanced in Chapter 3 is that change in immigration and economic contraction interact in affecting the rate of ethnic conflict. This claim was tested by adding the interaction effect of proportional change in immigration and real wages of common laborers that was added to the odd-numbered columns, as we discussed above. Recall that the argument in earlier chapters claimed that the interaction effect should affect the rate of ethnic conflicts in particular. This argument is not supported by the majority of likelihood ratio tests noted above.[12]

However, there is a significant positive interaction of the level of real wages and proportional change in immigration on the rate of ethnic protest (in column 6).[13] Taking the main and interaction effects of all three variables together simultaneously, this means that effect of higher wages on the rate of protests depends upon the level of proportional change in immigration, such that as both immigration and wage rise the rate of ethnic protest increases even more. This means that the estimated effects of proportional change in immigration, real wages of laborers and the interaction term must be taken together. The combined effects show that the rate of ethnic protest rises sharply when wages of laborers are high and change in immigration is high.

These results suggest that ethnic protest (rather than conflict) is sensitive to forces that are in turn affected by both high levels of wages in low-paying occupations and changes in supply of low-wage labor. This means that for protests the interaction effect is exactly opposite what the hypothesis made for ethnic conflicts. Why? One leading theoretical framework introduced above provides an explanation for these findings. Recall that resource mobilization theories suggested that the effect of immigration raises rates of ethnic protest particularly when real wages of those competing in the immigrant niche also rise. The results are consistent with the argument that ethnic protests depend upon rising numbers of immigrants and wages as ethnic resources.

But what about the opposing force, overall economic decline? Many theories of economic hardship claim that *all* types of economic contraction increase collective action and social turmoil. Is this true for this period? The answer is not straightforward. We address this question

---

[12]It may be important to recall, however, that the model assumes that the covariates affect the rate log-linearly. Such models already include multiplicative effects of the covariates.

[13]It is also significant in the analysis of all ethnic collective actions considered together (column 2). But because the interaction effect is significant for protests but not conflicts, the fact that the interaction term is significant in the second column should be interpreted only as it affects protests.

by including two measures of overall economic contraction in Table 5.2: change in business failure rate and depression year. For the two types of ethnic collective action combined and for ethnic conflicts, surges in business failures increase the rates significantly. For ethnic protests, the effect of business failures is negative, but it is small and insignificant. Interestingly, the effect of depression years is opposite that of business failures, suppressing the rate of conflicts but raising the rate of protests significantly. The time-series data on the independent variables used here show that business failures rise before serious depressions during the period of study. Such failures may signal to workers and employers that unemployment and other economic hardships are to follow. Seen this way the pattern of results for economic hardship makes sense in Table 5.2; that is, conflicts rise with the first sign of economic contraction. But when serious depressions set in, conflicts against others seem less likely. This explanation appears to hold, according to the effects in the third column.

Diffusion also has strong effects on the rates of conflict and protest. Recall that the analysis employs two different measures for the diffusion of events across the country: a monthly event count (updated with each event in the country as a whole) and a specification of monotonic duration dependence. It is clear from the last two rows of Table 5.2 that diffusion effects are powerful.

Consider first the monthly event count. In the second column, the coefficient of .178 implies that if an event occurred in the last month, the rate of ethnic collective action increased 10% when compared to a 30-day period with no event (because the estimated scale parameter is 1.81 and $.178 \div 1.81 = .098$, $\exp(.098) = 1.10$ and $\exp(0) = 1.0$). According to this estimate, spells that follow the observed peak number of events in a month have a three-fold higher rate than those that follow a month without an event. Protests show even greater sensitivity to the diffusion of ethnic events. At the observed peak of 11 events observed, the rate of protests is six times higher than the baseline of a 30-day period with no activity at all. These results suggest that contagion had potent effects on the future rate of events and that choice of a monthly event count has substantive meaning at the national level.[14]

Finally, consider time dependence in the rate. The evidence, reported as the effect of the scale parameter in Table 5.2, supports the

---

[14]Note that these findings support McAdam's hypothesis that a month's gap between events is a crucial one. The results shown here suggest that diffusion effects are most potent one day after an event, and decline sharply after one month, and nearly disappear after six months have passed.

contention that the rate of ethnic conflict varies with the recency of the last event. The estimated scale parameter always differs significantly from one, indicating time dependence in the rate. The estimated scale parameter in each column indicates that the rate *declines* with the time since the last event, since a scale parameter greater than one implies negative time dependence. Indeed the rates decline sharply with time since the previous event according to these estimates.

The two specifications of conflict diffusion produce surprising results. They imply that events in one city affect the likelihood of ethnic events elsewhere, even before the development of television, radio, and other modern communication links. The results show that for both types of collective action, bursts of *either* protests and conflicts raise rates of both kinds of ethnic collective action. Furthermore, the actual count in a previous month and the time span since the last event contribute to subsequent jumps in the rate.

Attacks on African-Americans, Chinese, and White Immigrants. Next we consider the causes of ethnic collective action by ethnic groups involved. There are several indications that differences by target might exist. Social histories of this period suggest that reactions to Chinese and African-American migrants in cities were far more virulent and hostile than reactions to the more racially familiar Europeans (see, for example, Higham 1955; Bodnar et al. 1982). Research on racial and ethnic differences in occupational attainment, residential segregation and ghettoization, and other measures of race differences in quality of life suggest that the reactions to Chinese and to African-Americans, who migrated from the rural south to northern cities, were not only more violent and oppressive, but were unrelated to measurable local differences in racial tolerance, education of residents, or some other factors associated with prejudice and ethnocentrism of all kinds (Lieberson 1980 provides a review). For these reasons, it makes sense to examine the underlying causal structure of ethnic collective action involving these groups separately.

Table 5.3 reports the results of the analysis broken down by the ethnic groups involved in conflicts. The structure is the same as that of Table 5.2, with one change. Because the interaction effect between real wages of laborers and proportional change in immigration was significant only for the rate of attacks on Chinese, they are reported solely for Chinese/white conflicts (column 2).

Evidently, the yearly surges in immigration had sharply divergent effects on rates of ethnic collective action depending on which groups were involved. Surges in immigration increased rates of conflicts involv-

TABLE 5.3

Effects of Immigration and Economic Conditions on the Rate
of Ethnic Conflict Involving Various Ethnic Groups
in 77 American Cities, 1877–1914

(Asymptotic Standard Errors in Parentheses)

	Black/White (1)	Chinese/White (2)	Other (3)
Intercept	−10.6*** (2.45)	16.4*** (4.04)	−6.91** (3.19)
Proportional change in immigration	1.75** (.754)	12.6*** (4.43)	.010 (1.25)
Real wage of common laborers	8.04*** (1.70)	−15.5*** (3.70)	4.06* (2.22)
Real wage*proportional change in immigration		−12.0*** (4.87)	
Change in business failure rate	.019*** (.006)	.018 (.018)	.010 (.013)
Depression year	−1.14** (.487)	−1.44 (1.09)	.360 (.743)
Number of events in previous month	.069 (.102)	.311*** (.109)	.345 (.295)
Scale parameter	1.95*** (.159)	1.93*** (.242)	1.77*** (.274)
Number of spells	263	263	263
Uncensored spells	90	39	27
Log likelihood	−279.21	−121.05	−114.98

* $p < .10$, ** $p < .05$, *** $p < .01$

ing blacks and whites significantly. And immigration significantly raised rates of attacks on Chinese as during this period.

Curiously, those who instigated the flow—European immigrants—were apparently not the target of conflicts during peak surges of immigration. This pattern suggests that the relationship between those who raise levels of competition and those who are targeted by hostility it generates is not a straightforward one. Evidently those who are victimized by ethnic attacks are not always the ones who generated the initial spark to competition. Rather it is those who are least powerful to fight back who encounter the most violence and conflict. This irony is one we will return to in other sets of analyses of ethnic conflicts in chapters that follow.

Real wages of common laborers (an indicator of immigrant well-being) has a positive and significant effect on the rate of black/white conflict (column 1) but (when taken together with the interaction effect) a negative and significant effect on Chinese/white conflict (column 2).[15] This means that as improvements in the bargaining position for those at the bottom of the occupational structure (who were predominantly foreign-born) raised the rate of antiblack conflict, they depressed the rate of anti-Chinese conflict. Why would this be the case? One possibility is that African-Americans were viewed as a continuing threat across the country, while the influx of Chinese affected perceptions of competition in a small number of cities. A second possibility is that after 1882, passage of the Asian Exclusion Act undercut anti-Asian social movements and sharply decreased the number of anti-Chinese events, even in San Francisco (Saxton 1971). Both of these accounts imply that competition forces would weaken rates of anti-Asian violence. Since nearly all anti-Chinese conflicts took place on the West Coast, further investigation of regional differences in employment and ethnic group distributions in the common laborer occupation may help to account for these patterned differences.

Consider next the interaction between proportional changes in immigration and real wages on the rate of attacks on the Chinese (column 2). The negative interaction effect means that, as the wage rate varies from its first-quartile level of 1.10 to its third-quartile value of 1.46, the impact of change in immigration on the rate is negative. Increasing wages for laborers decreases the competition force of immigration on the rate of anti-Chinese events. This result runs opposite what one version of competition theories would lead us to expect. When interpreting these results, a note of caution is probably wise, since these results may be due to the fact that nearly all anti-Chinese events took place during 1880–1882, when real wages of laborers were high and immigration was rising.

The absence of a significant interaction effect for black/white and other/white events is substantively interesting. Instead, the main effects take the center stage for these targets of conflict. For events involving African-Americans and whites and events involving European immigrants, the real wage of common laborers has a positive effect on the rates, as does immigration for antiblack events. So during economic recovery periods and periods of relative prosperity in the immigrant and minority niche, attacks on African-Americans and white immigrants rise.

It is informative to compare the effects of our measures of economic contraction across the three broad categories of ethnic and racial groups involved in events in Table 5.3. Change in the business failure rate has

---

[15] All but one black/white conflict was instigated by whites, and all Chinese/white conflicts were instigated by whites.

a significant positive effect on conflict involving African-Americans, but this effect fails to reach significance for the other two groups. Likewise, a depression year increases the rate significantly for conflicts involving white immigrants, but it does not have a significant effect on the rates for other groups. One way to understand these differences is to consider the ethnic and racial stratification ladder. African-Americans occupied the bottom rung and were the first group targeted with attacks when the first signal of economic decline appeared. Others have argued that African-Americans were affected more severely by economic decline because they were unprotected by ethnic ownership of family businesses, as some Asian groups were (Saxton 1971; Ichioka 1988; Nee and Nee 1986). If both claims are true, then antiblack conflict would have been more sensitive to the *initial* signals of economic hardship, as the pattern in the first column for business failures suggests.[16]

One unexpected difference among the types of events concerns the effect of depressions. Depressions decreased the likelihood of antiblack conflicts and anti-Chinese conflicts; but these effects are only significant for antiblack conflicts. The fact that business failures increase the rate of attack on African-Americans while depressions decrease it parallels the findings shown in Table 5.2. Above we suggested that business failures signal future economic hardship, which may be most likely to affect those with the least power.

Number of recent ethnic events (involving any ethnic or racial group) has a positive and significant effect on the rate of Chinese/white events. Perhaps once again we might argue that this effect of contagion is magnified because these events were geographically concentrated in San Francisco over this period. Somewhat surprisingly, this effect is smaller and insignificant for black/white conflicts. So it appears that contagion of events has potent effects which differ in strength when the targets of attack are taken into account.

This macro-level analysis of ethnic collective action using event histories from newspaper accounts shows a consistent pattern of results for this early period of American history. Immigration and economic well-being affect the response to immigrants and racial minorities in similar ways. However, events involving African-Americans or Chinese are far more sensitive to macro-economic variables than ethnic events involv-

---

[16]Other specifications of interaction effects were examined, including an interaction between the change in business failure rate and depression years, and an interaction of depression years with level of real wages of common laborers. The guiding hypothesis was that periods of extreme contraction may have had curvilinear effects, such periods of extreme economic difficulty that suppressed all kinds of attacks. None of the interactions was statistically significant.

ing other immigrants. These findings also suggest that while economic hardship increases the likelihood of events involving European immigrants, it decreased the likelihood for black/white confrontations. Economic prosperity or recovery, measured by the absence of depression, significantly raises rates of protest against discrimination. This finding runs contrary to many economic hardship models of collective action.

Conclusions

The findings reported in this chapter clarify the processes by which economic competition and immigration of nationality groups affected rates of ethnic conflict and protest. At the national level, immigration and business failures sharply increased rates of ethnic collective action, particularly black/white confrontations. These results indicate that ethnic competition resulting from a slack job market or from increases in the supply of (lower wage) immigrant labor increased rates of ethnic collective action.

One particularly intriguing pattern is the sequencing of racial targets. In the beginning of the period, first Chinese, then African-Americans are overrepresented as targets of collective action in this period of American history. We need to investigate whether similar patterns hold for competition effects at the local level in chapters which follow. A second avenue we will investigate is suggested by the analyses supporting competition arguments for black/white and Chinese/white events: are the causes of ethnic conflict directed against European or white immigrants substantially different in nature from those involving other race groups? The results show strong differences in the macro-economic indicators on events involving African-Americans, Chinese, and white ethnics. Attacks on African-American and Chinese targets seem particularly sensitive to wage fluctuations or to business failure rates. Events involving white immigrants are more sensitive to fluctuations in immigration, as might be expected. Yet events involving white immigrants increase during economic depressions (although not significantly so), while events involving others do not. Periods of high business failures—a signal that more bad times are coming—significantly increase black/white confrontations. And anti-Chinese events apparently depend in part on the number of attacks on Chinese in the previous month. This implies that confrontations with race groups have different thresholds of ignition than other kinds, which provides motivation for analyses that distinguish racial and ethnic targets. Finally, what ethnic population characteristics, such as income levels, mobility and other achievement characteristics, affect these rates of ethnic collective action? We take up these issues in the chapters that follow.

6

Labor Unrest and Violence Against African-Americans

This chapter examines links between labor unrest and ethnic/racial conflict over the period of interest (but beginning in 1880 rather than 1877 for reasons discussed below). It explores the hypothesis that the two kinds of collective action—strikes and ethnic/racial conflict—were linked by their joint dependence on two processes. In the first process, a rise in immigration led to an increase in ethnic/racial competition in labor markets which in turn raised rates of ethnic conflict, as the previous chapter demonstrated. In the second, immigration also led to the proliferation of national labor unions. Such organizations provided leadership and resources for organizing strikes and for efforts by higher-wage workers to resist the influx of foreign and African-American workers. Thus immigration produced a rising supply of low-wage labor as the growth of national unions allowed organized workers to combat competition from immigrants and African-Americans. Taken together these two processes increased rates of both strikes and ethnic conflicts.

Many documentary reports of racial confrontations suggest that strikes and ethnic/racial conflict were causally connected. For example, accounts of this period published in the *New York Times* suggest that the union activity of white workers often coincided with attacks on African-Americans. This was common when black strikebreakers were hired.[1] Consider an event in New York's garment district in the spring of 1913:

---

[1]Gompers (1925), Bruce (1959), Bonacich (1972), Wilson (1978), Foner (1982), and Fink (1983) discuss the effect of strikes on antiblack rioting and violence during this period. The extensiveness of the use of African-American and white immigrant strikebreakers has been much debated (Brody 1960; Ehrlich 1974; Higgs 1977; Davis 1980). The point made here is that peak periods of immigration made workers aware that employers could always hire African-Americans or white immigrants; the threat was there even if it was never actually implemented.

More than 100 negro women were at work in the white goods factory of Mitchell Brothers on the ninth floor of 543 Broadway yesterday when three men entered, drew revolvers, and fired at the ceiling ... The members of the firm said that the garment workers' union was responsible for the outrage. When their operators walked out in a recent strike they employed negro women as strikebreakers, and, when the strike ended, retained them. (*NYT*, April 15, 1913, p. 3)

Strikes were not the only precipitants of racial strife. It appears that conflicts against African-Americans occurred even without the presence of unions or strike activity. In some such cases, the precipitant was an event in another city, as was the case involving Chicago dock workers during the summer of 1908:

In a fight to-day between white and black dock laborers employed on the Western Transit Company's wharfs, growing out of antagonism which had developed since the Springfield riots, five men were injured and the police restored order only after a free use of clubs and threats to shoot. (*NYT*, August 20, 1908, p. 1)

Apparently attacks on African-Americans were likely when employers reacted to strikes or labor shortages by hiring African-American laborers. This chapter explores the mechanism underlying these patterns. It asks: how did the level of labor unrest influence the nature and frequency of racial/ethnic conflict? Little research has addressed this question, perhaps because researchers typically treat strikes and ethnic conflicts as forms of collective activity motivated by different interests. Strikes supposedly reflect economic interests while ethnic conflicts reflect "primordial," that is ethnic or national, loyalties. Sociological analyses of each type of collective action tend to ignore the other. This is surprising given the widespread agreement in the historical accounts that labor unrest and antiforeigner sentiment were related to the industrialization of production and the expansion of the work force (Commons 1918; Brody 1960; Foner 1947; Gordon et al. 1982; Fink 1983).

Increased activity of the labor movement could have affected rates of racial and ethnic conflict in at least two ways. One view that seems implicit in many historical accounts is that the unrest accompanying strikes caused ethnic conflict (Yellen 1936; Rudwick 1964). An alternative view, developed here, is that resources accumulated during the growth of national unions caused rates of strikes to increase during the same time that unions also encouraged ethnic conflicts.

Immigration, Labor Movement Activity, and Ethnic Competition

The heuristic model in Figure 6.1 provides one answer to questions about how labor unrest and ethnic conflict might be causally related. It sug-

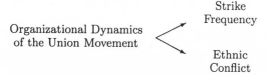

FIG. 6.1 Parallel Forms Model of Strikes and Ethnic Conflict

gests that the temporal covariation of labor unrest and ethnic conflict does not reflect any direct relation between the two, that strike activity per se does not cause ethnic conflict. Instead, it suggests that both forms of collective action depended upon the growth of unions, ethnic competition, and rising immigration. According to Figure 6.1, immigration encouraged ethnic competition and the growth of union organization. Growth of union organizations increased the frequency of strikes, as leadership and organizational resources enabled workers to express their grievances.

During this period, competition for jobs intensified when the supply of low wage labor due to immigration or African-American migration rose. Under such conditions of increased ethnic/racial competition, conflicts against the least powerful minorities erupted (Bonacich 1976; Higgs 1977; Olzak 1987). The two paths in Figure 6.1, which link the growth of union organizations to strike frequency and ethnic conflict, require some amplification, as they have not been analyzed in the sociological literature. This section reviews some of the historical evidence linking these processes.

In the decades between 1880 and 1920, rapid industrialization created an enormous demand for immigrant labor; and immigration flows rose to fill that demand. As the ethnic/racial diversity of neighborhoods and factories rose, immigrants came to be seen as less than desirable neighbors, coworkers, and citizens, and they became the object of numerous protests (Higham 1955).

This period also marked the end of Reconstruction in the South and the establishment of Jim Crow laws which once again formally separated African-Americans and whites into unequal worlds (Chalmers 1965; Woodward 1974; Wright 1986). In addition, this period witnessed a substantial increase in the demand for labor in the industrializing North. These changes apparently caused a flow of African-American migrants to northern cities,[2] where they were even less welcome than

---

[2]Wilson (1978: 67) notes that five of the largest population centers experienced significant increases in their African-American communities between 1910 and 1920. For instance, in this decade the African-American population of Chicago increased

foreigners. African-American migrants from the South encountered discrimination, segregation, and violence reminiscent of what they had tried to escape (Bodnar et al. 1982).

Conflicts involving native-born whites, white and Asian immigrants, and African-American migrants during this period initially took the form of sporadic clashes. Whites harassed and attacked African-Americans, Chinese, and recent European immigrants in cities where they were concentrated (Jackson 1967; Saxton 1971; Boswell 1986; Olzak 1987). Later, native whites organized sophisticated political movements, often with a national scope, such as the Workingman's Association and the Immigration Restriction League (Garis 1927; Higham 1955; Archdeacon 1983). These national social movements initially sought federal laws to end immigration from China. In 1924, a more general anti-immigration movement culminated in the passage of the National Origins Act, which restricted immigration by a system of national quotas (Keely 1979; Cafferty et al. 1983).

Increases in immigration also encouraged the founding of national labor unions during this period (Hannan and Freeman 1987). While national labor unions recruited and received strong support from various ethnic populations (Fink 1977), most unions participated vigorously in lobbying and campaigns designed to restrict further immigration (Garis 1927; Foner 1947). Union histories make clear that increasing immigration was sometimes met with swift, vocal resistance by national unions, most notably those in the A. F. of L. Some native-born white workers and white immigrants who arrived prior to 1880 saw national unions as organizations designed to protect their economic self-interest (Commons 1918; Gompers 1925; Higgs 1977). Exercising this protection led to policies that were antiforeigner and antiblack because it was usually African-Americans and recent immigrants who were willing to work for lower than the prevailing wages (Gompers 1925; Foner 1982).

Of course confrontations between labor and management were also common during this period. Expansion of unions encouraged strikes (Snyder 1975; Hibbs 1976; Edwards 1981). Workers of various ethnicities organized strikes and walkouts; employers often reacted with lockouts and offensives against unions (Powderly 1889; Commons 1918; Yellen 1936; Foner 1947 and 1964). The overlap between cycles of ethnic and

---

by nearly 150%, Pittsburgh by 117%, New York City by 66%, and St. Louis, by nearly 60%. In his analysis of the 1917 East St. Louis Race Riot, Rudwick (1964) claims that the black population grew from the 1910 census count of 5,882 to 10,617 in 1917 (as estimated from school, church, and draft records).

labor protest during this period suggests that the two patterns of unrest may have been related. This is because the rising numbers of immigrants fueled both strikes and ethnic conflict. A review of three interrelated lines of historical argument clarifies these links between immigration, competition and conflict.

Immigration and a Reserve Army of Labor. According to one argument, immigration provided a reserve army of low-wage workers whose presence undercut the power of unions and the effectiveness of strikes (Montgomery 1979; Davis 1980). Immigrants and African-American migrants diminished the power of unions directly when they served as strikebreakers. More subtle pressure on the labor movement came from the fact that migrant African-Americans and immigrants were willing to work for lower wages and/or for longer hours than native-born whites. T.V. Powderly, leader of the Knights of Labor, explained:

The opposition to the Hungarians in the coke regions amounted to hatred—a hatred which is liable at any time to burst forth in a blaze which may sweep them wholly out of that country ... Last Monday, the largest firm engaged in the manufacture of coke sent a force of Hungarians down into the mines and the men employed in the mines immediately quit work ... They work for little or nothing, live on fare which a Chinaman would not touch, and will submit to every indignity which may be imposed on them ... Before the Hungarian was imported the task for an ordinary man was to draw five ovens, but the Hungarian takes the contract for six ovens for less money than the American formerly received for five ... to the creature whose highest ambition is to work, work, without knowing whether he receives adequate compensation or not, I have no welcome and would prevent him from landing if I could. (Powderly 1884: 576–77)

Ethnic competition also caused antagonism toward Asians on the West Coast, even after Chinese immigration was stopped. For example, the San Francisco Labor Council described the "Mongolian Labor Curse," in the *American Federation of Labor Journal* (April 7, 1900), long after the Chinese Exclusion Act of 1882. African-American migrants too provided a reserve army of labor in the industrializing cities. Policies on membership of African-Americans in unions varied by location and period (Commons 1918; Foner 1947; Wright 1986). Yet most trade unions either ignored them or displayed open antagonism. According to Commons (1918: 135),

Clashes between black and white laborers were not infrequent ... When, during the same decade, the Negro began to invade the trades and superior positions, the opposition to him was no less strong ... The bricklayers' union in Washington D.C. forbade their men to work alongside coloured men. Four white union men were found to be working with some Negroes on government work, and the union decided unanimously to expel them from the union.

Ethnic Divisions Within the Working Class. A second view in labor history stresses that the division between skilled and unskilled workers also coincided approximately with ethnic/racial distinctions.[3] Because the alternative sources of labor were members of other ethnic or racial populations, economic self-interest often led to racist and antiforeigner hostilities. Native-born whites and earlier immigrant groups (such as Germans and Irish) were more likely to be part of the trade union movement than African-Americans and South-Central and Eastern Europeans (Foner 1964, 1982; Fink 1983; Ross 1985). "New immigrants" and African-Americans were also less likely to move into skilled occupations than were second-generation and third-generation immigrants and native whites (Thernstrom 1973; Lieberson 1980; Bodnar, Weber, and Simon 1982; Wright 1986; Gutman and Bell 1987). And finally, racial differences in industrial skills and experience played an important role in maintaining the gaps between whites and African-Americans in mobility and earnings, particularly in the textile, tobacco, and steel industries in the South during this period (Spero and Harris 1931; Wright 1986).

When employers hired new immigrants or African-American migrants, members of all-white unions tended to draw racial distinctions between members and nonmembers. During periods of labor unrest, minorities became convenient targets for hostilities. A revealing glimpse of official union views comes from a report on "East St. Louis Riots—Their Causes," by Samuel Gompers, founder of the A.F. of L.:

> ... the packing plants and stockyards of Armour, Swift, and Morris, the Aluminum Ore Company, the American Steel Foundry, the Commercial Acid Company and twenty-seven railroad lines ... employed many foreigners until workers were called home to their colors. They began the policy of negro importation from the south. Negro importation became a regular business— agents were sent throughout the south who collected groups of negroes and paid the railroad fare to East St. Louis ... As a result, East St. Louis became a sort of convention center for excited, undisciplined negroes who were intoxicated by higher wages than they had ever known. Some of these as in the case of the Aluminum Ore Company, were used as strikebreakers, and the element of racial industrial competition was added to other trouble-breeding influences. (*American Federationist*, 1917: 621)

Trade unionists, representing the so-called aristocracy of labor, fre-

---

[3]Fink (1983: xii) states that "While only 13 percent of the total population was classified as foreign-born in 1880, 42 percent of those engaged in manufacturing and extractive industries were immigrants. If one adds to this figure workers of foreign parentage and of Afro-American descent, the resulting non-native/nonwhite population clearly encompassed the great majority of America's industrial work force." See also Archdeacon 1983, Wright 1986, and Gutman and Bell 1987. Lieberson (1980) and Olzak (1989c) provide estimates of overlap in occupational distributions of foreign-born, native-born and blacks in this period.

quently opposed admitting as members those foreigners and African-Americans whose presence in urban labor markets undermined the power of skilled workers who had won the rights to closed shops and union bargaining (Fink 1983). Such attempts at exclusion caused ethnic antagonism to flare.

Deskilling, Strikes and Ethnic Conflict. A third historical perspective agrees with the first two but claims that it was mechanization that actually precipitated ethnic conflict. In this view, ethnic conflict was driven primarily by skilled workers' fears of deskilling rather than by racism (Gordon, Edwards, and Reich 1982). Skilled, unionized workers organized collectively in the face of threats of automation to prevent the employment of the *unskilled*, who happened to be disproportionately African-American and foreign-born.[4] The process of mechanization initiated fears of deskilling, while the presence of African-American strikebreakers and immigrants added credibility to fears that machines and unskilled operatives could be substituted for skilled, unionized labor. To the extent that these less-skilled workers were members of ethnic or racial minorities, strikes also encouraged ethnic/racial strife.

So far the discussion has emphasized that immigration and union organization provided skilled workers with the motivation and capacity to react to immigrants and African-American migrants. There is also another side to labor conflict. Employer resistance often succeeded in halting workers' movements to organize (Gompers 1925; Edwards 1981; Fink 1983; Griffin, Wallace, and Rubin 1986). It appears that immigration significantly increased employers' capacity to undermine unions. As Edwards (1981) and others argue, factors like immigration that increase the organizational resources of employers also increase the frequency of strikes. So, immigration fueled the motivation and capacity to engage in strikes for both partners to labor conflict during this period.

Ethnic Competition, Split Labor Markets, and Labor Unions

The historical evidence appears to imply that strikes and ethnic conflict are causally related. But closely examined, the historical expla-

---

[4]Several case studies of ethnic/racial communities provide evidence on this point. The wave of immigration beginning in the 1880s (especially of the South-Central-Eastern Europeans) provided a low-wage supply of labor characterized by high rates of illiteracy, low education, rural skills, and little industrial experience. The United States Bureau of Immigration (1901), Walkowitz (1978), Hershberg (1981), Fink (1983), and Gutman and Bell (1987) provide details of the immigrant experience during this period, and Spero and Harris (1931), Blassingame (1973), and Higgs (1977) document the African-American experience in the labor force during this same period. Saxton (1971) and Nee and Nee (1986) treat the experience of Chinese immigrants during this period.

nations suggest elements of two different models of collective action. On one hand, some of the accounts imply a direct causal relationship between strike activity and antiblack violence in instances where African-American strikebreakers were recruited. Alternatively, arguments emphasizing the role of the labor aristocracy and deskilling seem to imply that labor unions facilitated both strikes and ethnic conflict, but that the two forms of collective action are themselves unrelated. In order to clarify these issues, we must sharpen the distinctions between the two processes.

At least two sociological perspectives shed light on these issues: competition theory and resource mobilization theory. As previous chapters have discussed at length, each suggests that (1) ethnic competition, stimulated by economic depressions and immigration, raised rates of ethnic conflict and (2) increases in the organizational resources of the labor aristocracy raised rates of collective action, including ethnic/racial conflicts.

The reserve army and deskilling perspectives suggest that the influx of unskilled immigrants and African-American migrants encouraged both sides of labor conflicts to engage in strikes during periods of peak immigration. Why did *ethnic* conflict also erupt? The answer lies in combining these historical accounts with competition theory. Migration and immigration intensified competition for jobs with low pay and status.[5] As the threat from immigrant and other low-wage workers rose, the likelihood that white and native-born workers would retaliate with ethnic collective action against immigrants and African-Americans rose. One version of this general argument emphasizes that ethnic antagonism peaks under conditions of a split labor market.[6]

Another kind of competition argument claims that it was not a necessary condition that African-Americans and native whites and foreigners worked at the same jobs in the same cities (or were actually hired as

---

[5] How strongly did native whites, foreign immigrants, and African-Americans compete in job markets? While analysis of this question lies outside of the scope of this chapter, it is useful to note that occupational segregation for the foreign-born *declined* between 1870 and 1880 in a subset of the cities analyzed here, as Chapter 8 shows. This suggests that significant levels of competition for jobs existed among white foreign- and native-born even prior to the period studied here. Blassingame (1973: 61) claims for New Orleans that "Since foreign-born workers constituted 49 and 33 percent of the total number of laborers in New Orleans in 1870 and 1880, they represented the Negroes' chief competitors for jobs." (See also Higgs 1977 and Bodnar et al. 1982.) Lieberson (1980) also finds that occupational and residential segregation for South, Central, and Eastern Europeans declined from 1890 to 1920 while they increased for African-Americans.

[6] Bonacich (1972: 549) claims that ethnic/racial conflict occurred where there were two or more ethnic or racial populations "whose price of labor differs for the same work, or would differ if they did the same work."

replacement workers as in strikebreakers) for ethnic conflict to erupt. Rather, an awareness of the presence of such ethnic populations as potential low-wage competitors anywhere in the country, could elevate ethnic tensions and spark conflict (Olzak 1987). This chapter argues that labor unions played a crucial role in spreading such awareness and in facilitating collective action to focus attention on these competitive forces.

Organizational Resources: The Role of National Labor Unions. Resource mobilization theories hold that increases in resources controlled by collective actors raise their rates of collective action. The likelihood of collective action rises especially when the balance of power among competing groups shifts so that disadvantaged groups experience a rise in *numbers of organizations* and other strategic resources (Tilly, Tilly, and Tilly 1975; Jenkins 1983). Though such arguments are plausible, existing theory and research have not yet specified how shifts in organizational resources produce different forms of collective action, nor have they explained how labor and ethnic unrest might be causally linked. Surprisingly few studies have actually estimated the impact of organizations on the rate of collective activity (but see McAdam 1982, Jenkins and Eckert 1986, McCarthy et al. 1988). The following discussion attempts to sharpen distinctions between two kinds of resource mobilization arguments that have been conflated in studies of collective action.

This chapter argues that labor unrest and ethnic conflict are related only by their common dependence on variations in the organizational resources of the labor movement. In other words, labor unrest and ethnic conflict are "parallel forms" of collective action. One concrete source of the relationship between the two kinds of unrest is their common dependence on rising organizational resources represented by union structures.

According to Shorter and Tilly (1974), industrial conflict intensifies when the balance of power between management and workers changes. Outcomes of labor negotiations and strikes depend on the number of and access to *organizational* resources on each side of the conflict. An increase in strike frequency is commonly attributed to growth in the organizational capacity and resource base of labor unions (Snyder 1975; Wallace, Rubin, and Smith 1987).

Growth of labor unions has been affected by the economic and political environments (Hannan and Freeman 1987, 1989). Founding rates of unions rise during economic booms and fall during economic depressions (Hannan and Freeman 1987). Research on the life-histories of organizations within social movements appears to confirm the premise of the resource mobilization perspective that the organizational dynamics are key to a social movement's success. The number and scope of national organizations associated with a social movement increase the movement's ability to mobilize members, extend its longevity, resist failure, and influence national policy (McCarthy 1987; McCarthy et al. 1988).

But did unions encourage collective action against ethnic/racial groups in addition to mobilizing strikes and walkouts? Some historians have suggested that the labor movement's organizations, communication networks, and sometimes charismatic leadership also facilitated (and perhaps legitimated) collective actions against ethnic/racial groups as well (Foner 1982; Fink 1983). Victories in labor struggles may have encouraged labor leaders to consider all kinds of issues relevant to job security in closed shops, including national programs and campaigns to contain immigration and African-American migration (Foner 1964). Union structures were a resource to apply against threats posed by the presence of unskilled African-Americans and white ethnics in the labor force or community.[7] Thus the model in Figure 6.1 depicts the relationship between labor and ethnic unrest as "spurious." That is, this parallel-forms argument suggests that organizational growth of the union movement caused both kinds of collective action, but that the two types were not causally related. By implication, once the causes of strike frequency are controlled in analysis of ethnic conflict, the organizational base of the union movement will be associated with ethnic conflict but the relationship between strikes and ethnic conflict will diminish or even disappear.

An alternative to the model in Figure 6.1 can also be teased out of the historical accounts. This second model might be called a "causal chain" model of strike activity and ethnic conflict. It portrays the relationship of strike frequency and ethnic conflict as causal. It treats the occurrence of strikes as one stage of a social movement leading to a second stage of ethnic conflict. As the labor movement gains momentum, the likelihood of strikes increases. The occurrence of strikes builds further organizational momentum that union leaders could apply to ethnic or racial issues. In this view, strikes created communication links and associations that facilitated social protests. In this way, leaders, strategies, and

---

[7]Although there are examples of union organizations (notably the Knights of Labor prior to 1890) that did not exclude blacks (Wright 1986), exclusion of African-Americans by the A.F. of L., as well as other trade union movements around the turn of the century, has been well documented (Spero and Harris 1931; Yellen 1936; Higgs 1977; Foner 1982). According to Foner (1964: 239) this is particularly true for the railroad industry where African-Americans workers experienced a sharp reversal in fortunes around 1900 following unionization: "Before the formation of the Brotherhood of Engineers and Firemen, Negroes held many of the higher playing railroad jobs. Many were firemen and brakemen. After the formation of the Brotherhood, Negroes were pushed out of these positions, and were replaced by men who were eligible for membership in the all white Brotherhood."

Organizational Dynamics   ⟶   Strike   ⟶   Ethnic
of the Union Movement   Frequency   Conflict

FIG. 6.2   Causal Sequence Model of Strikes and Ethnic Conflict

repertoires from the labor movement spread to ethnic forms of collective action. Put differently, the alternative model of collective action suggests that labor unrest and ethnic conflict are linked by the process of diffusion. As the previous discussion indicated, the labor movement during this period often took action against European immigrants and African-Americans. The historical examples and quotes from labor leaders also suggest that the link between labor unrest and ethnic conflict was much stronger when African-Americans and immigrants were used as strike-breakers. Figure 6.2 depicts these relationships as a series of stages.

The processes depicted in both Figures 6.1 and 6.2 assume that immigration, ethnic competition, and the growth of national labor unions increased the frequency of strikes over this period. So these "background" factors must be included in any empirical tests of these arguments. The key difference is that the model in Figure 6.2 holds that strike frequency had an independent effect on the rate of ethnic conflict. It implies that strike frequency ought to affect the rates of ethnic conflict *directly*, net of the effects of union organization, business cycles, depressions, wage rates, and factors previously associated with the growth of the labor movement's organizational structure.

The empirical analysis reported below considers the implications of the models in Figures 6.1 and 6.2. If resource mobilization arguments that emphasize the importance of organizational structure are accurate, we would expect that any apparent empirical relationship between strike activity and ethnic conflict will be diminished in those models which include measures of the growth of national labor unions. Figure 6.1 suggests we should find clearcut and positive effects of the growth of national labor unions on rates of ethnic conflict. If, on the other hand, strike activity is instrumental in the mobilization of ethnic conflict, we should expect that there is a direct path between strikes and ethnic conflict, as Figure 6.2 suggests.

Research Design and Data

The previous chapter provided motivations for conducting analysis at the "national" level, that is, for the entire set of cities taken together. However, in the case of the issues addressed in this chapter, there are additional issues to be considered in deciding on an appropriate level of analysis. Historical accounts suggest that cycles of union activity and economic depression affected *national-level* rates of ethnic conflict. Some readers have suggested that the cities in the urban system were weakly connected during this period.[8]

Second, annual conventions of the Knights of Labor, A. F. of L., and individual national unions, which attracted officials and members from many cities during this period, routinely took up issues of national concern and policy. Information about local trouble spots involving immigrant or black strikebreakers were frequently the central topic of these conventions during 1880–1915 (Powderly 1884 and 1889; Gompers 1925; Garis 1927; Foner 1947). National lobbying organizations representing these union interests caused changes in the United States immigration laws throughout this period (Garis 1927; Keely 1979). During this period employer resistance to the labor movement also become organized on a *national* scale. Prominent examples include the Citizens Industrial Association, the American Anti-Boycott Association, and the National Council of Industrial Defense (Taft 1964: 212–229).

The analysis begins with 1880, the first year for which a consistent time series on strike frequencies is available. This year also marks the beginning of a significant rise in immigration. The analysis ends at the close of 1914, for reasons discussed in the previous chapter.

Independent Variables.   All economic variables were measured as changes in levels over the previous year in this chapter. This is because competition and resource mobilization theories stress the importance of *gains and losses* in resources. That is, such theories predict sudden or relative reversals to have more potent effects than the customary levels of these same indicators. Economic contraction, which signals worsening conditions (especially in low-skilled jobs) and diminished opportunities to open new businesses, is measured by change in the business failure rate per 1000 businesses (United States Bureau of the Census 1975) and economic depression.[9]

Changes in economic prosperity for the disadvantaged are measured

---

[8]It would be interesting to obtain data at the local level to see if the use of African-American strikebreakers led directly to attacks on blacks in the largest cities in the United States, or if union organizing was more likely in these urban settings. There are a few local-level data sets (from Massachusetts and New Jersey) on labor organizing for a subset of this same period, and data on locals organizations associated with the Knights of Labor is available for about twenty years beginning in 1880 (Carroll and Huo 1986, 1988). Unfortunately I know of no broad systematic source of information on the specific location of union organizing or strikes over the longer period studied here. Furthermore, to my knowledge, there is no systematic information on which local strikes were ethnically/racially motivated.

[9]Another indicator of economic hardship, the unemployment rate, is only available beginning in 1890, which means that ten years of information on events are lost when

by the change in the real wage rate for common laborers. Labor unrest was measured using yearly strike frequencies, a combined count of walkouts and work stoppages (Griffin 1939). And proportional change in immigration is measured as in the previous chapter.

This analysis uses two measures of organizational growth and success of the labor movement: the number of national unions and the number of union foundings (Hannan and Freeman 1987, 1988). It is more common to use the proportion of workers in unions, sometimes called "union density," in research on strike rates. Such studies assume that aggregate union membership drives the process of labor unrest and subsequent growth of unions. Hannan and Freeman (1988: Figure 1) show that the number of unions rose 25–30 years *prior* to the rise in the proportion of workers in unions. Whereas the number of unions reached a peak in 1890, proportion of unionized workers did not peak until the 1930s, suggesting that the rise in the number of unions caused growth in membership.[10] Between 1880 and 1915, the number of labor unions rose from 31 to 183 (which is close its historic high of 211). So this was the period in which the labor movement experienced its greatest organizational growth. Nonetheless, the yearly number of foundings fluctuated widely, ranging from 1 to 19, which suggests that there were large short-run fluctuations in the organizational capacities of the labor movement during this period. Both the number of union organizations and the founding rate provide potentially useful information on the organizational strength of the labor union movement.

There are also good theoretical reasons for focusing on organizational structures rather than membership in labor unions. Actual numbers of union organizations and foundings were used in the present analysis because resource mobilization theories clearly focus on the existence of organizational structures as sources of collective action (Tilly 1978; Jenkins 1983; Zald and McCarthy 1987).

Results

Figure 6.3 shows the covariation of number of ethnic conflicts, number of strikes, and immigration over the period. Note that both kinds of collective action followed similar trajectories across this period. Because

---

this indicator is included. Nonetheless when it is included in variations of the models whose estimates are reported here, it has no effect on any of the rates of conflict.

[10]Another reason for not using union membership is that it is available only from the year 1897. If the more commonly used measure of "union density" were used here it would sharply restrict the period under analysis. However, I did examine the effect of union membership on the rate for only eighteen years, 1897–1914. The effect of union membership on the rate of ethnic conflict was negative and insignificant.

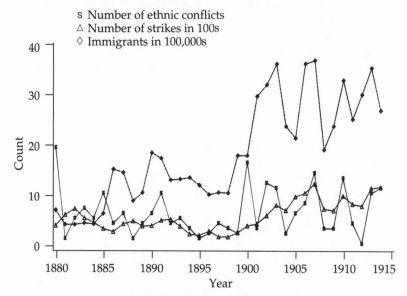

FIG. 6.3 Labor Unrest, Ethnic Conflict,
and Immigration, 1880–1914

the variation in all three curves is uneven, no simple time trend models
or explanations can account for the patterns.

Table 6.1 shows that two thirds of all conflicts from 1880 through
1914 were directed against African-Americans. African-Americans were
not only more likely to be the targets of conflict, but they were significantly more likely to be the targets of violence. Therefore, we devote
particular attention to the effects of covariates on the rate of conflict
directed against blacks.

Did the causes of violent events differ from the causes of nonviolent
ones and did the causes of conflicts against blacks differ from the causes
of conflicts against others? Tables 6.2–6.4 speak to these questions.
Table 6.2 reports ML estimates of the effects of covariates on *all* conflicts
(columns 1 and 2), *violent* conflicts (columns 3 and 4), and *nonviolent*
conflicts (columns 5 and 6). (In this and subsequent tables, the models
and estimator used are the same as those described in the previous
chapter.)

Table 6.3 contains estimates of the effects of the same covariates
on rates of conflicts against *blacks* (columns 1 and 2) and on rates of
conflicts against *other groups* (columns 3 and 4). Table 6.4 contains
estimates of the effects of these covariates on rates of *violence against*

TABLE 6.1
Ethnic and Racial Conflicts in 77
American Cities, 1880–1914

Conflict	Violent Conflicts	Nonviolent Conflicts	Total
Against African-Americans	75 (83%)	15 (17%)	90 (100%)
Against Others	26 (43%)	34 (56%)	60 (100%)
Total	101 (67%)	49 (33%)	150 (100%)

blacks (columns 1 and 2) and on rates of *violence against others* (columns 3 and 4).

Whether the number of union organizations and foundings alters the effect of strikes is a key issue here. Therefore, the results have been organized in pairs. In each analysis, results for models that include the effect of strike frequency, immigration, and economic conditions but exclude measures of the organizational dynamics of unions are found in the odd-numbered columns. The results for models that add the number of unions and union foundings are in even-numbered columns.[11]

We first performed tests to see if the various categories of conflicts must be analyzed separately: violence versus nonviolence, antiblack versus other targets, and violence against African-Americans versus violence against others. In each case there were good reasons to believe that the causal structure of events might differ by target and the presence of violence. This suspicion proved correct. In the first comparison in Table 6.2, a pooled model (adjusted for the appropriate number of spells)

---

[11]These are only two of the hierarchical models of possible interest. Readers might also be interested in the results comparing odd- and even-numbered columns that also exclude changes in immigration to the same models that include immigration. This comparison tests the hypothesis that the effect of change in immigration is "spurious" as well. According to likelihood ratio tests, excluding the effect of change in immigration always decreases the fit significantly. Moreover, the estimates of the effect of strike frequency is virtually unchanged from those reported in the odd-numbered columns in Tables 6.2–6.4 when change in immigration is excluded. In addition, models that exclude changes in immigration from the set of covariates in the even-numbered columns fared significantly worse for all conflicts, violent conflicts, antiblack conflicts, and antiblack violence. For all but one column in Tables 6.2–6.4, changes in immigration have more powerful effects on the rates of conflicts than any other variable. Finally, the effects of the key measures of union organization are larger relative to their standard errors when changes in immigration are *included* rather than excluded. For these reasons, we begin the hierarchical comparisons of models with and without union organization measures with models that include changes in immigration.

TABLE 6.2

Estimates of the Effects of Strikes and Union Organizations on Rates of All, Violent, and Nonviolent Conflicts in 77 American Cities, 1880–1914

(Asymptotic Standard Errors in Parentheses)

Independent Variables	All Conflicts		Violent Conflicts		Nonviolent Conflicts	
	(1)	(2)	(3)	(4)	(5)	(6)
Intercept	.584 (.389)	.478 (.502)	-1.44*** (.591)	-2.26*** (.823)	.717 (.541)	.940 (.609)
Number of strikes/10	.003* (.001)	.002 (.003)	.008*** (.002)	.001 (.004)	-.007** (.003)	.000 (.006)
Number of union foundings		.021 (.039)		.014 (.010)		.119* (.065)
Number of labor unions		.001 (.007)		.017* (.010)		-.023** (.011)
Change in immigration	2.14*** (.351)	2.20*** (.401)	2.23*** (.530)	2.66*** (.614)	1.40*** (.450)	1.17** (.512)
Change in real wage of laborers	-10.1 (6.35)	-10.7 (6.72)	-14.8 (9.17)	-11.6 (9.74)	-4.79 (7.81)	-9.80 (8.49)
Change in business failure rate	.014** (.006)	.014** (.006)	.018** (.007)	.018** (.007)	-.008 (.011)	-.013 (.013)
Scale parameter (σ)	1.93*** (.124)	1.93*** (.122)	2.06*** (.162)	2.07*** (.163)	1.63*** (.183)	1.61*** (.181)
Number of spells	253	253	253	253	253	253
Uncensored spells	150	150	101	101	49	49
Log-likelihood	-411.46	-411.32	-320.38	-318.76	-167.69	-163.59
Degrees of freedom	6	8	6	8	6	8

* p < .10,　** p < .05,　*** p < .01.

TABLE 6.3

Estimates of the Effects of Strikes and Union Organizations
on Rates of Attacks on African-Americans and Other Groups
in 77 American Cities, 1880–1914

(Asymptotic Standard Errors in Parentheses)

Independent Variables	African-American Targets		Other Targets	
	(1)	(2)	(3)	(4)
Intercept	−1.77***	−3.16***	.713	1.64***
	(.609)	(.897)	(.581)	(.659)
Number of strikes/10	.010	.000	−.008***	.003
	(.002)	(.004)	(.003)	(.006)
Number of union foundings		.108**		−.135
		(.046)		(.083)
Number of labor unions		.020**		−.020*
		(.010)		(.012)
Change in immigration	1.54**	2.27***	2.05***	1.48***
	(.604)	(.717)	(.490)	(.507)
Change in real wage of laborers	−15.7*	−17.3*	−5.17	−6.14
	(9.12)	(10.4)	(8.49)	(8.11)
Change in business failure rate	.016**	.019***	.002	.001
	(.007)	(.007)	(.012)	(.012)
Scale parameter (σ)	1.93***	1.94***	1.93***	1.90***
	(.158)	(.160)	(.200)	(.197)
Number of spells	253	253	253	253
Uncensored spells	90	90	60	60
Log-likelihood	−283.44	−279.28	−207.57	−204.81
Degrees of freedom	6	8	6	8

* $p < .10$,   ** $p < .05$,   *** $p < .01$.

shown in the first column (excluding the union variables) was tested against a pair of analogous models for violent and nonviolent conflicts in the third and fifth columns. Similarly, a pooled model in the second column in Table 6.2 including the two union organizations measures was tested against analogous models in the fourth and sixth columns. The resulting likelihood ratio tests of the pooled models of all conflicts versus the same models distinguished by violence and nonviolence reveal that models broken down by presence of violence fit significantly better than the pooled model.

The same kinds of comparisons were conducted in Tables 6.3 and 6.4. Once again the likelihood ratio tests justify the separation of analyses by racial target. For instance, Table 6.4 shows a breakdown of all violence events by target—antiblack violence versus violence against other

TABLE 6.4

Estimates of the Effects of Strikes and Union Organizations
on Rates of Violent Attacks on African-Americans
and Other Groups in American Cities, 1880–1914

(Asymptotic Standard Errors in Parentheses)

Independent Variables	Violence Against African-Americans		Violence Against Other Groups	
	(1)	(2)	(3)	(4)
Intercept	−2.93***	−4.72***	2.27*	−1.28
	(.767)	(1.16)	(1.25)	(1.46)
Number of strikes/10	.012***	.000	−.005***	.004
	(.002)	(.001)	(.005)	(.010)
Number of union foundings		.078		−.319
		(.051)		(.175)
Number of labor unions		.027**		.005
		(.011)		(.021)
Change in immigration	2.17***	3.10***	2.02**	1.49
	(.682)	(.838)	(.972)	(1.02)
Change in real wage of laborers	−18.2*	−18.0	−9.18	−1.10
	(10.9)	(12.0)	(17.6)	(16.6)
Change in business failure rate	.017**	.018**	.008	.004
	(.007)	(.008)	(.021)	(.018)
Scale parameter (σ)	1.93***	1.94***	2.48***	2.49***
	(.171)	(.173)	(.410)	(.409)
Number of spells	253	253	253	253
Uncensored spells	75	75	26	26
Log-likelihood	−242.79	−239.14	−125.72	−123.55
Degrees of freedom	6	8	6	8

* $p < .10$, ** $p < .05$, *** $p < .01$.

targets. The likelihood ratio tests conducted here also show that when the models in Table 6.4 that are broken down by antiblack and other targets fare better than a pooled model. Taken together these results indicate that events of each subtype should be analyzed separately.

Consider first the effect of economic conditions. Economic contraction has been found to depress strike frequencies (Griffin 1939; Edwards 1981). The previous chapter showed that it also raises rates of ethnic conflict and protest (see also Olzak 1987). As we discussed in Chapter 3, both competition theory and resource mobilization theory hold that collective action increases when resources become available to disadvantaged groups (Olzak 1983; Jenkins 1983). Economic contraction (decreases in laborers' real wages and increases in business failure rates) does increase rates of most types of ethnic conflicts. Change in real wages has the strongest effect on conflicts against blacks, as can be seen in the first and second columns in Table 6.3 and in the first column of Table 6.4.

Now we turn to the key issues regarding the relationships among immigration, labor unrest, and ethnic conflict, as summarized in Figures 6.1 and 6.2. According to theories of competition and split labor markets, increases in immigration, which swell the supply of low-wage labor, increase rates of ethnic conflict. Every column in Tables 6.2–6.4, save the fourth column in Table 6.4, shows strong and consistent effects of this measure of rising competition. That is, increases in immigration significantly increase the rates of all types of conflict.

The effect of strike frequency depends on the target and on the presence of violence. In the first column of Table 6.2 the estimated effect of strike frequency on the overall rate of ethnic conflicts is positive and significant. When violent and nonviolent conflicts are considered separately, however, strike frequency appears to have opposing effects: the strike rate significantly *increases* the rate of violent events but significantly *decreases* the rate of nonviolent ones.

Indications from labor history that waves of strikes and antiblack activity coincided appear to be corroborated here. The effect of strike frequency is strongest for violent antiblack events, as can be seen in the first column of Table 6.4. When the estimated effect, .0012, is divided by the scale parameter, 1.93, the result implies a 7.5-fold increase in the rate of violent antiblack conflicts as the strike frequency rose from its minimum of 476 to its maximum of 3724. This is because the effect at the maximum is $\exp(.0012/1.93 \times 3724) = 10.1$, while the effect at the minimum is $\exp(.0012/1.93 \times 476) = 1.34$. Taking a ratio of these effects yields an 7.5-fold increase in the rate as the strike frequency ranged from its minimum to the maximum over this period. For violence against blacks, then, strike frequency has potent effects. But we have not yet reached the end of the story.

Do these effects hold when measures of the organizational dynamics of the union movement are added to models? We turn now to a comparison of the odd- and even-numbered columns in Tables 6.2–6.4. Here the answer is straightforward. The estimated effect of immigration is unchanged by this addition. That is, in every even-numbered column the effect of changing immigration is significant and positive as it was in the odd-numbered columns. The situation is quite different for the effect of strike frequency which was significant in all seven odd-numbered columns. Adding number of unions and foundings does reduce the effect of strikes considerably. In fact, all seven estimates of the effect of strike frequency are insignificant once indicators of the organizational strength of the union movement are included in the models (in all even-numbered columns in Tables 6.2–6.4).

How did the organizational resources of the labor movement affect the rate of ethnic conflict? Likelihood ratio tests indicate that the joint null hypothesis that number of unions and foundings have no effect on the rates should be rejected for three types of events: nonviolent conflicts (column 6 versus column 5 in Table 6.2), antiblack conflicts (column 2 versus column 1 in Table 6.3), and antiblack violence (column 2 versus column 1 in Table 6.4).

The growth of unions affects attacks on African-Americans whether or not they are violent, and nonviolent conflicts no matter which ethnic group is the target. In the case of violence, in the fourth column of Table 6.2, the effect of the number of unions is positive and significant and the effect of the number of union foundings is positive though insignificant. (A likelihood-ratio test of the model whose estimates appear in the fourth column against the model whose estimates are in the third is also not significant.) According to Table 6.3, number of unions and foundings had a strong positive effect on the rate of attacks on African-Americans. The estimate in the second column in Table 6.3 implies that growth in the number of national unions from the minimum of 31 to a maximum of 183 produced a 4.6-fold increase in the rate of attacks on blacks. The estimated effect of the number of foundings implies that the rate of attacks on African-Americans increases 2.8-fold over the range of observed foundings, 1–19. In the case of violent attacks on African-Americans (the second column in Table 6.4), the effect of number of unions is even stronger. This rate rises over 20-fold as the number of unions rises from minimum to maximum. As the number of foundings rises from its minimum to maximum, the rate of antiblack violence rises roughly two-fold.

Turning to nonviolent conflicts in Table 6.2, the situation is more complicated. In this case the two union measures have significant effects in opposite directions. The number of foundings has a strong positive effect on the rate and the number of unions has a negative effect.

The effects of union organizations on conflicts against groups other than African-Americans are generally negative. The number of unions has a significant negative effect on the rate of conflict against other-than-black targets. And the number of foundings has a significant negative effect on the rate of violence against others. So union organization raised the rates of attacks on blacks while it depressed the rate of conflict involving other groups. This difference agrees with the common claim that attacks on African-Americans and attacks on immigrants had different sources.

Implications and Conclusions

The analysis suggests several implications for theories and research of collective action. This analysis lends credibility to the claims of resource mobilization theorists that the dynamics of organizations are key to understanding the waves of protest and conflict associated with social movements. It also adds credence to the growing suspicion that violence and protest are cyclical in nature and suggests that ethnic conflict—especially against African-Americans—diffused rapidly across late nineteenth century urban America.

Specifically, this chapter investigated whether labor unrest was causally related to ethnic conflict during an important period of American history. It distinguished two kinds of resource mobilization arguments: a "parallel forms" model and a "causal chain" model. The former argument receives support in analyses of rates of three types of events distinguished by violence and racial targets. That is, models that included measures of the numbers and foundings of unions improved over those that included only strike frequency for rates of *antiblack conflict, violent antiblack conflict, and nonviolent conflict.* Taken together, these findings suggest that conflicts against African-Americans and nonviolent conflicts were more sensitive to the growth and founding of national unions than were the other kinds of conflicts (attacks on other than African-Americans and violent attacks on any target).

The central claim of the chapter—that models that included measures of the organizational dynamics of the labor movement would temper any effects found for strike activity—was supported in the case of antiblack activity, whether it was violent or not. These findings suggest that antiblack activity coincided with the early takeoff period for the growth of American unions, which provided the organizational bases for other kinds of collective actions. Growth in the number of unions had an especially strong effect on the rate of violence directed against African-Americans. These findings strongly support one version of labor history that suggested that the early history of labor unions coincided with racial exclusion and discrimination.

Labor unions did not mobilize racial violence in a vacuum. Competition from newcomers added credibility to legislation and unions favoring labor protection against African-Americans and new immigrants. But the analysis also reveals that the source of competition was not invariably the target of hostility. The analysis also reveals that change of immigration (of mostly-white South, Central and Eastern Europeans) increased the rate of ͻntiblack events. In order to understand this relationship, we have to return to accounts of antiblack and anti-immigrant mobilization discussed at the outset. Historical accounts reveal that immigration did intensify competition in urban labor markets at precisely the same time that white workers were organizing unions. The present analyses suggest that whites reacted to competition differently according to the targets. While some conflicts were directed at foreigners, two-thirds of all collective conflicts and most of the violence was antiblack. So, even though immigration intensified competition levels among foreigners, native whites, and African-Americans, conflicts were more likely to be directed against African-Americans who had even less power to fight back.

This pattern suggests a provocative conclusion: although surges in immigration provided an initial shift in competition over jobs, the targets of ethnic hostilities were not inevitably the white immigrants who were the source of much of that competition. The groups that tip the threshold of ethnic competition are not necessarily the victims of the hostility that it generates. This conclusion is further supported by the consistently positive effects of changing immigration on all forms of conflict. Sharp increases in immigration have a stronger effect on rates of antiblack violence than on rates of violence against other groups or on rates of nonviolent events. Put differently, the findings suggest that resource mobilization models that include measures of organizational strength should also take levels of competition into account in analyzing the causes of collective action.

7

Lynchings and Urban Racial Violence

So far we have considered only urban racial and ethnic unrest. But there were rural instances as well during this period. How similar were the causes of rural lynching and urban violence against African-Americans in America at the turn of the nineteenth century? At first glance, the idea that lynching and urban violence against African-Americans share causes seems reasonable because both forms of collective violence sought to terrorize and repress mainly African-American victims. But on closer inspection, there appear to be sharp differences between the two processes governing racial violence. Their histories differ, especially regarding the location and timing of events. Lynching occurred mainly in the rural South; its frequency rose sharply after the Civil War and then declined considerably by 1905 (United States Bureau of the Census 1975). Urban violence against African-Americans occurred predominantly in the North and rose significantly only after 1900 (Wilson 1978).

Despite these differences, scholars of this period cite good reasons for suspecting that both types of racial violence had similar causes.[1] Both lynching and urban violence rose during periods of economic and political turmoil. Competition for jobs and other scarce resources in the United States rose in the North and the South, following the end of Reconstruction in 1877. Rising competition seriously threatened the job monopolies and other advantages enjoyed by native whites in both regions. And in both the North and the South, whites organized labor unions, lobbyist organizations, nativist political parties, and passed exclusionary laws to combat competition (Saxton 1971; Higgs 1977; Bennett 1988; Shapiro 1988). Under conditions of such intense competition, racial violence was common.

---

[1]For instance, see Blalock 1967, Woodward 1974, Boskin 1976, Inverarity 1976, and Corzine, Corzine, and Creech 1988.

Lynching and urban violence against African-Americans have been invariably analyzed separately. This chapter breaks with that tradition of keeping research questions and analytic models separate. Instead, it offers and tests the claim that similar macro-level processes sparked both forms of collective racial violence. The main reason for addressing this issue is to explore the generality of the claim that competition causes ethnic collective action. Thus the goal of this chapter is to examine whether similar competition processes also explain rural forms of racial violence.

Until recently, competition theorists have focused primarily on economic forces of competition. Various historical accounts suggest that the political context was just as important as the economic context in affecting lynching. In particular, these accounts suggest that lynching was related to the rise of southern Populism during the late 1880s. So any evaluation of these arguments about Populism requires that forces of political competition be considered in our analysis of lynching (James 1988).

This chapter applies arguments about political and economic competition to data on lynching and urban violence against African-Americans. In doing so, it explicitly tests the hypothesis that, despite differences in geographic concentration, the same competition processes were related to both forms of racial violence. Event-history and time-series analyses of data on the United States, 1882–1914, provide the bases for the analysis.

Perspectives on Lynching

This section first reviews several well-known arguments about the causes of lynching. We next examine how these arguments can be recast into a competition framework, noting at the onset that most scholars link the rise of lynchings during the years in question to a combination of economic and political changes in the South.[2]

Populist Challenge to White Supremacy. One explanation claims that the timing of the *Populist challenges* to the Democratic Party is related to the peaks in lynching in the South. This view emphasizes the role of this challenge to white supremacy, symbolized by the interracial Farmers' Alliance and the related success of the Populist movement during the 1880s and 1890s in the South. Historical accounts suggest that the brief period of southern Populism, which initially joined African-

---

[2]Excellent sources dealing with this period in the South include those by Woodward 1938, 1951, 1974, Kousser 1974, Schwartz 1976, and Hahn 1983. Empirical studies of lynching include Blalock 1957, Reed 1972, Inverarity 1976, McAdam 1982, Corzine, Creech, and Corzine 1983, Corzine, Corzine, and Creech 1988, and Tolnay, et al. 1989.

Americans and whites in the Farmers' Alliance, threatened newly established white supremacy organizations and longstanding rule by the white planter class (Inverarity 1976; Hahn 1983). For instance, candidates on Independent and Republican ballots for local and state-offices won from one-third to one-half of the votes in seven of eleven southern states in elections from 1880–84 (Kousser 1974). Though it was short-lived, political competition generated by southern Populism may have unleashed waves of racial violence and terrorism to repress this challenge (Schwartz 1976).

Several proponents of this view claim that economic changes facilitated the ability of Populism to recruit both African-American and white supporters. They argue that violence erupted because Populism challenged the racial power structure which was based on economic hegemony (James 1988). In this view, economic cycles and the commercialization of agriculture that changed the class structure in the South sparked class conflict between poor whites and landowning whites. This conflict spread and threatened the white planter class. In response, some white landowners countered such political movements by repressing and disenfranchising African-Americans (as well as many poor whites) throughout the South (Hahn 1983; James 1988).

Was the success of southern Populism connected to the rise of racial violence in the South? Woodward (1974: 62) suggests that it was: "In the campaign of 1892 a Negro Populist who had made sixty-three speeches for Watson was threatened with lynching and fled to him for protection. Two thousand armed white farmers, some of whom rode all night, responded to Watson's call for aid and remained on guard for two nights at his home to avert the threat of violence." But by the turn of the century, the conservatives had won and the southern Populists under Watson's leadership had turned against the African-Americans (Woodward 1938; Kousser 1974). If these accounts are correct, periods of strong challenges by Populists and other third-parties coincided with peak periods of lynching.

Fluctuation in the Cotton Economy. A second common explanation is that violence in the South during this period was directly related to the region's economic *dependence on cotton farming*. In one version of this view, growth in the price of cotton, beginning in 1900 and lasting through 1920, increased the South's dependence on this crop, which in turn increased white landowners' dependence on black laborers and sharecroppers (Wright 1986: 118–22). After the Civil War, African-Americans began to migrate to urban centers, first in the South, later in the industrializing North (Wilson 1978; Fligstein 1981; Wright 1986).

According to several economic historians and sociologists, the combination of out-migration of African-Americans and increasing reliance on cotton after 1900 caused white landowners to escalate repression and violence in order to maintain their control over the black labor force and to keep the cotton economy intact (Kousser 1974; McAdam 1982). These arguments suggest that lynching was linked to the rising prosperity of the cotton economy.

Increasing reliance on the cotton-crop economy also meant that cotton farmers were more vulnerable to economic forces outside the South, including small changes in the world price for cotton. A more immediate threat was the impact of better economic opportunities in the North leading to black out-migration (Fligstein 1981). Increases in migration may have in turn motivated landowners to control the supply of labor, through repression and intimidation. In this view, a rise in wages in manual labor jobs in the North may have caused rates of lynching to rise in reaction.

Psychologists and sociologists have suggested an alternative hypothesis, that the *declining price of cotton also increased racial tension in the South* (Hovland and Sears 1940; Hepworth and West 1988; Beck and Tolnay 1990). In their view, a downturn in cotton prices exacerbated racial tensions, leading to higher rates of lynching of African-Americans. This is because cotton prices provide a good measure of well-being in the South. As Wright (1986: 50) argues, for three-quarters of a century beginning with the 1870s, the price of cotton is the "main determinant of prosperity or depression for the South."

Urbanization of African-Americans. A third explanation holds that the initial process of *urbanization of African-Americans* signaled a reduction in the formerly rigid barriers to racial competition for jobs, housing, and political power in the North and the South. Apparently, urbanization of African-Americans also signaled a rise in prosperity for at least some African-Americans (Higgs 1977: Technical Appendix, p. 142–3). An influx of African-American migrants to urban centers may have elevated racial tension as a result (Jackson 1967; Wilson 1978). From 1880 to 1920, African-Americans living in urban places rose from 12 to 34 percent (United States Bureau of the Census 1975).

Wilson (1978: 56) claims that urbanization did change the context of race relations in the United States around the turn of the century:

During the last quarter of the nineteenth century, lower-class whites found themselves in increasing contact and competition with millions of freed blacks at the very time that a labor surplus developed in the face of enormous population growth in the South. The problem was especially acute in the Lower South. For the first time, African-Americans and working-class whites of the

Lower South, historically separated in the black belt (lowlands) and the uplands respectively were forced by economic conditions to confront one another, bump shoulders, and compete on a wide scale for the same jobs. Black youths gradually moved from the lowlands to the new mining and industrial towns of the uplands and found menial, dirty, low-paying work in tobacco factories, mines, and turpentine camps; meanwhile sons of white farmers, overwhelmed by debts and falling prices, sifted down from the uplands to the lowlands, where they settled for work in the textile mills or drifted into tenancy.

These three explanations of temporal variations in lynching suggest the idea that when a racially ordered system breaks down, competitive forces are released, as urbanization, upward mobility, and political mobilization by the disadvantaged take place. Since these forces threaten the prevailing power and class structure, the dominant racial group often reacts with threats of violence to maintain their dominance.

Some sociologists further distinguish between economic competition and "power-threat" (or political power) explanations of lynching (Blalock 1957, 1967). Blalock's (1957) claim that there would be a positively accelerated relationship between proportion black and the lynching rate has received some support. For instance, researchers from this power-threat perspective have found that a positive relationship exists between the proportion (and sometimes growth) of the population that was black and the lynching rate (Reed 1972; Corzine, Creech, and Huff-Corzine 1983; Corzine, Huff-Corzine, and Creech 1988; Tolnay, et al. 1989; but also see Mintz 1946;). According to the power-threat formulation, these results indicate that whites who lived in counties with high proportions of African-Americans perceived them as a threat to their dominance. Such threats were met by repressing African-Americans—until they were disenfranchised and Jim Crow laws were instituted in the South (Kousser 1974; Woodward 1974).

Competition and Split Labor Market Theories. Large-scale changes in the economy appear to have coincided with racial violence in both the North and the South during this period. By the 1880s, attacks on African-Americans were also becoming more frequent in cities in the North, as immigration, labor unrest, and urbanization created new frictions between residents and newcomers (Rudwick 1964; Boskin 1976; Bodnar et al. 1982). Although the economic and political structures of the North and South differed greatly in this period, the two regions were affected in similar ways by events in an increasingly integrated world economy.[3]   Both regions were also drawn into an increasingly

---

[3]For example, Kousser (1974), Hahn (1983), and Wright (1986) have documented that competition for cotton from Egypt and India wreaked havoc with cotton prices and thus the cotton economy in the South during the 1880s and 1890s. Transporta-

national network characterized by extensive flows of credit, goods, and labor. Changes brought about by large-scale immigration, extension of a national railroad system, and nationally-focused political movements, such as the extension of national labor unions affected all regions in the country (Bennett 1988). These facts suggest that attacks on African-Americans, whether perpetrated by rural mobs or urban race riots, could be related to the same structural conditions in both northern and southern settings.

Competition theories provide one way to understand the underlying causes of racial violence in various settings. As we have elaborated in earlier chapters, the key argument from a competition perspective holds that racial violence surges when interracial contact and competition intensifies. We have depicted race and ethnicity as forms of social organization whose boundaries are demarcated by skin color, language, and national origin. As Chapter 2 suggests, competition theorists maintain that race and ethnic conflict is minimized when groups occupy nonoverlapping occupations or *niches* (Barth 1969; Hannan 1979; Nielsen 1985). By this same argument conflict ensues under conditions of *niche overlap*. That is, conflict arises when groups come to compete for the same jobs, housing, or territory. Under conditions of niche overlap, competition among groups rises, which in turn encourages attempts to exclude the competitors. Such attempts often entail violent conflict. We now apply these ideas to other settings and types of racial violence in this chapter.

Results presented in Chapters 5 and 6 suggested that surges in immigration and unfavorable changes in economic well-being raised rates of racial and ethnic violence. The explanation for this pattern of results that was offered is that immigration and economic contraction raised levels of competition among the ranks of the less-skilled. Put differently, processes of immigration and economic contraction contributed to an increase in niche overlap between lower-class whites, immigrants, and African-Americans. First, immigration sharply intensified this competition because the supply of low-wage labor increased relative to demand (Wilson 1978; Lieberson 1980). Second, economic contraction shrinks the amount of available resources, so that competition greatly intensifies in niches most likely to be filled by African-Americans and immigrants.

Other researchers hold that roots of violence against African-Americans during this period can be understood by examining the emergence of a racially split labor market. A split labor market is one in which two or more racially distinct populations who are in the same labor market

---

tion and financial markets in the North were simultaneously affected by such price fluctuations, as the depressions of the 1890s indicate.

command different prices (or incur the same costs to the employer) for the same work (Bonacich 1972, 1976).

Unfortunately no reliable data on racial differences in wages within occupational categories are available for a large number of urban and rural settings prior to 1890, which would be needed to test specific predictions from split labor market theory directly.[4] Instead, we focus here on more general indicators of competition: economic prosperity and economic well-being of common laborers in the country as a whole. General formulations of competition theory predict that a decline in economic prosperity for laborers will raise levels of racial competition for jobs, housing, and other resources.

Fortunately, data are available that speak to the issue of labor market competition among native whites, immigrants, and African-Americans within the unskilled occupations beginning in 1890. The evidence suggests that immigrants and African-Americans commonly held laboring jobs when they first entered urban labor markets during this period.[5]

But did African-Americans and lower-class whites actually compete for the same jobs during this period? At least some scholars believe that they did (Higgs 1977; Bennett 1988). Consider Blassingame's analysis for New Orleans using data from the 1870 and 1880 manuscript censuses:

In spite of discrimination, blacks were able to garner a disproportionate share of certain skilled jobs. While Negroes constituted only 25 percent of the to-

---

[4]Some economic historians have found surprisingly small race differences in agricultural wages from this period. For instance, Higgs (1977: Table 4.2) used estimates of wages of agricultural workers and reported that for 15 southern states, the ratios of white to black wages ranged from a low of 0.98 in Kentucky to a high of 1.17 in Alabama. The white money wage exceeded the black money wage rate by only about 8 percent on the average. While this gap is not trivial, it is probably far lower than the conventional wisdom would expect. Even if the racial gap in wages for unskilled jobs in rural agriculture was small, the historical evidence suggests that occupational attainment of African-Americans was on the average below that of whites nearly everywhere in the United States at this time (Spero and Harris 1931; Lieberson 1980; Farley 1984).

[5]As Archdeacon (1983) reports, nearly 50% of all ethnic immigrants entering the United States after 1890 were more likely to state "laborer" as their former occupation. Spero and Harris (1931) have estimated that over two-thirds of blacks in manufacturing industries in 1920 were laborers, while less than 20% were skilled laborers. The Chinese, Japanese, and other Asians were apparently equally disadvantaged, at least initially (Saxton 1971; Loewen 1988). Lieberson (1980) has also documented that immigrants from southern, central, and eastern Europe and Asia were more likely to hold jobs as laborers and unskilled workers than were ethnic immigrants arriving prior to 1870 from different countries, such as Germany, Ireland, and Scandinavia.

tal labor force, they held from 30 to 65 percent of all jobs as steamboatmen, draymen, masons, bakers, carpenters, cigarmakers, plasterers, barbers, and gardeners in 1870. By 1880, though the percentages had changed, Negroes were still overrepresented in many of these occupations ... Since foreign-born workers constituted 49 and 33 percent of the number of laborers in New Orleans in 1870 and 1880, they represented the Negroes' chief competitors for jobs. (Blassingame 1973: 61)

It is hard to answer the question of how much actual competition took place between whites and African-Americans during this period with certainty. However, Bonacich (1972), Higgs (1977) and others argue that it is not necessary that many workers from different racial populations compete *directly* for exactly the same jobs in order for racial antagonism to flare. *Potential* competition can spark such antagonism before much direct (head-to-head) competition has occurred. For one thing, workers were well aware that employers could, and often did, substitute lower-wage or unskilled workers in order to maintain profits and subdue trade unions (or both). The implication is that the presence of a racially different unskilled labor force—raises the specter of racial competition for jobs.

By allowing for the possibility that it is potential rather than actual competition that matters, several empirical anomalies become understandable. That is, the evidence suggests that racial violence in response to potential competition was sometimes not directed against the new competitors. Anti-Asian sentiment flourished in regions with few Asians, and national union movements to exclude African-Americans met with success in many all-white communities (Bennett 1988). Those who ignite fears of competition are not always the targets of violence. For instance, recall that in Chapter 5 we saw that immigration of mostly-white Europeans affected the rates of attacks on African-Americans more than it affected rates of attacks on the same white immigrants, from the late 1870s through World War I. Evidently those who are victimized by racial attacks are not always the ones who generated the initial spark of competition. These results also suggest that it is important to look beyond local geographical boundaries and local job markets for causes of racial violence.

This chapter develops these implications of processes of indirect and potential job competition first by considering whether different levels of European immigration affected rates of racial violence. Such newly arriving populations were frequently viewed as potential competitors for low-wage jobs, as the discrimination against immigrants and African-Americans that characterized at least some trade unions suggests (Garis 1927; Foner 1982). According to labor historians, some labor leaders such as Gompers, Powderly, and others, viewed the rising number of un-skilled immigrants and African-Americans in the industrializing North as a threat to white (and more skilled) workers (Yellen 1936; Foner 1982; Gutman and Bell 1987). As discussed in Chapter 6, leaders organized rallies, circulated newsletters, and held labor conventions that intensi-fied perceptions of competition, which in turn may have raised the level of anti-immigrant and antiblack activity in the country (Garis 1927; Higham 1955; Bennett 1988). It is in this sense that we conceptualize African-Americans and whites as having been in labor market competi-tion. Thus when the influx of low-wage groups in a country or region rises—due to immigration and migration—so does competition for jobs, housing and other resources, at least initially.

Processes of both economic and political competition provide the the-oretical link between these structural changes and conflict. The funda-mental hypothesis is that *rates of racial collective action rise when inter-racial contact and competition intensifies.* This means that changes ac-companying urbanization of African-Americans, immigration, and eco-nomic decline increased rates of both types of racial violence and that political challenges to white supremacy in the South and contraction of the cotton economy increased the number of lynchings. In order to see if economic and political competition can explain the two types of racial violence, I test arguments using event data on lynching and urban violence from the exactly the same historical period.

Research Design and Methods
At what level of analysis should one test these arguments? Past research has analyzed lynching using either national-level or county-level data. As in all research, there are trade-offs to be weighed when choosing a unit of analysis. Each choice involves some degree of aggregation over time or space. The majority of studies on lynching contain cross-sectional designs of lynching (e.g., Reed 1972; Corzine et al. 1983; Corzine et al. 1988; Tolnay, Beck, and Massey 1989). That is, these researchers have aggregated lynching counts across many years which contain consider-able variation and related them to covariates at one point in time. In some cases this decision to rely on cross-sectional data had the conse-quence of choosing independent variables measured decades *after* the de-pendent variable of lynching counts began. Such a strategy casts doubt on the causal sequencing of these models. In contrast, this chapter uses a strategy of applying time-series and event-history methods that maxi-mize variation in annual observations on economic and political variables (see Chapter 4 for an extended discussion of these trade-offs).

The decision made here is a pragmatic one based on competition arguments. The theory informs us that large-scale processes—urbaniz-ation, level and rate of immigration, economic depressions, wage fluc-tuations—affected *national-level* rates of two kinds of racial violence in the United States during this period.[6] Such assumptions are routinely used in analyses of other forms of collective action, including African-American insurgency, strikes, and other forms of unrest (McAdam 1982; Tarrow 1983; Tilly, Tilly, and Tilly 1985; Jenkins and Eckert 1986; Ru-bin 1986). A related issue is that previous empirical analyses suggest that events diffuse from one region to another—that racial violence and social movements such as the KKK were often national in scope. Hy-potheses about national-level diffusion can be modeled straightforwardly using the Weibull models of duration dependence, as we do below.

There are also pragmatic reasons to analyze national-level data on lynching. It makes sense to begin first at the national-level, where com-parable lynching and urban violence data are readily available.[7] This way, we can determine whether the enormous effort that would be re-quired to test these arguments at the local-level using the appropriate longitudinal data is warranted.

Answering questions about the causes of rural and urban violence against African-Americans requires a research design that incorporates changes in the economy and social structure. It also requires a focus on specific regional differences in economic factors. The analysis re-ported here begins in 1882, the first year for which national-level data on lynching are available (United States Bureau of the Census 1975). It also roughly coincides with the beginning of an enormous surge in immigration, which did not decline until World War I (see Figure 7.1 below). It ends at the close of 1914, the beginning of World War I, to be consistent with other analyses presented in this book.

Dependent Variables. There are two dependent variables. The first is the yearly count of lynchings in the United States (United States Bureau of the Census 1975). It is important to note that few sources

---

[6]Of course, the strategy to begin this comparative analysis with national-level data does not preclude analysis at the local level. This chapter represents only a beginning exploration of competition arguments about trends in immigration and economic fluctuation at the national level, where such trends are meaningful. The stand taken here is that several levels of analysis involving collective action (e.g., national and city-levels) should be empirically investigated to see if any processes suggested by the available theories hold at multiple levels of analysis. For analysis of urban events conducted at the city level, see Chapters 8 and 9.

[7]Tolnay, Beck, and Massey (1989) reported that they have begun a large project to collect and validate local-level accounts of lynchings in the South using a variety of archival and newspaper accounts. Some of this data has been analyzed and published in Beck and Tolnay (1990).

of data on lynching are without flaws (see Tolnay, Beck, and Massey 1989). To minimize some error, we have separated lynchings by race of the victim, since not all lynchings were of African-Americans. For instance, Wilson (1978) reports estimates that while only 10% of the 300 lynching victims between 1840 and 1860 were African-American, the vast majority of lynchings after that point had African-American victims and took place in the South.

The second dependent variable is the rate of occurrence of urban violence against African-Americans. This rate is estimated using event histories coded from microfilms of daily accounts in the *New York Times* (Olzak and DiGregorio 1985). Note that these data pertain to only *urban* events: these histories were coded only for public events not regularly scheduled and which occurred in any of the 77 largest cities as reported in the 1880 Census (Appendix B provides a list of cities). Information on two broad kinds of ethnic collective actions were collected from the *New York Times*: civil rights protests and inter-group conflicts. Recall that ethnic protests were defined in Chapter 6 as collective actions that articulate a claim for civil rights or a grievance on behalf of (usually) one ethnic or racial group. Ethnic conflicts are confrontations between two or more racial or ethnic populations.

Conflict was coded as violence against African-Americans if two or more persons engaged in threatening or actual violent behavior directed against African-Americans using racial epithets or symbols. A conflict was distinguished as *violent* if anyone was killed or injured or if guns, knives, bricks or some other weapons were deployed or used to threaten victims. Thus, random, interracial crimes, strikes by (ethnically homogeneous) workers for higher wages, and domestic violence are excluded from the set of events analyzed here.

Independent Variables. Independent variables include three measures of economic conditions. The real wage of common laborers, discussed in Chapter 5, (coded from David and Solar 1977) indicates variation in well-being for the lowest status occupations, the ones most likely to be held by recent immigrants or African-Americans.[8] An index of years of economic depression, coded from the time series of depressions,

---

[8]The foreign-born comprised nearly 60% of the common laborers in these 77 cities in 1880 (United States Census, 1880), while they were only 20% of the labor force on the average in these same cities. Spero and Harris (1931: 85) report: "There were 825,321 Negroes employed in manufacturing industries in 1920. Only 16.6 percent of them were skilled workers, 67.9 percent of them were laborers, and 15.5 percent were semi-skilled." Lieberson (1980) and Olzak (1989a) provide evidence regarding levels of occupational segregation of the foreign-born and African-American population in cities, from 1880 through 1920.

recessions, and recoveries by Thorp and Mitchell (1926), distinguishes years of extreme economic contraction. The real price of cotton (United States Bureau of the Census 1975) measures economic conditions in the South, as was described above.

Some readers have questioned the rationale for including change in immigration and change in laborers' wages in analyses of lynchings on the grounds that lynchings took place primarily in the rural South while immigrants and others who worked for wages settled mainly in the urban North. The major justification for including immigration and real wages of common laborers in models of lynching is theoretical. The hypothesis from competition theory advanced here is that rise in real wages of laborers ought to affect levels of competition among racial groups, whether or not wage labor is a dominant feature of the economy. It is, however, important to note that wage labor was by no means absent in the South. Historians claim that wage labor increasingly characterized both the southern and northern economy during this period. Higgs (1977: 93) finds that although the southern economy was based on agriculture, wage labor was an important feature of both agriculture and the growing urban industries in the South during this period.

Less well known is the fact that immigrants were the targets of hostility in the South as well as the North (Bennett 1988). There is good evidence that the presence of immigrants affected racial violence and lynching there as well. Even though immigrants were concentrated initially in the Northeast, European and Asian immigrants were not absent from the South (Garis 1927; Higham 1955; Wright 1986). Analyses of specific southern communities (e.g., Loewen 1988), and of immigrant employment in southern coal mines, shipping, and other industries suggest that white immigrants were often active participants in racial incidents throughout the South (Blassingame 1973). Even the Populist leader Tom Watson from Georgia had harsh words for the foreign white immigrant:

The scum of creation has been dumped on us. Some of our principle cities are more foreign than American. The most dangerous and corrupting hordes of the Old World have invaded us. The vice and crime which they have planted in our midst is terrifying. (Quoted in Hofstader 1955: 82)

There is another advantage to including immigration and real wages in models of lynching as well as models of urban violence. The advantage is that it affords direct comparisons and contrasts. Only by providing similar specifications of models including the same measures can such speculations be evaluated. If the results for the two types of racial violence are substantively different, then we will have shed new light on the debate.

In an event-history analysis of urban events, these covariates are measured for the year in which a spell begins (denoted by t in the tables). In the time series analysis of yearly counts of lynchings, covariates are measured for the previous year (denoted by $t - 1$ in the tables).

Measures of political challenge include a dummy variable that indicates years of Populist electoral contests (coded from the summary in Schlesinger 1983 and Bureau of the Census 1975 reports of voting results). Another dummy variable distinguishes those years in which a presidential election occurred. And "percentage of splinter party vote" is the fraction of votes in national elections received by parties in an election year for other than Republican and Democratic parties. These indicators refer to the current year in the analysis of lynchings.

Diffusion of Racial Violence. Processes of contagion are specified in several ways in the analysis of urban violence. First contagion is represented as a form of time dependence in the rate of occurrence of racial violence: the hypothesis is that the rate declines with the duration (in days) since the previous event in the system against any target. A second specification uses a covariate that indicates whether the most recent event was an attack on African-Americans. A third approach specifies that the occurrence of lynchings and urban violence against African-Americans are jointly dependent, affected by common unobservables.

Methods of Analysis. Until recently, analyses of longitudinal and quantitative data on collective action have relied almost exclusively on time series data and methods. Event-history analysis, which uses information on the exact timing of events, allows researchers to exploit all of the information available about sequences of collective action. As Chapter 4 argues, using all of the available information carries an important advantage when the number of events is small, as in the case of urban violence in the period of this study. Moreover, these methods are particularly useful in analyzing the effects of time dependence, over periods shorter than the conventional one-year lag in time series analysis of collective action (Tuma and Hannan 1984). By using continuous-time models of time dependence, effects of cycles of violence can be determined empirically, not assumed a priori, as was shown in Chapter 4.

Event history methods are used here in analyzing rates of urban violence for which the exact sequences and timing of events are known. An alternative strategy would have been to aggregate the event-history data to yearly counts and perform the same time-series analysis on both data sets. For the urban violence data, this results in small annual counts, causing problems for time series estimation. In addition, using time series methods would discard potentially useful information about the duration and sequencing of events of urban violence.

In order that our results could be compared with those of McAdam (1982) and others who have analyzed national-level lynching data, we chose the most widely available analyzed national-level data set on lynching, published by race of victim in the *United States Historical Statistics, Colonial Times to 1976*. We did not use the NAACP's *Thirty Years of Lynching*, because it begins in 1889, seven years after the event-history data do. So for comparability and widest available time span, we use national-level time-series data.

Event History Analysis. The models used in analyzing urban violence assume that the rate of urban violence against African-Americans depends log-linearly on the observed covariates described above. They also assume that the rate depends on the waiting time since the most recent event in the set of cities.

An important research decision concerns the definition of spells. Should we define durations between conflicts only? Or between any type of ethnic confrontation and protest? Research reported in Chapters 5 and 6 found that the occurrence of *either* a conflict or a protest affected the rate of subsequent conflict. The explanation offered is that the occurrence of an ethnic event in the country, even during this early historical period, affected the salience of ethnic boundaries, making future clashes among ethnic and racial populations more likely. To take these prior results about contagion into account and to facilitate testing such hypotheses here, spells are defined as the waiting times between any event, either attacks on African-Americans, or some other type of ethnic collective action. This period experienced 231 events, of which 73 were attacks on African-Americans. The spells include a left-censored spell beginning on January 1, 1882, and ending at the time of the first observed event anywhere in the country. So the waiting times (spells between events) begin just after an outbreak (against any ethnic or racial victim) occurs *anywhere in the country*. In formal terms, let T_n denote the random variable that tells the time of the nth event of ethnic collective action in any city in the system. The duration (or waiting time) from the $(n-1)$th to the nth event is $U_n = T_n - T_{n-1}$.

Though this analysis focuses on violence against African-Americans, it uses information on the timing of all kinds of ethnic and racial collective actions to define durations between attacks on African-Americans. As noted above, because the occurrence of urban ethnic collective events other than violence against African-Americans may have affected the rate of this particular form of violence, waiting times are defined using all racial and ethnic conflicts and protests. Each analysis also includes a dummy variable that tells whether the previous event in the system was violence against African-Americans.

As in previous chapters, the urban events analysis treats events in different regions and involving different racial targets statistically as "competing risks" (Tuma and Hannan 1984). Durations of spells that end in protests, conflicts against some target other than African-Americans, or violence against other than African-American targets were treated as censored on the right. In the analysis of southern cities, durations of spells that end in an attack on African-Americans in the South are the dependent variable, while all other durations are treated as censored on the right. In the analysis of Northern cities, the durations of spells ending in an attack on African-Americans constituted the uncensored spells, while all other kinds of events that happen outside the North are censored on the right.

In Chapters 5 and 6 we found that the rate of urban violence against African-Americans varied with U_n and that this dependence was negative. This meant that the rate declined as the most recent event receded in time. We interpreted this time dependence substantively as reflecting a process of diffusion of ethnic conflicts (see Chapter 6). Inspection of cumulative hazard functions of the data on urban racial violence suggests that such negative time dependence does characterize the rate of occurrence. The rate appears to drop sharply (and monotonically) with the waiting time since the previous event. Based on the shape of these cumulative hazard functions, I again apply a Weibull model to represent the functional form of time dependence in the rate. The generic form of this model with effects of measured covariates is,

$$r(u_n) = \exp\left(\beta' \mathbf{x}[t_{n-1}]\right) \cdot u_n^{\rho-1}, \tag{7.1}$$

here $r(u_n)$ is the rate of urban violence against African-Americans at waiting time u_n, t_{n-1} is the historical time of the previous event in the country, $\mathbf{x}(t_{n-1})$ is a set of covariates measured at the beginning of the spell (the time just after the previous adjacent event has occurred), and ρ is the parameter that indexes time dependence. If $0 < \rho < 1$, then the rate declines with passage of time since the previous event.

It is convenient when estimating the Weibull model to express it as a regression model for the log of the waiting time in years (time that has passed since the previous event anywhere in the country). The regression model actually estimated (using PROC LIFEREG in SAS) equivalent to (7.1) above is

$$\log U_n = \beta^{*'} \mathbf{x}(t_{n-1}) + \sigma W, \tag{7.2}$$

where $\beta^* = \beta\sigma$, W has an extreme value distribution (Kalbfleisch and

Prentice 1980), and σ is a scale parameter. Recall that the scale parameter is the inverse of the parameter that indexes duration dependence in the Weibull model, that is, $\sigma = \rho^{-1}$. The tables report maximum likelihood (ML) estimates of the parameters of the model in the form of equation (7.2). The tables report the negative of the regression coefficients, that is $-\beta^*$, so that the sign is the same as the effects on the rate.

Time-Series Analysis. The time-series models used in analyzing lynchings assume that a set of yearly counts, $y_1, \ldots, y_T$, is a realization of a discrete-time process and that y_t is a function of a set of covariates lagged one year, x_{t-1}, and of changes in the covariates over the subsequent year, $\Delta x_t = x_t - x_{t-1}$. Some previous analyses of counts of collective actions also specified that y_t is a function of y_{t-1}, the lagged dependent variable. This is tantamount to forming a model of change in the dependent variable (see, for example, Tuma and Hannan 1984). Although such an approach may have merit in analyzing lynchings, it would complicate comparisons with results of event-history analysis of urban violence. As we discuss below, the event history analyses seek to explain variations in the rate of occurrence. That is, they treat the rates that control occurrences—rather than changes in levels of occurrences—of urban violence. So comparable time-series analyses should analyze the causes of counts of lynchings rather than changes in counts from year to year.

Since the number of lynchings per year is by definition nonnegative, it makes sense to use models that constrain the predicted number of lynchings to be nonnegative. We do so here by using log-linear models of the general form,

$$\log y_t = \beta_1' x_{t-1} + \beta_2' \Delta x_t + v_t \,, \tag{7.3}$$

where v_t is a stochastic disturbance term. Preliminary analyses revealed that this log-linear model produces better fits than linear models of lynchings.

As is well known, autocorrelation of disturbances may present serious obstacles to efficient estimation in models like (7.3). Analysis of (log) counts of lynchings revealed possible first-order autocorrelation of disturbances. In particular, Durbin-Watson test statistics fall in the range of indecision.[9] In order to take autocorrelation into account, generalized

---

[9]Specifically, the Durbin-Watson level for the OLS model in Table 7.2 model (1) was .817 and in Table 7.2 model (2), OLS results showed a Durbin-Watson level of 1.36. Since these fall out of the suggested range of acceptability for applying OLS, the GLS results were instead reported in these tables. Note that in Olzak (1990),

least squares (GLS) estimators were used (Judge et al. 1985). In forming GLS estimators, we assume that the disturbance process is first-order

$$v_t = \phi v_{t-1} + e_t, \qquad (7.4)$$

where ϕ is the autocorrelation coefficient for disturbances and e_t is a random disturbance that is assumed to be uncorrelated over time and with the regressors.

In every GLS time-series model shown, several specifications of the lagged error structure were conducted in addition to the first-order autoregressive models presented here. None differed significantly from those presented, and additional spectral analysis (also conducted using SAS software) for periodicity revealed that no periodic waves could be identified in the lynching data. Moreover, the estimates are stable across a wide variety of specifications. Nevertheless, a time trend variable was entered in all equations to test for the alternative hypothesis that the covariates merely declined in parallel with lynching over time. In both the event-history and time-series analyses, omission of either immigration or economic measures significantly decreases the fit of the model, but does not appreciably affect the size or the direction of any of the other coefficients, lending further credibility to the models shown below.

Results

Figure 7.1 shows the temporal variation in lynching and urban violence against African-Americans during 1882 through 1914. The zero-order correlation between lynching and urban violence against African-Americans is negative: peak periods of lynching fall between 1890 and 1902, while urban violence against African-Americans appears to rise only after 1900. It will turn out that the association is positive once we use controls for relevant covariates.

Urban Violence Against African-Americans. We turn first to the effects of these variables on the rate of collective violence against African-Americans in the set of all large cities in the United States. Each of the models whose estimates are discussed in this section includes a dummy variable for whether or not the previous event in the country was an instance of violence against African-Americans. They also include a specification of Weibull duration dependence in the rate.

---

only the OLS results were reported for a model that is similar to that shown in Table 7.2 (model (2)). OLS was used because the Durbin-Watson level was not outside the range. The OLS and GLS results are not substantively different, however. The autocorrelation coefficient for disturbances that are autoregressive, ϕ, is reported in Tables 7.2 and 7.3.

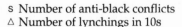

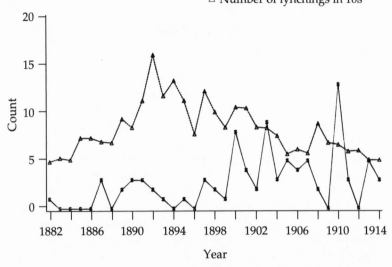

FIG. 7.1 Lynchings and Urban Antiblack Conflict, 1882–1914

First consider the effect of change in immigration. As in Chapters 5 and 6, change in immigration has a significant *positive* effect on urban rates of violence against African-Americans (column 1). In the case of all cities, the estimated effect of proportional change in immigration is 4.94 and the estimated scale parameter is 1.92. Taking the ratio 4.94/1.92 gives 2.57. Changes in immigration ranged from a minimum of −.39 to a maximum of .47 during this period. To calculate the effect of this variable at its the maximum, the estimated effect of change in immigration is exp(2.57 × 0.47) = 3.3. At the minimum, this effect is exp(2.57 × −0.39) = .37. The ratio of these effects tells that the implied rate of violence against African-Americans when immigration rose most steeply was about nine times higher than when immigration fell most steeply. To use a different comparison, the rate of violence against African-Americans in urban settings was over three times higher when immigration surged than in the period when immigration remained unchanged from year to year, because exp(0) = 1.

Past research finds that both levels and changes in immigration can be important (Olzak 1986). Because the *level* of immigration might also affect the rate, net of the theoretically relevant effect of *change* in immigration, I repeated the analyses reported here with both levels

TABLE 7.1

ML Estimates of Weibull Models of Effects of Economic Conditions
on the Rate of Violence Against African-Americans in All Cities,
Southern Cities, and Northern Cities in the U.S., 1882–1914

(Asymptotic Standard Errors in Parentheses)

Independent Variables	All Cities (1)	Southern Cities (2)	Northern Cities (3)
Intercept	−713 (698)	−1862 (1195)	770 (962)
Change in immigration(t)	4.94*** (1.19)	8.67*** (2.66)	3.76*** (1.37)
Real wage of laborers (t)	19.1** (8.99)	18.9 (15.5)	17.2 (11.0)
Change in real wage (t)	−25.8*** (11.5)	−6.37 (18.7)	−26.8*** (13.3)
Depression year (t)	−0.98 (0.49)	−0.89 (0.97)	−.52 (0.75)
Proportion of African-Americans in cities (t)	65.6 (58.3)	167.* (93.8)	−58.3 (80.0)
Previous event involved violent attack on African-Americans	1.64*** (0.49)	2.30*** (0.83)	1.66*** (.57)
Number of lynchings (t)	0.03** (0.01)	0.03 (0.02)	0.04* (0.02)
Time trend	−0.40 (0.38)	−1.02 (0.65)	0.40 (0.52)
Scale parameter	1.92*** (0.17)	1.84*** (0.31)	1.77*** (0.19)
Number of spells	231	52	179
Uncensored spells	73	26	47
Log-likelihood	−220.18	−70.21	−140.63
Degrees of freedom	10	10	10

$^{*}\,p < .10,$ $^{**}\,p < .05,$ $^{***}\,p < .01.$

and changes in immigration as covariates. Interestingly, these analyses, (which are not reported here) reveal that the level of immigration does not affect the rate significantly.

When both level and change in wages are included in the same model (as in column 1) the *level* of real wages of common laborers also has a significant positive effect on the rate of violence against African-Americans. In periods when wages of laborers were high, the rate of urban violence against African-Americans was also high. However, *change* in real wages has a significant *negative* effect on the rate of urban violence against

African-Americans. Rising wage rates of laborers decreased rates of violence against African-Americans in urban settings.

How can the opposing effects of levels and changes in wages be interpreted? Consider again the historical setting. Racial competition was particularly intense within low-paying, unskilled occupations, such as laboring (as Wilson (1978) suggested). Competition intensified only insofar as labor supply exceeded demand. But years in which wage rates of laborers increased were presumably times of low levels of competition in the labor markets facing unskilled workers. An increase in wages (whether or not they were at high or low levels) indicates that the demand for labor has temporarily outstripped the supply of laborers. Such an increase in this group's wages might have temporarily dissipated racial tensions between white and African-American workers. The finding that increases in the wages of laborers depressed the rate of violence against African-Americans is consistent with the view that racial competition declined with an upward shift in wages for laborers and increased when wages shifted downward.[10]

Note that the indicator of depression years does not have a significant effect on the rate. This finding is not what many historians and sociologists studying racial competition would have expected. Apparently, levels and changes of wages for those at the bottom affected racial violence more than overall contraction in the economy. An alternative explanation of the pattern of estimated effects of wage rates and economic depression is that these results reveal differences in the short-run and long-run effects of economic contraction. That is, in the short-run, economic decline increases rates of racial conflict, but protracted economic depression undercuts the ability of all collective actors to mobilize, thus depressing rates of racial conflict (and other types of collective action). Though this alternative was not anticipated, the results pertaining to effects of levels and changes in wage rates are consistent with it.

Urbanization of African-Americans did not affect the rate of urban violence significantly. This result does not support the historical and sociological arguments outlined above. Nor is it consistent with the hypothesis that violence directed at African-Americans increased as African-Americans became urbanized and began to compete with whites for jobs with low pay.

---

[10]Some readers have suggested that because the real wage index adjusts for price fluctuations, its use might mask effects of prices on these outcomes. To examine this alternative hypothesis, I estimated effects of both components—nominal wages and prices—the effect of prices on the rate of violence against African-Americans does not differ significantly from zero.

Contagion also affected the rate of urban violence against African-Americans. The estimated scale parameter in column 1 is 1.92, which implies that $\rho = .52$. This means that the rate drops sharply with the passage of time since the previous event, as expected. Specifically, the implied rate after a full year with no event is one-seventeenth as large as the implied rate just after an event has occurred anywhere in the country on the previous day.

The model whose estimates appear in the first column of Table 7.1 contains an additional specification of target-specific diffusion of urban violence: a dummy variable that equals one for spells that follow an event of violence against African-Americans. The significant positive effect of this indicator tells that the rate of violence against African-Americans rises following the occurrence of such events. The estimated effect is obtained by dividing the coefficient by the scale parameter, $(1.64/1.92 = .854)$. Then we can see that the rate $(\exp[.854] = 2.35)$ rises over twofold in periods following other acts of collective violence against African-Americans. This result is net of other effects found. So it appears that specific targets of attacks affect the rate in addition to the timing of events.

Did the number of lynchings affect the rate of urban violence against African-Americans? It is interesting to note that, although the time-series plots in Figure 7.1 suggest a negative relationship, when a full model is specified, the relationship is positive. The results in the first column for all cities and in the third column for northern cities in Table 7.1 suggest that lynchings affect the rate of urban violence against African-Americans. The effect of number of lynchings in the same year is positive and significant. The point estimate (divided by the scale parameter) is $.03/1.92 = .016$ for lynchings (column 1), implying that the rate of urban violence rose six-fold as the number of lynchings varied from its minimum to maximum over this period. This result suggests that rural and urban violence against African-Americans were related during this period and that this effect was especially significant in the urban north.

Southern and Northern Cities Compared. Combining southern and northern cities (as in column 1) might mask effects of enormous differences in historical traditions of slavery, Jim Crow laws, and related differences in the political economies of the North and South. In order to examine regional differences in the causes of urban violence against African-Americans, we next consider estimates of separate models for each region. Column 2 reports estimates using data for the ten cities (in which durations are calculated for southern cities alone) in the South that were classified as large urban centers by the 1880 Census.[11] The remaining cities were classified as northern (see Appendix). So the analysis whose results appear in columns 2 and 3 of Table 7.1 replicates that of column 1 except that the observations are restricted to *southern* and *northern* cities, respectively.

Compare next the results of columns 1, 2, and 3. Effects of change in immigration, level of real wages of common laborers, change in real wages, and contagion are essentially the same (although the effects are not always significant in column 2 because the number of spells is so much smaller).[12] As hypothesized, the effect of urbanization of African-Americans is positive and significant (although only at the .10 level).

One regional difference appears: the effect of changes in real wages is insignificant in the southern city analysis in column 2, while it is positive and significant in the northern city analysis, as seen in column 3. There are several plausible explanations for this difference. First, as noted above, the number of spells ending in urban violence against African-Americans in the South is small. Second, as many have argued, wages of laborers may have been less salient in the South compared to the North.

The results from all three columns suggest there is an effect of recency of past racial violence on the rate of urban violence during this period. Urban violence against African-Americans apparently diffuses rapidly across the country affecting rates of subsequent urban violence in both the North and the South during this period. That is, when a previous ethnic event that occurred anywhere in the country was an attack on African-Americans (compared to some other target), the rate of racial violence against African-Americans increased significantly in the South and in the North. Peak periods of lynchings also increased the urban rate, significantly so in the North. But although the effect of lynching is not statistically significant in column 2, the point estimate is positive. This coefficient (divided by the scale parameter) indicates that the rate of urban violence in the South rose threefold over the observed minimum of 49 and maximum number of 161 annual lynchings during this period.

---

[11]The 10 cities are Atlanta, Baltimore, Charleston, Memphis, Nashville, New Orleans, Richmond, San Antonio, Washington D.C., and Wilmington Del. (see the Appendix). Although other criteria certainly would be plausible (such as cities within states below the Mason Dixon line) these cities were designated as belonging to the South because they have been historically categorized as such in the United States Census (United States Bureau of the Census 1975 Vol I, p. 5). Eliminating Wilmington from the set of southern cities does not change the results appreciably.

[12]This is because this analysis in column 2 uses durations between only southern events in estimating the rate of urban violence against African-Americans. Likewise, the analysis in column 3 uses durations between only nonsouthern cities.

Lynching. Column 1 of Table 7.2 reports GLS estimates of a model for lynchings that parallels the models used in Table 7.1 in analyzing urban violence. Due to the differences in the structure of the data noted above, the parallel is not exact. Because this lynching data set does not contain exact dates of events, we cannot estimate time dependence and effects of the form of the previous event.

We can now compare the results in Tables 7.1 with those in column 1 of Table 7.2. The effects of change in immigration, level of real wages, and change in real wages are significantly different from zero in the case of lynchings and agree in sign with the estimated effects for urban violence. It is revealing that stereotypes of the South as unaffected by wage labor and immigration are not always upheld.

By estimating similar models for lynching and urban violence, two other comparisons may be made between Table 7.1 and column 1 in Table 7.2. As was the case for urban violence, urbanization of African-Americans does not have a significant effect on lynchings. However, the effect of economic depression is opposite for the two forms of racial violence. The frequency of lynchings increased significantly during depressions.

The model whose estimates appear in the first column of Table 7.2 contains an effect relevant to diffusion across the two types of violence: the number of urban attacks on African-Americans in the previous year. Interestingly, the estimated effect is *negative* and significant. So, while the count of lynchings has a positive effect on urban violence, the count of events of urban violence has a negative effect on lynchings. This difference suggests that the direction of contagion is from rural to urban areas, where perhaps communication channels are more densely connected to one another. An alternative hypothesis which needs exploration is the possibility that diffusion from urban to rural regions is more rapid (or even instantaneous) than the one-year lag suggested by the analysis reported in Table 7.2, column 1.

Political and Economic Competition and Lynchings.

Column 2 in Table 7.2 reports estimates of a model specifying effects relevant to understanding the impact of features of the social structure of the South. The additional variables are the (lagged) price of cotton, change in the price of cotton, presidential election year, Populist electoral challenge, and percentage of votes obtained by splinter party or third party presidential candidates.

Four variables whose effects have been considered above—immigration, level of real wages, change in real wages, and depression year—have significant effects in column 2. The signs of these effects agree with those

TABLE 7.2

GLS Estimates of Effects of Social, Economic, and Political
Variables on the Log of Yearly Counts of Lynchings

(Asymptotic Standard Errors in Parentheses)

	(1)	(2)
Intercept	.021	0.21
	(2.72)	(1.07)
Change in immigration $(t-1)$	0.23*	0.24*
	(0.12)	(0.12)
Real wage of laborers $(t-1)$	4.86***	4.55***
	(1.48)	(.938)
Change in real wage $(t-1)$	−3.72***	−3.37***
	(1.01)	(.063)
Depression year $(t-1)$	0.18**	0.22***
	(.07)	(0.06)
Price of cotton $(t-1)$		−8.89***
		(3.17)
Change in price of cotton (t)		7.24***
		(2.45)
Populist electoral contest (t)		0.30**
		(0.11)
Presidential election year (t)		−0.33***
		(0.09)
Percentage of votes to third parties (t)		1.91***
		(0.64)
Proportion of African-Americans in cities $(t-1)$	−6.26	
	(13.7)	
Number of attacks on African-Americans $(t-1)$	−0.02*	
	(0.01)	
Time trend	0.05	0.07***
	(0.05)	(0.01)
Number of observations	33	33
R^2	0.78	0.83
ϕ	0.59	0.31

* $p < .10$,   ** $p < .05$,   *** $p < .01$.

in column 1. So adding measures that are arguably more relevant to
events in the South does not diminish the effects of national conditions
on lynchings. Indeed, this addition actually strengthens the effects of
national conditions.

How does our hypothesis regarding the effects of southern social
structure and political process fare? First consider the effect of cotton prices. Both the lagged price of cotton and the year-to-year change

in the price of cotton have significant effects on the frequency of lynching. But the effects differ in sign. Lynching declined during periods of peak cotton prices. But when the annual cotton price rose, lynchings surged. Why would this be the case? To answer this question, we must return to the historical speculations about the impact of economic prosperity on the rates of racial violence in the South: the greater the prosperity, the greater dependence on King Cotton. By this argument, economic prosperity increased the need to exert social control over the sources of cheap labor in the South, the African-Americans. The positive and significant effect of annual changes in cotton prices suggests that short-term economic shocks had direct effects on lynching.

All three indicators of political challenge are significant and in the direction suggested by historical accounts of the Populist challenge to white supremacy and one-party rule in the South. As noted above, economic historians and sociologists have claimed that the political challenge of Populism was met with swift and violent resistance by the white power structure. One method was to impose widespread terror with lynchings. The results in column 2 of Table 7.2 are consistent with this key historical claim. During years of Populist electoral challenges and years in which splinter candidates competed well in presidential elections, the frequency of lynchings rose. Interestingly, years of presidential elections with no Populist challenge had significantly lower levels of lynching than nonelection years. So it appears to have been the Populist challenge per se rather than electoral politics that sparked increases in lynching.

Conclusions

Were the causes of lynching and urban violence against African-Americans the same in turn-of-the-century America? It appears that economic slumps, particularly those that affected the least skilled workers, increased rates of both forms of racial violence, as did rising competition from immigration. But lynching also appears to have been sensitive to political and economic upheavals in the post-Reconstruction South connected with Populism and the changing fortunes of the cotton economy. Nevertheless, even when these indicators of such upheavals are included in analyses, competition processes remain strong.

This comparison of two settings of racial violence in America speaks to the debate about the generality of theories of collective action with respect to types of events and historic periods. At the outset, we noted the vast differences in the timing of peak periods and location of urban racial violence and lynchings. Yet the results show patterns of striking similarities, despite these obvious differences. Specifically, a rise in the intensity of racial competition indicated by increases in the supply of low-wage labor and economic contraction raised rates of both urban and rural violence against African-Americans. Moreover, periods of economic recovery, as measured by increasing wages for laborers at the very bottom of the occupational structure, had low rates of urban violence against African-Americans and lynching.

Yet economic competition provides only a partial explanation for the rise and fall of racial violence in the rural South during this period. These results also support contentions by historians that the short-lived Populist challenge to white supremacy intensified racial terror and violence. Put differently, political competition also appears to have affected racial violence. Indicators of Populism's political challenges to one-party rule are associated significantly with levels of lynching, even when indicators of national and regional prosperity are included in the analysis. By including measures of both facets of competition, this analysis has added empirical support for these arguments. The results all point to competition as a fundamental mechanism of mobilization.

8

The Changing Job Queue

Research on the late nineteenth and early twentieth century finds that the structure of opportunity for African-Americans in the United States deteriorated sharply just as occupational mobility for white immigrants improved.[1] We know little about the mechanisms that produced these paths of opportunity, despite the fact that they undoubtedly have consequences for today's gaps in occupational attainment between African-Americans and whites (Farley 1984). In order to explore these issues, this chapter analyzes data on changes in levels of occupational segregation of the foreign-born population in cities in the late nineteenth century.

Lieberson (1980) proposed an intriguing explanation for the divergence of African-American and white experiences which deserves further empirical attention. Gaps in occupational attainment between whites and African-Americans, which were evident as early as 1900, only partly reflected differences in statuses and skills according to Lieberson. Equally important was a queue process. The queue process implies that a group's median level of attainment is constrained by its position in the hierarchy and its size relative to the size of other groups. African-Americans and white immigrants tended to fill the jobs at the bottom and next-to-last rung on the occupational queue respectively. But when the number of good jobs expands, a queue process generates upward mobility even for those at the bottom:

If the group at the bottom of the ethnic-racial hierarchy amounts to Q percent of the population, then it will find the Q least desirable positions available ... If Q is large, then the group will have opportunities higher on the occupational hierarchy because the more highly ranked groups are not pushing as far down ... Insofar as the queuing effect operates (and obviously it is not the

---

[1] For evidence on this point, see Thernstrom 1973, Walkowitz 1978, Wilson 1978, Hershberg 1981, Bodnar et al. 1982, and Archdeacon 1983.

only factor), the group at the bottom of the ethnic-racial ranking can only go upward occupationally when there are fewer of the other groups around. (Lieberson 1980: 297–98).

However, the existence of a queue does not alone explain why African-Americans became more segregated and the foreign-born became less so during this period. To address this question we turn to theories that take the dynamics of segregation into account explicitly. Another explanation of changes in racial segregation suggests that changes in the population composition affect job competition which in turn affects segregation. So competition theories of racial conflict might account for these early patterns of desegregation of the foreign-born in the United States around the turn of the century. Chapter 5 showed that rising levels of competition from increasing numbers of immigrants raised rates of racial conflict and violence against African-Americans when compared to conflicts against the foreign-born.

But racial violence and conflict were not the only means by which African-Americans have been oppressed. By increasing levels of segregation of African-Americans, whites suppressed the threat of job competition from African-Americans. A rise in the levels of occupational segregation of African-Americans meant that native-born whites were able to maintain their advantages in the labor force. This argument also has implications for the opportunity structure for the (mostly white) foreign-born as well. It suggests that levels of occupational segregation for the foreign-born declined because limitations on opportunities for African-Americans allowed the foreign-born to disperse throughout the occupational hierarchy more freely.

Efforts at learning whether the opportunity structure facing African-Americans and (mostly white) immigrants was affected by a job-queue process have been hampered by scarcity of data on occupational distributions by race for the earliest periods when industrial labor markets took shape. Existing research begins with conditions in 1900, when processes of discrimination and allocation of African-Americans to the bottom of the job queue were well underway. The purpose of this chapter is to investigate the determinants of occupational segregation in an earlier period. It considers the causes of changes in occupational segregation for the foreign-born using evidence from the period 1870 to 1880. The decade is interesting because it comes just before the great surge in immigration to the United States.[2] This chapter focuses on the effects

---

[2]Prior to 1880, there were three sizable waves of immigration that correspond to peak periods of immigration by country of origin. They were foreign-born from Ireland (peaking in 1845–1855), Germany (peaking 1850–1855), and China (1869–

of numbers and changes in the sizes of ethnic/racial groups on changes in occupational segregation of the foreign-born in 30 cities during this decade. Understanding how the process worked during the early stages of the great wave of immigration can perhaps clarify the causes of the apparent divergence in opportunities of African-Americans and white immigrants in subsequent periods.

In addressing these issues, this chapter offers two innovations. It shows that the isolation index (or P^* index) which was developed for analyzing residential segregation can be applied usefully in analyzing occupational segregation. Second, unlike previous research on occupational segregation in this early period which has analyzed levels of segregation at one point in time, this research treats causes of changes in occupational segregation.

Choice of an index of segregation is crucial in analyzing ethnic/racial differences in distributions. Recent investigations of race/ethnic differences in geographic mobility have demonstrated the usefulness of the isolation (or P^*) index developed by Bell (1954).[3] Although the merits of the isolation index and the more common index of dissimilarity continue to be debated, an emerging consensus regards the isolation index as preferable when there is strong reason to believe that *proportions* affect the outcomes of interest (Coleman, Kelly, and Moore 1982; Lieberson and Carter 1982; Stearns and Logan 1984; White 1986; Massey and Denton 1989). A major advantage of the isolation index for studies of race/ethnic relations is that it reflects the relative sizes of groups in a population (Lieberson 1969). This advantage is especially relevant when the relative size of a group affects subsequent levels of isolation for that group.[4]

Another advantage is that P^* is an *asymmetric* measure. Lieberson

---

1877), according to analysis of census data by Archdeacon (1983: 39, 120). However, it was from 1880 to 1920 that the largest number of immigrants arrived. During these decades, an estimated 23 million immigrants came from mostly South, Central and Eastern European origins (Easterlin et al. 1982). During the years 1890 to 1915, yearly immigration flows averaged nearly one million (United States Bureau of the Census 1975).

[3]See Farley 1977, Lieberson 1979, 1980, Lieberson and Carter 1982, Massey 1978, Massey and Blakeslee 1983, Taeuber and Taeuber 1976, Winship 1978, and White 1986 for empirical analyses of various indexes applied to spatial segregation.

[4]For example, the proportions of blacks or foreigners apparently affect rates of inter-ethnic interaction on the job and in the neighborhood (Lieberson and Carter 1982). Others have found that proportions of race/ethnic populations even affect rates of interracial crime and lynching (Blau and Schwartz 1984; Reed 1972). Coleman, Kelly, and Moore (1982: 177–79) also claim that the sociological evidence weighs heavily in favor of using the P^* index (over the dissimilarity index) in analysis of school segregation. Economic models that use similar measures to estimate

(1969: 859) noted that this makes it useful when population sizes are expected to influence the amount of interaction or isolation of groups in a system. In comparison, the more commonly-used index of dissimilarity can generate a similar index value for two cities having different proportions of minorities in them, for example. According to Lieberson, the solution is to use a measure of ethnic interaction, like P^*, that takes into account both the pattern of dissimilarity and population composition.

This chapter departs from the traditional uses of the isolation measure by exploring applications to *occupational segregation*. Given widespread interest in differences in opportunity for various race/ethnic groups during the period of industrialization, it is surprising that this measure of segregation has rarely been applied to distributions of occupations.

Occupational Segregation and the Job Queue

Though Lieberson's analysis concerns models of a group's proportion in the population and in selected occupations, this chapter considers how these arguments have implications for dynamics of changing population sizes and how they might affect segregation levels. For a group concentrated at the bottom of the job hierarchy, decreasing occupational segregation means upward mobility. Lieberson (1980) applied his arguments about the queue process to an analysis of occupational attainment and dispersion of African-Americans compared to South, Central, and Eastern (SCE) European immigrants in 1900. In order to draw the implications of a job hierarchy for the analysis of levels of occupational segregation of immigrants, a connection between occupational segregation and occupational status must first be established.

Upward Mobility and Occupational Segregation. If the evidence shows that African-Americans and foreign-born were initially segregated at the bottom of the occupational queue, then a decline in occupational segregation for some group suggests that upward mobility occurred as well.[5] Historical studies of the relationship between occupational status and levels of occupational segregation during this period speak to this issue. Immigrants and African-Americans entered urban labor markets

---

how varying numbers of African-Americans moving into a neighborhood affect blockbusting and "white flight" can be found in Schelling (1973).

[5]Without a systematic analysis of individual mobility of individual members of the foreign-born and native-born African-American population followed over time, we are unable to determine whether declining job segregation always meant upward mobility, as the queue model would indicate. While historians have attempted to use retrospective family histories to reconstruct such data (see Bodnar et al. 1982), such analysis is outside the scope of this chapter.

in the North in the United States with similarly low levels of skills and education (Higham 1955; Saxton 1971; Bodnar et al. 1982; Gutman and Bell 1987). Not surprisingly, both immigrants and African-Americans were overrepresented in unskilled positions (laborers and domestics) and semi-skilled occupations in manufacturing and extractive industries. Immigrants as well as African-Americans entered the urban labor force in Northern cities after 1870 at the bottom of the occupational queue. For example, an analysis of occupations of entering immigrants shows that

[from the mid 1840s through 1890] ... the proportion of unskilled persons categorized as laborers showed the most dramatic rise. After the mid 1840s, laborers were consistently the most numerous group among each year's immigrants ... [between 1860 and 1890] readings in the 40 percent range became more frequent than lower ones and the 50 percent mark was passed four times. (Archdeacon 1983: 133)

How did the position of African-Americans and Asians compare with that of European immigrants? Because the census did not report data on racial distributions in occupations prior to 1890, we must rely on later data. It appears that African-Americans and Asians also entered the occupational structure at the bottom. Spero and Harris (1931: 85) report that, for blacks in manufacturing in 1920, "Only 16.6 percent of them were skilled laborers, [and] 67.9 percent of them were laborers ..." From 1900 to 1920, African-Americans had higher rates of downward mobility and increasing occupational segregation than did those born in Italy, Austria-Hungary, and Poland in northern cities (Lieberson 1980). Entry positions for Chinese immigrants in West Coast cities were apparently no better. Saxton (1971: 7) reports:

In summary, the Chinese during the seventies and eighties comprised about one-twelfth of the inhabitants both of California and of San Francisco. Having earlier been largely occupied as placer mining, they were moving now into heavy construction and farm labor, and into manufacturing ... In the hinterland, Chinese were generally restricted to unskilled positions as agricultural and construction workers; in the city they were generally restricted to 'sweated' trades ...

So most native-born African-Americans and foreign-born immigrants apparently initially took jobs as domestics, laborers and semi-skilled occupations that were concentrated at the bottom of the job queue.[6]

---

[6]The data from 1880 analyzed here are consistent with these historical accounts. The foreign-born comprised nearly 60% of the common laborers in these 30 cities in 1880, while they were only 20% of the total labor force in these same cities. In Philadelphia, for example, in 1880, over one-third of all domestic servants were born in Ireland, while those born in Ireland were only one-tenth of the labor force in general.

Hence decreasing levels of segregation for the foreign-born means upward mobility.

Dynamics of the Queue Process. According to Lieberson (1980), urban labor markets in the United States operated according to a job queue stratified by ethnicity and race as early as 1900. He assumes that employers shared racial/ethnic prejudices and exercised them when dealing with a large, racially diverse labor force. In particular, employers preferred whites of any ethnicity to African-Americans. The queue process is one in which employers fill jobs at higher levels with persons from favored ethnic/racial groups first and employ disfavored groups in such jobs only when the numbers of jobs exceeds the number of favored workers available. So concentration of groups in jobs of differing quality depends on the number of jobs, preferences of employers, and on the relative sizes of race/ethnic groups.

As presented by Lieberson (1980), a pure queue process implies that an increase in the number of the foreign-born in a city may decrease their occupational segregation but it cannot increase it. That is, as the foreign-born move from 10 to 20 percent of the population they will disperse into jobs other than those where they were concentrated and their median level of attainment rises, all else being equal (see Lieberson 1980: Table 12.3). To the extent that foreign-born enter the job queue at the bottom, or even middle levels, this also means that they will be more dispersed. If only a pure queue model were at work, then, an increase in the numbers of foreign-born in a population would decrease their levels of occupational segregation.

But two other processes might be operating. First, if members of some ethnic group continue to arrive and if they tend to be initially concentrated at the bottom of the job hierarchy (as the historical evidence suggests), then new arrivals of immigrants may undercut any decreases in segregation implied by a strict queuing model. Thus Lieberson (1980: 380) also claims,

Sizable numbers of newcomers raise the level of ethnic and/or racial consciousness on the part of others in the city; moreover, if these newcomers are less able to compete for more desirable position than are the longer-standing residents, they will tend to undercut the position of other members of the group.

There are several reasons this might occur. First, new arrivals provide an increase in the supply of low-wage labor, which employers may prefer to hire over higher-price labor. Second, new arrivals may have initially low levels of skills which restrict them to unskilled occupations. Third, evidence from studies of past and present ethnic enclaves suggests that newly arriving immigrants are most likely to concentrate in jobs and industries where their compatriots are already located (Light 1972; Hareven 1982; Aldrich et al. 1985; Portes and Bach 1985). This too would encourage high levels of occupational segregation. In fact, if new arrivals greatly outnumbered those already in residence, we might expect segregation levels for the foreign-born to increase overall, at least initially. So a second prediction of a queue model would be that *growth* in the number of immigrants increases the occupational segregation of this group.

Finally, prejudice and racism affect segregation. The queue model holds that if newcomers arrive who are ethnically/racially distinct and less-preferred than those groups already in residence so that they enter only at the bottom of the job queue, then any expansion of jobs will allow those groups just above them to disperse throughout the job hierarchy. According to Lieberson this was what happened in the 1920s and 1930s in the United States, when immigration had slowed while the enormous migration of African-Americans to northern cities had begun:

... increases in the African-American component would upgrade the new Europeans at a more rapid rate as long as the queuing process remains intact. In effect, this queuing notion is compatible with the long-standing ladder model that holds that increases in a lower ranked population would tend to upgrade populations above them. (Lieberson 1980: 377–78)

So the queue process contains an explanation for three offsetting effects of rising numbers of newcomers on the levels of occupational segregation of immigrants. First, the foreign-born disperse as their proportions in the population rise. Second, their segregation level increases if new immigrants enter only at the bottom of the hierarchy. Third, a rise in the numbers of a racially-distinct and less-preferred group would allow those in the middle-ranked population to disperse during times of economic expansion.

Effects of Timing of Entering the Job Queue. Another reason why the foreign-born may have benefitted from the existence of a racial job queue was that the arrival of the foreign-born in urban labor markets preceded the largest wave of African-American migration to northern cities. Because they entered urban labor markets prior to the rise in migration of southern African-Americans, the foreign-born were able to take advantage of the initial expansion of jobs in skilled and craft industries that occurred. For example, Thernstrom (1973) and Hershberg (1981) have documented that white native-born and foreign-born persons tended to monopolize jobs in skilled occupations in the expanding industries. One explanation for this advantage is that they arrived in industrial centers before most African-Americans did. Such skilled occupations were also the first to be organized by trade unions (Commons 1918). Others have claimed that such monopolies over skilled jobs enjoyed by white native-born and foreign-born workers in trade unions encouraged racial conflicts (Wilson 1978; Foner 1982).

Historical case studies also point to several ways in which the timing of immigration of some groups affected their occupational attainment. Early waves of immigrants may have obtained initial advantages in obtaining skilled jobs and by building ethnic institutions when compared to later arrivals (Thernstrom 1973; Hareven 1982). The earlier white immigrants—principally those from Northern Europe and Great Britain—also entered trade union organizations, which may have also been used to keep other nationalities and races from entering skilled occupations or closed shops (Commons 1918; Wilson 1978; Foner 1982). Bodnar et al. (1982: 65-6) indicate that the *timing* of immigration affected attainment even when nationality of different cohorts is held constant:

Time of migration, however did seem to influence occupational differences among the various Polish groups. On the average, Poles from Prussia arrived in America six years before the Russian Poles and eight years before those from Austrian territory. Moreover, fully one-third arrived before 1885. This group had been in Pittsburgh for at least fifteen years by the 1900 census. Their ability to secure better occupations no doubt contributed to their longevity in the community.

Expanding the Model of the Queue Process
The point that labor market expansion and contraction would alter effects of employers' preference orderings means that factors in addition to the queue can affect changes in occupational segregation. At least three other fields of research have implications for the processes under discussion: economic theories of immigration cycles and expansion, human capital theories, and theories of ethnic/racial competition and conflict.

Economic Expansion and Immigration. Expansion and contraction of industries across cities evidently affected segregation and dispersion in occupations after the turn of the century (Easterlin et al. 1982). But economic expansion may have had two different effects on occupational segregation, depending on the characteristics and composition of groups involved. Initially, upward swings in local economies may have encouraged ethnic segregation into just a few occupations (whether or not they are low-status jobs), as groups were recruited by nationality or region. This was often the case for "contract" labor, recruited from designated regions overseas where firms had previous luck finding workers (Commons 1918; Barton 1975). But continuing growth in jobs may have encouraged desegregation, as the queue process outlined above suggested.

Human Capital Factors. Differences in education and skills among groups cannot be ignored when considering the job allocation process. Ethnic/racial populations with few skills experienced more segregation at the bottom of the job queue, at least initially (Lieberson 1980; Bodnar et al. 1982). Newly arriving ethnic/racial groups filled the niches that their education, training, and experience allowed.

But each entering group's characteristics can also affect the chances for others to move out of segregated niches. If Lieberson is correct, then migration of largely uneducated African-American workers to some northern cities prior to 1880 would have subsequently increased the likelihood that white ethnics moved out of laborer and domestic jobs into semi-skilled and skilled occupations. Lieberson's queue process suggests that cities with substantial populations of uneducated African-Americans had lower than average levels of segregation for the foreign-born (whatever their level of education). According to this perspective, the rank ordering of ethnic and racial groups by employers would ensure this fact, even if white foreigners had equally low levels of education (see also Becker 1973).

Competition and Occupational Segregation. We know that white ethnic groups had higher illiteracy rates than African-Americans in the same cities (United States Census 1870). The more educated African-Americans could have moved up the queue as less educated whites moved into the unskilled jobs. But recent analyses show that African-Americans fared far worse then the white immigrants by 1920. What happened? Competition explanations of racial conflict suggest that when African-Americans and white ethnics came to compete for the same jobs, skills mattered less than racial boundaries did.[7] And they also suggest that efforts to contain this competition arose where and when African-Americans successfully competed with white ethnics for the same jobs. Prior research along with the research in previous chapters suggests that racial conflict occurred when ethnic and racial competition rose during this period. Here we suggest that the occupational segregation (or in some cases re-segregation) of African-Americans was also invoked to contain competition from African-American workers. The result was that whites were able to move out of segregated occupations

---

[7]This proposition depends upon there being a polyethnic social system in which race boundaries attach to occupational boundaries so that when competition over jobs arises, ethnic boundaries are mobilized.

during expansionary periods in the economy, while African-Americans became more concentrated in the lower-status occupations.

What were some of the mechanisms that caused the reversal of conditions for African-Americans? Competition theories hold that direct competition among ethnic populations tends to ignite conflict among those groups. No simple correspondence between an ethnic/racial group's initial and subsequent levels of attainment assures continued upward mobility in the job queue. In fact, competition theories suggest that *desegregation* of African-Americans into formerly all-white occupations sometimes activated racial antagonism and movements designed to contain African-Americans. That is, racial antagonism increased the occupational segregation of African-Americans during this period (Woodward 1974). Desegregation intensified competition over jobs between whites and African-Americans, resulting in an increase in discrimination (and perhaps also violence) against African-Americans, as we have seen in previous chapters.

Rising numbers of African-Americans may have triggered the predispositions of whites to maintain a fixed distance from African-Americans in terms of rates of interaction in occupations. An influx of African-American migrants temporarily increases racial diversity in job markets. If whites were to maintain fixed levels of social and physical distance from nonwhites, African-Americans must become more segregated in occupations. This is because rates of interaction between majority and minority groups (by definition) increase with a rise in the size of a minority population if no barriers exist between them (Schelling 1973; Blau and Schwartz 1984; Lieberson 1980). An increase in the numbers of African-Americans represented a threat to white isolation to which whites responded by increasing their social distance from African-Americans. The result was that African-Americans became increasingly segregated into low-paying occupations (Spero and Harris 1931).[8]

Research Design and Analysis

This chapter pursues the arguments drawn above using data from an earlier period than previously analyzed. It asks: *Did the sizes of the*

---

[8]This discussion is drawn from Lieberson's analysis of residential segregation. According to Lieberson, an increase in the numbers of African-Americans represented a threat to white isolation to which whites responded by increasing their social distance from African-Americans. The result was that African-Americans became increasingly segregated into deteriorating neighborhoods. Though arguments presented here hold that the process of competition and racial discrimination could affect both kinds of segregation in the same ways, analysis of factors affecting residential segregation is outside of the scope of this chapter.

immigrant and African-American populations affect change in levels of occupational segregation for the foreign-born? One answer suggested by the queue process is that higher proportions of foreign-born in cities decrease their level of segregation. On the other hand, newly arriving foreign-born might also have been highly isolated in occupations in cities where they were especially high or growing in number. By this argument, high concentrations of immigrants also produced dense ethnic enclaves (Light 1972; Portes and Bach 1985). An argument drawn from Lieberson suggests that large numbers of racially different newcomers decrease the levels of segregation for those just above them in the job queue. We ask if this relationship might not also hold for a much earlier period in which the sizes of the African-American population and foreign-born was much smaller.

Did educational levels affect a change in levels of segregation of the foreign-born? The human capital and queuing arguments reviewed above suggest that opportunities for the foreign-born improve and their segregation declines where the size of the uneducated African-American population was large. But in this period the foreign-born had low levels of education, indicated by high rates of illiteracy (United States Census 1870). So we might expect segregation of the foreign-born to increase or at least remain unchanged when their educational attainments were low. Such theories might not expect the size of African-American and illiterate populations to affect segregation levels of the foreign-born at all. On the other hand, if competition and queuing arguments hold, we would expect that the size of the African-American illiterate population should decrease segregation levels of the foreign-born.

Did changes in the composition of foreign-born and African-Americans in cities cause the occupational segregation for the foreign-born to diminish? At least one version of the queuing process discussed above leads one to expect that foreign-born residents would have experienced desegregation in cities where African-Americans moved in to fill the least skilled jobs. So places with increasing African-American populations should have decreasing levels of foreign isolation. Segregation of the foreign-born would also decrease in settings with expanding opportunities in general. Based on historical evidence on the establishment of ethnic enclaves during this period, we would expect that larger cities and cities attracting higher numbers of immigrants would (at least during this early period) increase the levels of segregation of the foreign-born.

Time Frame. Data for the period 1870 to 1880 are used here. This starting point was chosen because immigration began to increase sharply around 1880, slowing only with World War I and nearly ceasing with the

1924 Immigration Act (United States Bureau of the Census 1975; East-erlin et al. 1982). According to the historical accounts cited earlier, groups who entered expanding urban economies and skilled occupations early had a high rate of mobility from highly segregated and low-paying jobs. In particular, immigrants who entered prior to the larger waves beginning in 1890 experienced considerable movement out of laboring and unskilled occupations. But Lieberson and others began their analysis of segregation and mobility decades later, after considerable immigration and mobility had taken place. By starting in 1870, the first year for which city-level data are available, we can uncover the early part of the historic process.

The ending point of 1880 was chosen for two reasons. First, racial categories used in reporting occupational distributions in the 1870 and 1880 censuses differ from those used in 1890 and subsequently. In 1870 and 1880 tabulations on occupational distributions, the categories foreign-born and native-born were not distinguished by race. This means that levels of segregation for native-born whites and African-Americans cannot be distinguished for 1870 and 1880. The category of foreign-born is also not distinguished by race in 1870 and 1880. So these two census periods are difficult to compare with data from later ones and are therefore analyzed separately in this chapter. Fortunately, data on the sizes of African-American, Asian, foreign-born and native-born populations are available at the city-level for this period. Of necessity, the focus will be on testing the implications from arguments described above to analyze changes in the levels of ethnic segregation for the *foreign-born* from 1870 to 1880.

A second reason that this analysis ends in 1880 is that the number and type of occupations changed considerably after 1880. This change further complicates efforts at subsequent comparisons.[9]

The Isolation Index. The analysis reported below uses data from the largest 30 cities for which information on occupational distributions and population composition exist for both 1870 and 1880. Even the calculation of one P^* index for a broad category such as "foreign-born" for this period requires a large investment in data collection and computation. The number of foreign-born in each of 171 occupations for 30 cities must be coded for each period (see Appendix A for a list of occupations included in the index). The index implies a nativity group's

---

[9]For instance, occupations such as farm laborer, livery-stable and hostlers, steamboatmen, blacksmiths, and wheelwrights engage a tiny number of persons in cities after 1880, while clerks, stenographers, mill and factory operatives, and laborers rise in number of persons so employed.

isolation with its own members within an occupational category, that is, the probability of finding another worker in that same occupation who is foreign-born.

Ideally it would be useful to examine patterns of segregation separately by nationality group, since the category of foreign-born is obviously heterogeneous. However, data from 1880 on occupational distributions are only distinguished for the foreign-born from Ireland, Germany, Great Britain, Sweden and Norway, Canada, and Other Countries. In some ways the least detailed category is sociologically the most interesting, since we have information that Germans, Irish, and Northern Europeans had higher levels of occupational mobility and lower levels of segregation by 1900 than did other groups born in the Austro-Hungarian empire, Poland, Italy, and other countries (Archdeacon 1983). Some account for these relative advantages of Northern Europeans in the job queue by citing the relatively early arrival of Irish, German, and other Northern Europeans, when compared to the SCE groups. Unfortunately, the aggregate data that is available does not allow us to tease out effects of the timing of entry by cohort and country of origin at the city level. Moreover, the detailed nativity categories are not uniform across all cities or when categories of nativity in 1870 and 1880 are compared. So analysis of changing levels of segregation by specific nativity group over the decade cannot be conducted with these data. For these reasons, it makes sense to focus on segregation levels for the foreign-born category as a whole for this decade in order to capture the changes in the levels of segregation for the foreign-born.

The P^* index is defined as:

$$P^* = \sum_{k=1}^{K} \left(\frac{n_{ijk}}{n_{ij.}} \cdot \frac{n_{ijk}}{n_{i.k}} \right). \tag{8.1}$$

where the . notation means summation over the index and n_{ijk} is the number of members of the foreign-born population j in occupation k in city i. So $n_{ij.}$ is the total number of workers in the foreign-born population j in city i, and $n_{i.k}$ is the number of workers in occupational category k in city i. K is the number of occupational categories. The index gives the probability that a randomly-chosen worker in any of the 171 occupations listed in Appendix A would belong to the same foreign-born population as another randomly-chosen worker from that same occupation. High levels of P^* indicate that the foreign-born are highly concentrated in just a few occupations.

A Model of the Relative Odds of Isolation. Because the index is a probability, it must fall in the [0–1] range. In order to deal with this limitation, I analyze levels of segregation using logistic regression analysis (see Hanushek and Jackson 1977: Chapter 7). Using a logistic regression model is more efficient than using a linear probability model, which is important given the small sample analyzed.

According to the logistic model, the log odds of isolation, $\log(P^*/Q^*)$, is a linear function of a set of covariates: $\log(P^*/Q^*) = \mathbf{x}'\beta$, where $Q^* = 1 - P^*$, $\mathbf{x}$ is a vector of observations on K covariates, and β is a vector of effects to be estimated. Alternatively, the model can be written as:

$$P^* = \frac{1}{1 + \exp(-\mathbf{x}'\beta)} \ . \tag{8.2}$$

A key factor expected to effect the level of isolation of a group in 1880 is its prior 1870 level of isolation. One useful way to build dependence of past isolation into the model is by considering the *log of the relative odds of isolation in the two periods* as a function of covariates measured at time 1. This can be written as,

$$\log\left(\frac{P_2^*}{Q_2^*} \div \frac{P_1^*}{Q_1^*}\right) = \mathbf{x}_1'\beta \ , \tag{8.3}$$

where $\mathbf{x}_1$ contains observations on city characteristics for the first period and β indicates the effect of these characteristics on the relative odds of occupational isolation at the second period (P_2^*) versus that in the first period (P_1^*). Because the distribution of occupational isolation may shift over time, it is preferable to use a generalization of (8.3):

$$\log\left(\frac{P_2^*}{Q_2^*} \div \left[\frac{P_1^*}{Q_1^*}\right]^\alpha\right) = \mathbf{x}_1'\beta \ . \tag{8.4}$$

Here α is a scaling factor which accounts for possible shifts in the distribution over time. Rearranging the terms in equation (8.4) gives us:

$$\log\left(\frac{P_2^*}{Q_2^*}\right) = \alpha \log\left(\frac{P_1^*}{Q_1^*}\right) + \mathbf{x}_1'\beta \tag{8.5}$$

The model of the log odds of isolation as represented in (8.5) tells that a vector of covariates, $\mathbf{x}_1$, affects the relative odds that two randomly selected workers in an occupation in a city will be from the same occupation at time 2 *relative* to the odds of the same event in the same city at time 1. If segregation for the group has increased the odds will be higher at the second time. So any covariate that has a positive effect on the relative odds increases segregation over the period.

The independent variables concerning population composition include the sizes of the labor force, the foreign-born population, the African-American population (nonwhite and non-Asian), and Asian population (Chinese plus Japanese) all are taken from the 1870 and 1880

Censuses, as are the occupational distributions for 30 cities. Data on literacy (available only for 1870) include measures of the number of foreign-born and African-Americans who cannot write in any language.

Because the isolation index includes the number of foreign-born in 1880 as part of its numerator and denominator, including the size of a city's foreign born population 1880 as an independent variable would be meaningless. For this reason only the 1870 foreign-born population size and changes from 1870 are included in models estimating the log odds of segregation in 1880.[10]

Results

Table 8.1 reports the means, standard deviations, and ranges of the variables used in the analysis. The mean level of occupational segregation of the foreign-born decreased from .57 in 1870 to .49 in 1880. This represents a 14 percent decrease in the level of segregation for the foreign-born, which is considerable for such a short period of time. The segregation index ranges from a relatively low level of segregation for the foreign-born of 0.23 (in Washington D.C. in 1880) to a peak of 0.74 (in San Francisco in 1880). The rankings of cities by level of segregation is relatively stable over this decade: San Francisco had the highest level of occupational segregation for foreign-born in both 1870 and 1880, while Washington D.C. had the lowest level in both years.[11]

During this period, cities with large African-American populations were located in the South (United States Census 1880). Even though a large northern migration of African-Americans had not really begun by 1880, some northern cities did experience significant increases in the size of their African-Americans populations.[12] In addition, only San

---

[10]This research also analyzed determinants of native-born isolation in occupations across 30 cities for which data exists. Because the information on occupational distributions at the city level combines whites and nonwhites into the category of "native-born," it is difficult to make any inferences from analyses conducted using this index. That is, high levels of isolation of the native-born in 1870 might mask the fact that African-American or white natives (or both) were not only highly segregated from the foreign-born but were also segregated from each other. Another reason that the analysis was restricted to the analysis of segregation of foreign-born is that in the case of analysis of segregation of two groups, one index can be mathematically derived from the other (see Lieberson 1980: 257). This would mean that the two indexes would not be independent of each other. Still, it is interesting to note that while average foreign- and native-born segregation levels are approximately the same in 1870 (both groups are in occupations that are about 57% foreign-born or 59% native-born) by 1880, the average level of foreign-born segregation declines to less than 49%, while native-born segregation increases to 62%.

[11]In Chapter 9, Table 9.1 compares levels of occupational segregation from 1880–1910 for the foreign-born in the largest cities.

[12]While it is difficult to estimate the exact size of African-American migration

TABLE 8.1

Means of City Characteristics, 1870 and 1880

(Standard Deviations in Parentheses)

	1870	1880	1880–1870
Occupational segregation of the foreign-born	.573 (.137)	.489 (.128)	−.084 (.051)
Occupational segregation of the native-born	.594 (.158)	.624 (.143)	.030 (.097)
Size of labor force	.625 (.713)	.901 (1.08)	.276 (.379)
Size of foreign-born population	.204 (.267)	.261 (.359)	.057 (.101)
Size of African-American population	.094 (.136)	.124 (.167)	.029 (.038)
Size of Asian population	.004 (.021)	.008 (.040)	.003 (.018)
Foreign-born illiterates	.070 (.108)		
African-American illiterates	.042 (.070)		

Note: All figures for sizes of populations and sizes of illiterate populations are in 100,000s. Literacy data are not available by race and place of birth for 1880.

Francisco had a significant Chinese or Japanese population, although Chinese and Japanese were found in New York, Chicago, St. Louis, and elsewhere in small numbers. The size of a city's labor force is correlated to be 0.9 with its growth over a decade. Furthermore, the size and growth of a city's labor force is correlated to be over 0.9 with the 1870 size of the foreign-born population and the number of illiterate foreign-

to specific cities prior to 1900, Archdeacon (1983: 131) estimates that while 90 percent of all African-Americans lived in the South following the Civil War, by 1880, 60,000 African-Americans had migrated North or West. Wilson (1978: 66) reports demographic estimates of net migration from the South of 71,000 during the 1870 to 1880 decade. The United States Bureau of the Census (1975: 95) estimates at the state level find that during 1870–80 the South and South-Atlantic states experienced a net loss of African-American migration (with the exception of Mississippi, Florida, and Washington, D.C.) while northern states nearly all experienced a rise in African-American net migration. These state-level data concur with the data on sizes and growth in African-American populations in the 30 cities analyzed here. After 1890, the rate of African-American migration intensified, as an estimated 200,000 African-Americans moved north from 1890 to 1910. Archdeacon (1983: 131) claims that the African-American population of New York City tripled over this latter period, and nearly tripled in New Jersey, Philadelphia, and Chicago.

born. Such high collinearity means that any models that include pairs of highly correlated variables will have large standard errors. As might be expected, the size and growth of the African-American population and the size and growth of the Asian population are also highly correlated. The choice of models attempts to minimize effects of multicollinearity, using only one indicator for a highly correlated pair in each model.

However, the log odds of segregation of the foreign-born is only weakly correlated with size of foreign-born population in 1870 ($r = .35$), but it has a strong, negative correlation with the size of the African-American population in 1870 ($r = -.63$). This suggests that it is not merely the size of a city's foreign-born population which determines its level of segregation in occupations.

Effects of Population Composition in 1870. Consider first the issue of the sizes of the relevant racial populations in Table 8.2. The odd-numbered columns report estimates of models that include the lagged dependent variable (the log of the odds of isolation in 1870), and the sizes of the labor force, African-American population, and Asian population in 1870. Models in the even-numbered columns replace the size of the labor force with the size of the foreign-born population (for reasons of multicollinearity discussed above). The first two columns include results for all 30 cities taken together, while the last two columns report results for the 26 northern cities alone. In each model the independent effect of each subpopulation size is estimated net of the effects of the size of other subpopulations (compared to the more common method of estimating the effect of "percent black," and so forth). This was done so that any effects of size of the labor force could be discerned from effects of the population composition effects on segregation. Also raw size variables are more appropriate for this analysis because percent measures might introduce multicollinearity with the components of the segregation index, as occurs when the constituent parts of ratio-dependent variables are introduced as independent variables in an analysis.

Did the sizes of ethnic populations affect the changing odds of isolation for the foreign-born? Table 8.2 reports estimates of the relevant models. The lagged dependent variable alone accounts for 86% and 79% of the variance in segregation in 1880 in all cities and in the North (estimates not shown). Nonetheless, adding measures of population composition to models containing only the lagged dependent variable does improve the fit of the models significantly. In cities with large African-American populations, the odds of isolation of the foreign-born declined as predicted. Size of the African-American population has a significant negative effect on change in segregation of the foreign-born over the

TABLE 8.2

Effects of Size of Labor Force and Population Composition
on the Log-Odds of Occupational Segregation of the Foreign-Born
in 30 American Cities and 26 Northern Cities in 1880

(Asymptotic Standard Errors in Parentheses)

	All Cities		Northern Cities	
	(1)	(2)	(3)	(4)
Intercept	−.229***	−.219***	−.214***	−.203***
	(.057)	(.058)	(.065)	(.064)
Log-odds of segregation	.640***	.628***	.626***	.611***
in 1870	(.086)	(.091)	(.100)	(.118)
Size of labor force	.110*		.101*	
in 1870	(.054)		(.058)	
Size of foreign-born		.284*		.266
population in 1870		(.149)		(.161)
Size of African-American	−1.04***	−.991***	−.962***	−.928***
population in 1870	(.359)	(.355)	(.421)	(.418)
Size of Asian population	3.02*	2.97*	2.09*	3.07*
in 1870	(1.63)	(1.65)	(1.76)	(1.77)
Number of cities	30	30	26	26
Adjusted R^2	.89	.89	.82	.82
F-test with 4 d.f.	61.2	59.9	30.1	29.7

* $p < .10$,   ** $p < .05$,   *** $p < .01$

decade in all columns in Table 8.2. This effect is significant even when
the sizes of the labor force or the foreign-born and Asian-born populations are taken into account. This result supports the queue hypothesis
that desegregation of foreign-born was in part related to the presence of
a sizable African-American population.

According to the estimated effect in column 1 in Table 8.2, the effect
of doubling the African-American population in a city, as Chicago, New
York, Detroit and others experienced a few decades later, is a shift of the
mean of the segregation index for the foreign-born from 0.49 to 0.46, a
5.3% decline.[13] But does this relationship also hold in the North, where
only a few African-Americans resided in 1880?

Because most African-Americans resided in the South and few immigrants did, these effects might have varied by region. Perhaps because

---

[13]Because of the nonlinear form of the logit model, the effect of a covariate on the
probability of isolation depends on the level of all covariates (including the lagged
dependent variable). To calculate these effects, I used the estimated model to obtain
an estimate of $\widehat{P^*} = 1/[1 + \exp(-\bar{\mathbf{x}}\widehat{\beta})]$, where the covariates are evaluated at their
means.

of this geographical isolation, we might have expected that the process of interracial competition would not affect desegregation of the foreign-born this early in America's immigration history. But the results in column 4 in Table 8.2 show that the relationship between size of the African-American population and segregation of the foreign born is significant and in the expected direction for northern cities as well. In the North, a doubling of the African-American population in a city would decrease the level of segregation of foreign born from 0.52 to 0.50, a 4% decline. This absence of a regional interaction supports the idea that, although the initial distributions of race and ethnic groups were quite different in the North and South during this period, the sociological mechanisms underlying changes in segregation for the foreign-born did not differ fundamentally by region.

The claim that cities with large foreign-born populations in 1870 would have increasing segregation for the foreign-born over the decade receives only partial support in Table 8.2. The effect of the size of the foreign-born population is significant only in column 2. It not significant in column 4, in the model for northern cities, which is important because it is in the North where the effect of large numbers of immigrants might have been expected to raise segregation levels for that group. However, the size of the Asian-born populations had a positive effect on segregation of the foreign-born over this decade, suggesting that they faced more discrimination than did other foreign-born residents.

The size of the labor force appears to have affected changes in segregation for the foreign-born, as can be seen in the first and third columns of Table 8.2. It was the largest cities that experienced increases in segregation of the foreign-born over this decade. These findings support the queue hypothesis that cities having larger populations tend to increase segregation for that group.

As noted above, data limitations preclude analysis of changes in levels of occupational segregation for specific ethnic or nationality groups. However, we address this issue in another way, using information about the urban concentrations of specific nativity populations in cities to test a substantively interesting hypothesis. It is reasonable to assume, for instance, that Chinese were even more concentrated in occupations such as domestic and personal services than other groups born outside of the United States in 1880 (Saxton 1971). This suggests that the Chinese constitute a special case. Do the effects of population size remain when the Chinese are removed from the segregation index? Though the distributions of Chinese into specific occupations listed in this book's Appendix A are not available in these censuses, the Chinese were only present in this data in significant numbers in one city, San Francisco.

TABLE 8.3

Effects of Population Composition and African-American Illiteracy on the Log-Odds of Occupational Segregation of the Foreign-Born in 30 American Cities and 26 Northern Cities in 1880

(Asymptotic Standard Errors in Parentheses)

	All Cities			Northern Cities		
	(1)	(2)	(3)	(4)	(5)	(6)
Intercept	-.229*** (.054)	-.240*** (.057)	-.251*** (.059)	-.210*** (.060)	-.224*** (.062)	-.191** (.069)
Log-odds of segregation in 1870	.629*** (.078)	.639*** (.084)	.637*** (.092)	.601*** (.092)	.615*** (.096)	.563*** (.106)
Size of Afr. Amer. pop. in 1870	-.861*** (.301)			-.784** (.349)		
Number of illit. Afr. Amer. in 1870		-1.53** (.637)			-1.31* (.741)	
Growth of Afr. Amer. pop. 1870–1880			-2.64** (1.29)			-2.27* (2.09)
Size of Asian Amer. pop. in 1870	2.26 (1.51)	2.43 (1.59)	1.89 (1.60)	2.45 (1.62)	2.58 (1.70)	1.94 (1.65)
Growth of foreign-born population, 1870–1880	1.00*** (.346)	.842** (.352)	1.29*** (.431)	.977*** (.369)	.830** (.377)	1.53*** (.506)
Number of cities	30	30	30	26	26	26
Adjusted R^2	.91	.90	.89	.85	.84	.84
F-test with 4 d.f.	70.9	56.3	61.7	36.0	32.9	34.5

$*p < .10$, $**p < .05$, $***p < .01$

So models similar to those in columns 1–4 were conducted omitting San Francisco (and leaving out the size of the Asian population in 1870). They show no significant differences.

Adding Effects of Growth of the Foreign-Born. One set of arguments cited above suggested that newly arriving immigrants undercut the position of earlier arrivals, leading us to suspect that an influx of foreign-born would increase occupational segregation for that group. Others suggested the opposite hypothesis, that growth of a population decreases segregation levels, when all else is equal. Does adding growth of the foreign-born population over this decade alter the effect of the size of the African-American population? This question is explored in three different models in Table 8.3 which include three measures of the size of the African-American population in cities along with the growth of the foreign-born population.

The answer is straightforward. All six columns in Table 8.3 show a significant negative effect of the size, illiteracy, and growth of the African-American population on the levels of segregation of foreign-born over the 1870–80 decade. These relationships hold even when previous levels of segregation, the size of the Asian population, and growth of the foreign-born population are taken into account. And as expected by a variant of the queue model, growth of the foreign-born also increased segregation for that group. This too is the case in all six columns in Table 8.3.

Consider the effects of African-American population size. The coefficients in the first column of Table 8.3 for all cities can be used to estimate the effects of even larger increases than those observed by 1880. What would happen if the African-American population of an average city grew suddenly, as it did for so many cities in the 1890–1930 period? The estimates in column 1 (evaluating all other variables at their means) imply that by tripling the observed mean increase in number of African-Americans in a city, the level of isolation of the foreign-born would decline by 8 percent. In northern cities, tripling the African-American population would produce a decline in segregation of the foreign-born of five percent on the average.

Table 8.3 also shows that growth in the foreign-born population had a substantial positive effect on the change of that group's occupational segregation. That is, cities that attracted more foreign-born also experienced significant increases in their segregation level, even when the size and growth of the labor force is controlled. Using the same calculation as described above, the estimates for growth in the foreign-born population in the sixth column show that a doubling of the size of the foreign-born population in northern cities would increase their level of segregation by an estimated 4.6 percent.

The number of African-American illiterates had a significant negative effect on change in occupational segregation of the foreign-born, even when the size of the foreign-born population is taken into account. In Table 8.3 this relationship is upheld for all cities and for northern cities. How can we interpret such effects? In the North particularly, a large number of illiterate African-Americans indicates not only educational disadvantage, but perhaps also recent rural migration of African-Americans to those cities, since rural African-Americans were far less likely to be literate than urban ones (Lieberson 1980; Wright 1986).

But the number of illiterate foreign-born might also have affected segregation of immigrants. In models (not shown) analogous to those seen in Table 8.3, the number of illiterate foreign-born was included and the growth of the foreign-born population excluded due to multicollinearity. Number of foreign-born illiterates did not affect change in occupational segregation significantly, once the size of the African-American population was taken into account. Surprisingly, African-American illiteracy affected occupational segregation of the foreign-born more than the illiteracy of foreign-born did. Taken together, these results suggest that occupational segregation depends upon the size and characteristics of other groups in the same labor market, especially those at the very bottom, indicated by the number of illiterate in a city.

Growth of the African-American population had the same negative effect as size on change in segregation of the foreign-born, as can be seen in columns 3 and 6 of Table 8.3. Given the high correlation between size and growth of the African-American population, this result is not surprising. This finding agrees with competition theory and the queue hypothesis that an increase in the size of an easily identified and ethnically different population intensifies racial competition, and may have led whites to repressive actions against African-Americans. If such repression had been successful, segregation of the foreign-born may have declined as opportunities for African-Americans deteriorated even further.[14]

The effect of a growing African-American population is also statistically significant when only northern cities are analyzed, as can be seen

---

[14] As in Table 8.2, the models whose estimates appear in columns 1–3 of Table 8.3 were estimated for all cities other than San Francisco, in an effort to test whether there was an effect specific to that city's concentration of Asians. When San Francisco is omitted from all three models, the effects of the size and growth of the African-American population and size of the illiterate and African-American are also negative and the effect for size of the African-American population is significant at the .01 level.

in the sixth column of Table 8.3. As noted above, because most African-Americans lived in the rural South, few northern cities experienced any substantial growth in African-American population over this decade. This suggests no effects would be found for such small increments in the size of the African-American population over this decade. Nonetheless, the estimated effect of growth in the African-American population for only northern cities is negative and slightly greater in absolute value than the estimate for all cities.

The models for northern cities alone provide more rigid tests of the competition argument than do the models for all cities, since it is mainly in the northern cities that competition over jobs among foreign-born and African-Americans would occur. So the fact that these patterns of effects for the African-American population hold when northern cities are analyzed separately in columns 4, 5, and 6 provides strong support for these arguments. Despite their relatively small numbers in most cities during this period, initial and rising numbers of African-Americans affected segregation levels in the North, where competition with the foreign-born was greatest.

Because the period of analysis ends prior to the enormous wave of northern migration of African-Americans, any conclusions about the effects of increasing the size of the African-American population after this point awaits analysis of subsequent decades. However, the results are suggestive of a queue process that held that growth in the size of the African-American population, particular those entering at the very bottom of the skill or education latter, would be related to desegregation in occupations for the foreign-born.

Discussion and Conclusion

The results of this analysis of change in segregation in 30 cities contribute to our growing knowledge about the dynamics of segregation and population growth in occupational structures. This chapter began by suggesting that the isolation index commonly used to analyze residential segregation could be usefully applied to occupational segregation of immigrants in late nineteenth-century America. The results are consistent with these more traditional applications of the isolation index. Cities experiencing a higher influx of foreign-born (especially Asians) have growing levels of segregation in occupations over a decade, but cities with relatively larger numbers of illiterate African-Americans, a larger than average African-American population, and growing numbers of African-Americans, showed a decrease in segregation in occupations for the foreign-born.

Most of the evidence presented here also gives credibility to the notion that an ethnic and racial job queue underlay the dynamics of job segregation and mobility in American cities during this early period. Cities that had initially large and growing numbers of African-Americans had decreasing levels of occupational segregation for the foreign-born. Most of the evidence reported here also agrees with Lieberson's (1980) analysis of a later period for a narrower set of occupational categories. His argument was that as flows of African-Americans, Asians, and whites who were foreign-born entered urban labor markets, native whites in particular sought to maintain a constant (or perhaps even increasing) level of distance or isolation from newcomers. The analysis reported here supports the contention that a similar dynamic decreased the level of isolation for the foreign-born in occupations. Not only did the presence of numerous illiterate African-Americans decrease levels of desegregation for foreign-born, but so too did an overall increase in numbers of African-Americans into the cities during this decade. Surprisingly, once a city's population composition was included in models of occupational segregation of the foreign-born, the number of foreign-born who were also illiterate appears to be unrelated to that group's segregation level.

The results for the effects of the size of the illiterate populations add to a growing uneasiness with usual explanations for the decrease in segregation for the foreign-born and increasing segregation for African-Americans in occupations at the bottom of the status hierarchy (Sowell 1975). Such explanations usually rely on differences in skills, literacy, or education among ethnic and race groups as a proxy for productivity or marketability. Such productivity differences are then implicated in models of initial differences that multiply the advantages or disadvantages over time. But in many cities analyzed here, the illiteracy rate for the foreign-born was substantially higher than that of African-Americans, as Lieberson (1980) noted was the case for later decades. The results reported here indicate that the numbers of African-Americans who are illiterate, not the numbers of foreign-born who are illiterate, affect the segregation levels of immigrants. This raises many questions about assumptions that it is merely differences in human capital accumulation that affect the dynamics of occupational segregation and dispersion. The analysis presented here implicates one possible advantage enjoyed by foreigners over African-Americans that does not rely on differences in productivity. It involves taking the changes in population composition and migration of African-Americans into account in evaluating the opportunity structure at the local level. Was there a queuing process at work that resulted in advantages for the white ethnics who entered American cities earlier than the African-American migrants? The research reported here suggests that just such a process was beginning in the decade between 1870 and 1880. As less-skilled African-Americans entered urban labor markets and white ethnics moved up the job queue, so too were native-born whites upwardly mobile during periods of economic boom. But such upward movement was not inevitable for each new ethnic or racial group. Increases in mobility for newcomers—both residential and occupational—affect patterns of housing, jobs, and marriages, which in turn affect later levels of discrimination and/or movement through the opportunity structure.

9

Local Job Competition and Ethnic Collective Action

This chapter further explores how *city* characteristics affected the rate of ethnic collective action. The analyses reported in Chapters 5 and 6 found that the *national*-level covariates—immigration, business failures, and growth of organized labor unions—affected levels of ethnic competition and conflict. It is likely that local characteristics affect competition even more powerfully, since it is within local labor markets that groups compete most intensely for jobs. So in this chapter we test the competition theory hypothesis that cities with *low* job segregation experience higher rates of ethnic collective action.

Again the key argument is that integration of the foreign-born and nonwhites in occupations elevates the level of competition, which in turn increases the rate of ethnic conflict and protest. In Chapter 8 we examined causes of changes in occupational segregation in cities, using an indicator of ethnic occupational isolation as the dependent variable. In this chapter, the level of competition in cities is measured with this same P^* index calculated over a much longer time period. We expect this index to be inversely related to rates of conflict and protest. That is, we assume that high isolation of the foreign-born and nonwhites implies weak competition.[1]

In the foregoing chapters we also found support for arguments from competition theory and resource mobilization theory about the relationship of economic hardship and ethnic collective action. In particular, fluctuations in the national economy produced ethnic conflict and

---

[1] Recall that the P^* for nonwhites is the probability that a randomly chosen worker who is nonwhite will be working alongside a similarly chosen nonwhite in the same occupation. High levels of P^* for nonwhites indicate that nonwhites are highly concentrated into a small number of occupations in that city.

protest. These national-level analyses found that an increase in the prevalence of business failures increased rates of conflicts, while competition, indicated by higher wages for common laborers and high levels of immigration, increased rates of protests against discrimination.

Were analogous economic processes at work at the local level? Competition theory arguments lead us to suspect that cities with higher numbers of unskilled immigrants and/or nonwhite minorities will have experienced high rates of ethnic conflict. Ideally, it would be best to have measures of absolute income or wealth by race and ethnicity to investigate this question. Unfortunately, no broad data on income distinguished by race or ethnicity exist for as far back as 1880. However, we have some indirect measures of education or skill levels for given categories at the city level over this period. These are measures of the prevalence of illiteracy in various populations. We use these data to measure skill and education. Holding size of population constant, the greater numbers of illiterates in a population, the more intensely the population competes for low-wage jobs. Competition theory arguments introduced in Chapter 3 suggest that rates of ethnic conflict will be highest in cities with much labor market competition. In addition to the total numbers of illiterates in a city, we also include as covariates the numbers of foreign-born and nonwhite populations who are illiterate to indicate competition from these two groups. Thus, we predict that the number of illiterates in ethnic and nonwhite populations has a positive relationship with the rate of ethnic conflict (holding constant the size of the populations involved).

Because information on occupational segregation is not comparable across the entire 1877–1914 period, analysis must be conducted for two subperiods, 1877–89 and 1890–1914. The analysis in this chapter addresses the hypothesis that the ethnic composition of the local labor market affects rates of ethnic conflicts and protests during both periods. They address two questions. First, *did ethnic job segregation affect rates of ethnic collective action?* And second, *did levels of illiteracy affect rates of ethnic collective action during this period?*

Occupational Segregation and Ethnic Conflict

As pointed out in Chapter 2, the cultural division of labor perspective suggests that extreme labor-market segregation of ethnic groups produces social organization, ethnic solidarity, loyalty, and motivation for ethnics to act collectively. According to Hechter (1975), a cultural division of labor emerges in underdeveloped regions that are exploited by other regions, as in the case of internal colonialism. In this view, internal colonialism perpetuates unequal ethnic differences between the region's natives and colonists. The result is that patterns of income, education, and occupational attainment, and other opportunities diverge along ethnic lines.[2] Thus, this line of argument implies that occupational segregation of ethnic groups has a *positive* effect on the rate of ethnic collective action.

In contrast, competition theory contends just the opposite. Competition theory arguments hold that a division of labor that is highly segregated along ethnic lines reduces ethnic contact and competition. That is, competition theory holds that segregation has a *negative* effect on the rate of ethnic collective action.[3]

A key proposition of cultural division of labor theory is that economically disadvantaged ethnic groups are more likely than advantaged ones to engage in ethnic collective action, because they have higher group solidarity (Blauner 1971; Hechter 1975: 43). One implication of this theory is that racial unrest should have disproportionately erupted in regions and cities where African-Americans were especially disadvantaged. However, much evidence suggests otherwise. For example, analyses of racial turmoil in the 1960s suggests that cities with more poverty and racial deprivation were less likely to experience race riots (McPhail and Wohlstein 1983). Reviews of research on race riots suggest that ethnic mobilization would be more likely in cities where opportunities and skill levels are *rising* and competition among groups is greatest (Lieberson and Silverman 1965; Spilerman 1971 and 1976). Furthermore, evidence on the civil rights movement in America leads McAdam (1982), Morris (1981), and others, to infer that rising resources in African-American communities also contributed to the occurrence of black insurgency of the 1950s and 1960s. Such findings are consistent with both resource mobilization and competition theories developed in earlier chapters.

Ecological Models of Competition and Conflict
Our key competition argument follows general ecology theory in claiming that competition intensifies under conditions of *fundamental niche*

---

[2]Recall from Chapter 2 that an internal colony refers to a situation in which a rich, culturally dominant core region dominates and exploits an ethnically different periphery.

[3]Earlier versions of competition theory reviewed in Chapter 2 were applied mostly to specific ethnic targets. Two prominent examples that have used competition arguments included analyses of middleman minorities and racial minorities exploited in split labor markets. Blalock (1967), Light (1972), Bonacich (1973), and Loewen (1988) provide good expositions of the middleman minority theory, and Bonacich (1972 and 1976) and Boswell (1986) offer arguments and evidence in support of split labor market theory. Here the goal differs from past theoretical work in that I provide a general model applicable to ethnic collective action involving *any* ethnic targets or protesters.

overlap (Gause 1934; Hutchinson 1957). The relationship of ethnic populations and the resource environments which they exploit constrains (or releases) ethnic competition. To the extent that ethnically distinct populations exploit different features of the environment, stable ethnic relations can result and persist. But when ethnic populations attempt to exploit the same set of resources, they compete and ethnic relations become unstable.

Following Barth, and others, I argue that competition for resources leads to attempts at exclusion of one group by another. Barth also suggests that such exclusion attempts produce periods of ethnic instability and conflict. His theory suggests that under conditions of (realized) niche overlap, competition among groups intensifies, which in turn encourages attempts to exclude the competitors. Attempts at exclusion often entail violent conflict. In multiethnic societies, niche overlap increases as ethnic segregation in specialized niches (or occupations) declines (Barth 1969: 1–19).

In Chapter 3 we suggested that these ecological principles could be extended to apply to modern industrial societies. In particular, we argued that occupational categories can be analyzed as habitats, in the sense that each can potentially be exploited by one or more groups. In this view, high levels of ethnic segregation in occupations imply that groups are exploiting different realized niches. Low levels of segregation indicate that niche overlap exists. Segregation indexes provide a useful ways to summarize the degree of ethnic concentration and dispersion from an occupational niche (White 1986).

To recall our argument, we assumed competition within a fundamental niche intensifies as ethnic groups come to compete for the same jobs. Two hypotheses from competition theory follow. First, ethnic segregation ought to be inversely related to rates of ethnic conflict. Second, to the extent that a disadvantaged ethnic group becomes less segregated in jobs, the level of ethnic competition rises. In this view, an increase in competition causes ethnic conflict.

But we have not yet specified what factors disperse disadvantaged ethnics from less skilled occupations: What processes increase niche overlap? One version of the competition arguments tested in Chapters 5 and 6 identified one especially potent causal factor: ethnic collective action rose sharply with immigration during this period. In the national-level analyses reported earlier, high levels of immigration and increases in immigration produced increases in the rate of ethnic conflict (Olzak 1986, 1987). We argued that these results indicated that competition from immigrants sparked ethnic unrest. Because surges in immigration tend to increase the supply of low-wage labor, less-skilled newcomers become seen as a threat to the standard of living to native residents. Sometimes these threats were met with hostile attacks.

Do the same forces operate when cities are compared? This chapter explores and tests several specific hypotheses using an analogous argument with city-level measures. The hypotheses suggest that we employ models of ethnic conflict which include the size and well-being of the foreign-born and minority populations, in addition to measures of occupational segregation and dispersion of these groups. Specifically, this chapter tests the hypotheses that cities with higher levels of occupational desegregation of foreign-born and nonwhite minorities will experience higher rates of ethnic collective action. Similarly, we test the competition hypothesis that cities with higher numbers of illiterates experience more intense ethnic competition in less-skilled occupations, which in turn raises rates of ethnic conflict and protest.

Research Design and Methodology

The city-level analyses reported here were limited by the fact that data on occupational distributions by race are available for cities only from 1890. Because of this constraint, the analysis of city differences is split into two parts. The first begins in 1877, with the Presidential administration of Rutherford Hayes and the recovery from a national depression. It ends in 1889 so that definitions of occupational segregation by nativity are comparable across this 13-year period.

The analyses of the second period, 1890–1914, have the same structure, but for this period include a measure of the level of occupational segregation of African-Americans for 77 cities.

Estimation: Weibull Model of Duration Dependence. As in previous chapters, we estimate regression models that compare to the accelerated Weibull models. But this chapter uses data at the city level. So the regressions have the form:

$$Y = \log U_{in} = -\beta^{*\prime} \mathbf{x}_i(t_n) + \sigma W, \qquad (9.1)$$

where i denotes city. Recall that $\sigma = 1/\rho$. As in the national level analysis, we compute maximum likelihood (ML) estimates of the parameters of model with this form. As in earlier chapters, the tables report ML estimates of the scale parameters and of the *negative* of the regression coefficients, $\widehat{\beta^*}$, because we are interested in the effects on the rate.

Estimating Weibull duration dependence at the city level requires a slight modification of the approach used at the national level. The modification is required because many durations at the city level exceed one year while almost none do at the national level. This makes a difference if one includes time-varying covariates as we do here. We use the standard strategy of "spell splitting." That is, we break spells into subspells whose length coincides with the interval measurement of the covariates—one year in this case. So a spell is broken into yearly segments and each subspell has associated with it the appropriate values of the changing covariate. Each subspell but the last for any complete spell is treated as censored on the right (Tuma and Hannan 1984). As a result, at the national level, spell splitting was fortunately unnecessary, but for the city-level analysis reported in this chapter, this spell splitting produces a minor inconvenience. The software used (PROC LIFEREG) treats the duration of each subspell as a complete spell, beginning at zero duration. This is a appropriate for only the first spell.

In order to describe the procedure precisely, let τ_p denote the beginning of the pth subspell $(p = 0, \ldots, P)$ and let u_p denote the duration of the full spell at the beginning of the pth subspell, that is at τ_p. And let u_p^* denote the duration of the subspell that begins at τ_p. We adjust for the durations that exceed a year by introducing u_p as a covariate in the model. That is, we express the accelerated Weibull model as

$$
\begin{aligned}
r(u_p^* \,|\, u_{p+1} \leq u_p^* < u_p) &\approx \exp(\beta' \mathbf{x}(\tau_p) + \theta \log u_p) \cdot u_p^{*\rho-1} \\
&\approx \exp(\beta' \mathbf{x}(\tau_p)) \cdot u_p^\theta \cdot u_p^{*\rho-1}
\end{aligned}
\tag{9.2}
$$

Note that the second approximation holds because $\exp(\theta \log u_p) = u_p^\theta$. The specification in (9.2) approximates duration dependence as a step function in duration over subspells. If this approximation is a good one, then $\theta \approx \rho - 1$. In the parallel regression models for log duration, the specification is

$$
Y \equiv \log u_p^* = -\beta' \mathbf{x}(\tau_p) - \theta \log u_p + \sigma W.
\tag{9.3}
$$

Independent Variables. Independent variables measured at the *city level* in both periods include the log of population size and percent non-white and two measures of job segregation for native-born and foreign-born, and (where possible) nonwhite populations, using the index of isolation discussed in Chapter 8. Table 9.1 reports isolation indices for the foreign-born over the period of interest.

Competition theory implies that cities with high isolation indexes have *lower* rates of ethnic collective action than those with low isolation indexes. Two specifications of the effects of occupational isolation and population size were tried with these data. They included a log-linear specification of the effects of the isolation indexes on the rate and a "power-law" specification. The latter, which provided a better fit, has the form

$$
r(u_p^* \,|\, u_{p+1} \leq u_p^* < u_p) = I_{ip}(N)^\alpha \, I_{ip}(F)^\beta \, S_{ip}^\gamma \, N_{ip}^\delta \cdot u_p^\theta \cdot u_p^{*\rho-1}
\tag{9.4}
$$

TABLE 9.1
Indices of Occupational Segregation of the Foreign-born,
$I(F)$, in American Cities, 1880–1910

	1880	1890	1900	1910
Albany N.Y.	.46	.43	.36	.34
Allegheny Penn.	.45			
Atlanta Ga.	.11	.15	.14	.14
Baltimore Md.	.31	.36	.36	.37
Boston Mass.	.58	.56	.58	.58
Bridgeport Conn.			.54	.55
Brooklyn N.Y.	.58	.56	.59	.62
Buffalo N.Y.	.54	.59	.54	.47
Cambridge Mass.	.57	.61	.56	.52
Camden N.J.	.26	.24	.26	
Charleston S.C.	.32	.22	.22	
Chicago Ill.	.65	.65	.61	.58
Cincinnati Ohio	.46	.42	.35	.28
Cleveland Ohio	.63	.63	.59	.56
Columbus Ohio	.34	.27	.19	.18
Dayton Ohio	.45	.29	.25	.21
Denver Colo.	.42	.36	.34	.33
Des Moines Iowa		.29	.25	
Detroit Mich.	.63	.62	.56	.49
Duluth Minn.			.65	
Elizabeth N.J.			.54	
Erie Penn.			.43	
Evansville Ind.		.29	.22	
Fall River Mass.	.70	.69	.62	
Grand Rapids Mich.	.50	.50	.48	.45
Harrisburg Penn.			.13	
Hartford Conn.	.52	.48	.52	
Hoboken N.J.			.66	
Indianapolis Ind.	.33	.26	.21	.16
Jersey City N.J.	.61	.57	.55	.51
Kansas City Misso.	.34	.28	.22	.22
Lawrence Mass.	.61		.58	
Los Angeles Calif.		.35	.30	.31
Louisville Kent.	.37	.29	.24	.20
Lowell Mass.	.57	.58	.55	.61
Lynn Mass.	.37	.36	.40	
Manchester N.H.			.51	
Manhattan N.Y.			.69	.72

(cont.)

TABLE 9.1 (cont.)

	1880	1890	1900	1910
Memphis Tenn.		.25	.19	.17
Milwaukee Wis.	.64	.68	.58	.52
Minneapolis Minn.		.64	.56	.50
Nashville Tenn.		.17	.15	.10
New Bedford Mass.			.50	
New Haven Conn.	.50	.54	.52	.52
New Orleans Louis.	.33	.30	.25	.23
New York N.Y.	.64	.66	.65	.68
Newark N.J.	.53	.53	.55	.55
Oakland Calif.			.44	.39
Omaha Neb.		.42	.40	.36
Paterson N.J.	.50	.56	.54	.60
Peoria Ill.			.27	
Philadelphia Penn.	.42	.44	.43	.44
Pittsburgh Penn.	.51	.54	.49	.43
Portland Oreg.			.29	.32
Providence R.I.	.50	.50	.52	.54
Queens N.Y.			.55	.52
Reading Penn.	.20	.19	.17	
Richmond Va.	.30	.15	.15	.15
Rochester N.Y.	.49	.50	.44	.47
Salt Lake City Utah			.44	
San Antonio Tex.			.34	
San Francisco Calif.	.74	.47	.48	.47
Scranton Penn.	.53	.54	.47	.42
Seattle Wash.			.31	.42
Somerville Mass.			.48	
Springfield Mass.			.41	
St Joseph Misso.		.26	.17	
St Louis Misso.	.48	.45	.37	.35
Staten Island N.Y.			.52	.47
St Paul Minn.		.66	.52	.46
Syracuse N.Y.	.43	.43	.42	.40
Toledo Ohio	.49	.51	.41	.35
Trenton N.J.		.47	.45	
Troy N.Y.	.54	.51	.45	
Washington D.C.	.21	.19	.20	
Wilkes-Barre Penn.			.38	
Wilmington Del.	.26	.27	.25	
Worcester Mass.	.49	.55	.53	.54

Note: See Chapter 8 for a definition of the index of isolation, $I(F)$.

where $I_{ip}(N)$ is the isolation index[4] for native-born for city i in year p, $I_{ip}(F)$ is the isolation index for foreign born in that city in that year, S_{ip} is the city's population, and N_{ip} is percent nonwhite. In analysis of the earlier period, 1877–89, each of these variables is fixed at the 1880 value for each city. In the 1890–1914 analysis, the indexes of occupational segregation for nonwhites and for the foreign-born were measured for four census years, 1890, 1900, 1910, and 1920, and then interpolated between census years to update the analysis each observation year. Recall that covariates are attached to the beginning of a spell in a city. The version of competition theory discussed in Chapters 2 and 3 implies that

$$\alpha < 0 \quad \text{and} \quad \beta < 0, \tag{9.5}$$

in which case the rate declines at a decreasing rate as each population becomes more isolated (conversely, it grows at an increasing rate as each population becomes more integrated in the occupational distribution).

A second theoretical claim involved the impact of illiteracy in the population. From a competition perspective, high levels of illiteracy are expected to produce higher rates of ethnic collective action. The percent illiterate is defined as the percent over 10 years of age who cannot write in any language or "inability to write regardless of ability to read" (from United States Bureau of the Census 1870, 1880, and 1890, and the retrospective account of the years 1900–1920, found in the United States Bureau of the Census, 1930, volume II, p. 1219).[5]

Other independent variables include measures of the population size and ethnic and racial composition interpolated across census years. Following the work of Spilerman and others who analyzed race riots during the 1960s, there is good reason to suspect that the proportion of African-Americans and white immigrants in cities affects the rate of ethnic collective action. Applying this argument to our city-level data, we would expect attacks on African-Americans to be concentrated in cities where they are most numerous. Using the same argument, we expect the rate of attacks on foreign-born whites was greatest in cities where they are concentrated.

---

[4] We have changed notation here slightly so as not to complicate the expression of equations. In the usual representation of the P^* index of isolation, $I(F) = {}_F P_F^*$.

[5] As in all data, this information on literacy undoubtedly contains measurement error. For instance, analysts have suggested that perhaps the definition of "ability to write" varied from census taker to census taker. Since no tests of ability were actually administered, it seems plausible that literacy and English language facility might be confounded in this period of peak immigration. It is heartening, however, that as early as 1870, census takers were instructed to require more than a signature as evidence of literacy, as well as to ask whether a respondent was literate in English or even his or her spoken language, if it was other than English.

Results For 1877–1889

Table 9.2 reports estimates of the effects of occupational segregation and illiteracy on the rate of ethnic collective action at the city level for the 1877–89 period. Estimates use data on all 48 cities for which information on labor force participation and literacy was available. Models 1–3 contain estimates of the effects of the size of the African-American population and the numbers of them who are illiterate (cannot read and write). Models 4–6 differ in that they contain instead the size of the foreign-born white population and the numbers of them who are illiterate.

Effects of Levels of Occupational Segregation. How does the competition hypothesis fare? The answer can be found by turning to the results of the two isolation index measures in the models in columns 1 through 6 in Table 9.2. In all but two cases, the point estimates for the effect of the isolation indexes are negative, as predicted.[6] Furthermore, the effect of occupational segregation for the native-born is significant and in the predicted negative direction in all six models and the effect of occupational segregation of the foreign-born is significant and in the expected direction in models 5 and 6 (which control for San Francisco and New York effects, respectively). This implies that the rate of ethnic collective action was higher in cities in which white and black native-born residents were more integrated in occupations with the foreign-born.[7] Put differently, these results show that cities with low levels of isolation of foreign-born or native-born have higher rates of ethnic collective action than do cities with ethnic populations in highly segregated occupations.

Just how big are these effects of occupational segregation? The estimated effect for the occupational isolation of the native born is −14.9 (divided by the scale parameter 2.47) from column 1 tells us that as segregation levels decline from the third highest to lowest quartile, the rate of ethnic collective action rises nearly 100%.

Effects of Illiteracy. Columns 1 through 6 include several specifications of the effect of illiteracy on the rate of ethnic collective action. In columns 1 through 3, the effect of number of African-Americans who are illiterate in a city is positive, as expected. Moreover, these estimates imply that the effects of illiteracy on the rate are substantial. For instance, taking the coefficient for African-American illiteracy in column 1,

---

[6] A comparison of the fit of the models in columns 1 and 2 shows that adding the isolation indexes improves the fit significantly in every meaningful model that was tested. The likelihood ratio test of the null hypothesis that both isolation effects are zero is 78.3 with two degrees of freedom, which is significant at the .001 level.

[7] These large effects do not disappear when national-level characteristics or interaction effects are introduced.

the coefficient 3.32 (which is then divided by the scale parameter) indicates that as illiteracy rises from the lowest to the third quartile, the rate of ethnic collective action is increased 11-fold. Note also that adding the effect of black illiteracy does not diminish the effect of segregation of native-born, despite the fact that blacks were highly segregated in just a few occupations in cities prior to 1890.

Scholars remind us that during this period immigrants from some countries were even *less* likely to be able to read and write than were American-born blacks (Lieberson 1980; Bodnar et al. 1982). This suggests that the size of the illiterate foreign-born population might also affect the rate of ethnic collective action. Columns 4 through 6 replace the size of the African-American population that is illiterate with the size of the foreign-born population that is illiterate. This effect is significant and in a positive direction as predicted in all but the last column. Finally, the effect of the illiterate foreign-born population is not significant in column 6. Nevertheless, in all six specifications in Table 9.2, the effect of low levels of segregation for the foreign-born remains potent and in the expected direction. This suggests that upward mobility of the foreign-born, out of segregated occupations, had a greater effect on the rate than did overall size of the foreign-born population or the number of illiterate foreign-born.

Control Variables. Other variables in the model behave in a predictable manner. Specifically, the measures of population size and composition show patterns that are highly consistent with Spilerman's (1971, 1976) research on racial turmoil in contemporary America. Here we interpret these coefficients as indicating that competition is intensified in larger and racially diverse cities. The results in Table 9.2 also show that large cities and cities with a higher proportion of blacks are more likely to experience ethnic collective action than are smaller ones and those with less racial diversity. The estimates for the effect of the percentage of blacks in a city raise the rate thirty percent from the lowest to third highest quartile over the range of this variable. If we compare this effect of racial diversity across a variety of specifications found in the columns 1 through 6 in Table 9.2, we see that racial and ethnic diversity increase the rate significantly.

It seems reasonable to consider the fact that race relations in the South during this period differed considerably from those in the North (James 1988). Not only were there strong institutional affects of Jim Crow laws, but there was a considerably larger concentration of blacks in urban areas in the South compared to the North in this early period of American history. Column 1 contains a positive and significant south-

TABLE 9.2

Effects of Occupational Segregation and Illiteracy on the Rate of
Ethnic Collective Action in 48 American Cities, 1877–1889

(Asymptotic Standard Errors in Parentheses)

	(1)	(2)	(3)	(4)	(5)	(6)
Intercept	−23.4** (9.84)	−29.8*** (9.03)	−22.1** (11.0)	−13.8 (9.73)	−22.1** (10.7)	−24.4*** (10.9)
Log of native-born occup. segregation	−14.9*** (5.53)	−17.3*** (5.21)	−17.5*** (5.75)	−36.6*** (10.1)	−22.1** (10.0)	−36.2** (9.25)
Log of foreign-born occup.segregation	5.32 (6.25)	−2.03 (5.07)	3.27 (5.75)	−2.84 (3.93)	−8.40** (3.71)	−7.79** (3.69)
Log of population (100,000s)	.724** (.369)	.817** (.366)	.250 (.541)	.178 (.587)	.126** (.623)	−.493 (.601)
% African-American	12.2** (5.35)	13.1** (5.39)	13.9*** (5.32)			
% Foreign-born (whites)				.001** (.000)	17.3 (24.5)	−47.2** (23.3)
African-American illit. (100,000s)	3.32*** (1.24)	2.38** (.099)	3.41*** (1.08)			
Foreign-born illit. (100,000s)				.718** (.350)	.656* (.370)	.001 (.001)
Southern Region	4.31** (1.70)			6.65*** (1.90)		
San Francisco		.817 (.853)			2.53** (1.29)	
New York City			1.66 (1.30)			1.43 (4.17)
Log of time since last event in city	−.396*** (.090)	−.409*** (.091)	−.411*** (.090)	−.408*** (.092)	−.411*** (.095)	−.454*** (.094)
Scale parameter	2.47*** (.262)	2.47*** (.264)	2.48*** (.266)	2.49*** (.265)	2.48*** (.265)	2.50*** (.269)
Number of spells	643	643	643	643	643	643
Uncensored spells	71	71	71	71	71	71
Log likelihood	−280.9	−283.9	−283.5	−283.5	−290.8	−292.8

* $p < .10$,   ** $p < .05$,   *** $p < .01$

ern regional effect. More precisely, the log-likelihood ratio test for the significance of the addition of the regional effect of southern cities is significant at the .05 level. But it is theoretically important that adding the effect of being in the South does not alter the direction or the significance of any other effects reported in Table 9.2 (when compared to models without the effect of the South). That is, the effects of low levels of occupational segregation, percent black, and literacy hold even when a control for southern region is included. This means that the relationships hold despite the fact that southern location of a city independently affected the rate of ethnic collective action.

Despite these strong effects, skeptics might raise several questions about the presence of unobserved heterogeneity, perhaps caused by city-differences that could be related to a particular city's machine politics, its organizational or religious culture, or some other unmeasured factors that remain constant over time and that directly influence race relations. Because San Francisco contributes 24 of the 71 uncensored spells in Table 9.2, a question arises about the undue influence of a "San Francisco effect."[8] That is, we ask, to what extent do the effects of the high numbers of Chinese, or occupational segregation of that group (or some other factors) present in San Francisco dominate the model? To examine this, column 2 includes a dummy variable for the city of San Francisco and column 5 includes this same dummy variable for San Francisco in a model that includes the percent foreign-born in a city (replacing percent black). When we control for a San Francisco effect, the effects remain exactly the same. So when this "outlier" effect of San Francisco is controlled (as in the second column) the effects of competition remain potent, as do the effects of all other covariates.[9] The relationship between covariates and the rate of ethnic collective action remain strong, even in column 5, where there is a strong positive effect of San Francisco city on the rate. This suggests that the effects of competition are not limited to one city or region.

There are equally good reasons to investigate whether there is an effect of New York City. First, and most important, is the question of whether there was a regional bias in newspaper reporting. Many critics of newspaper data have claimed that there would be an overrepresentation of news in general about New York in the *New York Times.* So these models may reflect a pure "New York effect." A second and related issue is that because so many European immigrants first arrived in New York, there was a an extremely high residential concentration of foreign-born

---

[8]Historical accounts also prompt us to consider this question. Available case studies of San Francisco and other West Coast settings during the 1880s have also found that this city witnessed extremely high levels of occupational segregation of Chinese as well as high rates of ethnic conflict directed against the Chinese (Saxton 1971; Nee and Nee 1986).

[9]Other specifications of this hypothesis about the high levels of segregation of the Chinese in San Francisco show exactly the same pattern. For instance, a model similar to the one in column 1 (not shown) was examined that included the percentage of Asians in a city. The results were nearly identical to those shown in column 2. In addition, I found that the percentage of Asians in a city and the level of segregation to be greatest in San Francisco across this period, suggesting strong confirmation of the historical accounts of the Chinese experience.

in this city. Such a concentration, however temporary, may have raised rates of conflict independently of occupational considerations. Third, because so many events occurred in New York, the relationships between characteristics of New York and a higher rate might be really due to the concentration of population, ethnic diversity, and collective action of all kinds that take place in the country's largest city. To begin to take some of these arguments into account, models 3 and 6 include a dummy variable for spells that occurred in New York. Somewhat surprisingly, this effect does not significantly affect the rate and the effects reported for lower occupational segregation, illiteracy, and population composition were evidently not due to the dominating presence of New York City in the event data.

Earlier we suggested that diffusion may affect the rate of conflict. In this chapter we suggest that this hypothesis can be restated as one which investigates whether time dependence affects the rate. If time dependence is present, then the rate would decline as the amount of time since the previous event elapses. Is this true? In Table 9.2, we can observe two different measures of this effect. At the bottom of column 1 we can examine the theoretically important effects of diffusion as measured by both the log of the time since the last event and scale parameter (time dependence within yearly spells). In model 1, for instance, the estimated effect of the log of time since the last event in a city implies that $\hat{\sigma} = 2.47$ which means that $\hat{\rho} = .40$. Such a result indicates extremely strong dependence of the rate on the waiting time (no matter if the durations are split into yearly spells or measured in time since the last event). In other words, the rate shortly after the occurrence of an event in a city is much higher than it is sometime later. If a city had an event on the previous day, the rate is 10 times higher than would be the case with the same levels of all covariates if the most recent event had occurred a year previously. Once a week passes with no event, the multiplier drops to 4.90; and it drops to 1.32 after six months have elapsed since the previous event.

Analysis of events during 1877–89 shows that competition for jobs between these two groups sharply raises rates of ethnic conflict and protest, while high levels of segregation decrease the rate. This means that for this period, cities in which foreigners were concentrated in just a few occupations also experienced significantly *fewer* ethnic attacks, protests, and unrest.

Results For 1890–1914
The results for the second period parallel those for the first period, but they have two important advantages. First, the results for 1890–1914 include an indicator of occupational segregation of nonwhites. Sec-

ond, information on covariates was available for interpolating across four decades (1880–1920) of the census, so all covariates are updated yearly in Tables 9.3 through 9.5.

Results for 1890–1914 that parallel those in Table 9.2 for 1877–89 appear in Table 9.3. It is interesting to compare the two sets of findings. First, the theoretically important levels of occupational segregation have strikingly similar effects on the rates of ethnic collective action. In both tables, the levels of occupational segregation for the foreign-born and nonwhites (native-born in Table 9.2) consistently have effects in the expected negative direction. For the latter period, occupational segregation of the foreign-born significantly depresses the rate of ethnic collective action. For the earlier period, occupational segregation of the native-born depresses the rate significantly. Although not all point estimates of effects of occupational segregation are significant, the coefficients are negative for both measures of occupational segregation in nearly every specification for both periods.

Comparison of the likelihood ratio test statistics across columns in Table 9.3 suggest that the model in column 3 fits the data better than all of the others. This model differs from the others in that it contains a measure of the total number of illiterates (rather than illiteracy broken down by race or nativity, as it is in columns 4 and 5), and it contains the percentage of blacks in the city, which is highly significant in all models in which it is included. The model in column 3 tells us that as the occupational segregation of the foreign-born declines from the third quartile to the lowest quartile, the rate of ethnic collective action rises fifty percent.

The effects of time dependence on the rate are also robust and in the predicted negative direction in all models in Table 9.3 as well. The estimated scale parameter in column 1, 1.69, implies that the rate is 3.4 times higher one day after an event occurred in a city when compared to a lapse of one year since an event occurred. After six months without an event, the rate is increased by only 1.15 times the rate.

Other results in Table 9.3 parallel those found in Table 9.2. For instance, the effect of population is consistently positive and significant, as is the effect of the size of the nonwhite population. Illiteracy has somewhat weaker effects in the latter period. The illiteracy rate for the population as a whole has a strong positive effect on the rate (column 3), as it does in the earlier period.

Conflicts and Protests, 1890–1914. Because there were more events during 1890–1914, we can analyze conflicts and protests separately and conflicts separately by racial targets. We do so in Tables 9.4 and 9.5, respectively.

TABLE 9.3

Effects of Occupational Segregation, Population Composition,
Literacy, and Contagion on the Rate of Attacks on Blacks
and Other Groups in 77 American Cities, 1890–1914

(Asymptotic Standard Errors in Parentheses)

	(1)	(2)	(3)	(4)	(5)
Intercept	−10.2***	−7.74***	−11.5***	−11.8***	−8.72***
	(1.60)	(2.00)	(1.74)	(2.02)	(2.17)
Log of non-white	−.662	−.274	−.206	−.953*	−.210
occup. segregation	(.459)	(.448)	(.509)	(.499)	(.451)
Log of foreign-born	−1.52*	−1.55	−2.77***	−1.92**	−1.72
occup. segregation	(.838)	(1.02)	(.992)	(.917)	(1.03)
Log of population	2.17***	2.26***	2.37***	2.40***	2.23***
(100,000s)	(.241)	(.247)	(.267)	(.300)	(.246)
% Black	8.54***		−2.29		7.07***
	(2.47)		(4.89)		(2.72)
% Foreign-born		−5.39			−4.81
(whites)		(3.44)			(3.46)
Total illiterates			24.5***		
per 1000			(9.05)		
Black illiterates				4.24	
per 1000				(2.75)	
Foreign-born illit.					7.41
per 1000					(6.08)
Log of time since last	−.210***	−.231***	−.190***	−.199***	−.228***
event in city	(.032)	(.032)	(.033)	(.033)	(.032)
Scale parameter	1.69***	1.71***	1.70***	1.71***	1.71***
	(.117)	(.118)	(.117)	(.118)	(.118)
Number of spells	1449	1449	1449	1449	1449
Uncensored spells	170	170	170	170	170
Log likelihood	−611.41	−615.82	−607.63	−610.23	−615.09

* $p < .10$,   ** $p < .05$,   *** $p < .01$

Table 9.4 speaks to the question of whether the causal structure underlying conflicts is similar to that of protests. The answer is that the effects are surprisingly similar. Looking across the columns, it appears that the pattern of effects in equivalent models for conflicts and protests is identical. In both cases, segregation of the foreign-born decreases the rate, while population size and illiteracy rate increase the rate. Apparently competition, indicated here by declining segregation and high rates of illiteracy, increases rates of both kinds of ethnic collective action.

When we examine the model in column 1 closely, we note that the co-

TABLE 9.4

Effects of Occupational Segregation, Population Composition,
Literacy, and Contagion on the Rate of Ethnic Conflict and Protest
in 77 American Cities, 1890–1914

(Asymptotic Standard Errors in Parentheses)

	Conflicts		Protests	
	(1)	(2)	(3)	(4)
Intercept	−10.3*** (2.13)	−7.80*** (2.54)	−16.1*** (3.29)	−11.9*** (3.52)
Log of non-white occup. segregation	.419 (.708)	.077 (.642)	.446 (.784)	−1.19 (.647)
Log of foreign-born occup. segregation	−2.23* (1.15)	.981 (1.26)	−3.96* (2.04)	−.348 (1.91)
Log of population (100,000s)	2.18*** (.341)	2.20*** (.327)	2.84*** (.448)	2.52*** (.414)
% Black	1.37 (5.62)		16.3 (10.7)	
% Foreign-born (whites)		−8.28* (4.70)		−5.94 (4.5)
Total illiterates per 1000	12.5 (10.7)	15.5*** (5.57)	52.1*** (17.9)	30.5*** (9.24)
Log of time since last event in city	−.243*** (.044)	−.242*** (.043)	−.114** (.049)	−.113** (.049)
Scale parameter	1.72*** (.159)	1.70*** (.156)	1.70*** (.175)	1.67*** (.171)
Number of spells	1449	1449	1449	1449
Uncensored spells	96	96	74	74
Log likelihood	−409.62	−408.09	−301.77	−302.33

* $p < .10$, ** $p < .05$, *** $p < .01$.

efficient for the effect of segregation of the foreign-born has the expected
negative and significant effect on the rate. Using the same metric of comparisons as we have in other tables, as we decrease the level of segregation
over the third to first quartiles of the range, the rate increases about forty
percent. The effect of illiteracy is equally strong. For example, over the
first to third quartile of the range of number of illiterates in a city, the
estimates from column 3 tell us that the rate increases a full 200%.

Targets of Conflicts: Attacks on African-Americans and Others. Do
the effects of occupational segregation, illiteracy, and time dependence
on the rates of conflict vary by ethnic and racial targets? We already
have some indications that causal patterns differ with respect to targets of the ethnic attack. For instance, in Chapter 6 we saw that the

TABLE 9.5

Effects of Occupational Segregation, Population Composition,
Literacy, and Contagion on the Rate of Attacks on Blacks
and Other Groups in 77 American Cities, 1890–1914.

(Asymptotic Standard Errors in Parentheses)

	Attacks on Blacks		Attacks on Others	
	(1)	(2)	(3)	(4)
Intercept	−15.3***	−15.5***	−8.41***	−8.79***
	(3.55)	(4.09)	(3.64)	(3.93)
Log of non-white occup. segregation	−.418	−.793	−.772	−.863
	(1.08)	(1.08)	(.857)	(.863)
Log of foreign-born occup. segregation	−3.09*	−2.78*	−1.09***	−1.26
	(.562)	(.616)	(1.85)	(1.87)
Log of population (100,000s)	2.64***	2.63***	1.80***	1.79***
	(.562)	(.616)	(.399)	(.400)
% Black	8.83	12.8***		
	(7.09)	(4.41)		
% Foreign-born (whites)			.156	.820
			(6.72)	(6.88)
Total illiterates per 1000	10.6		2.98	
	(13.5)		(9.01)	
Black illiterates per 1000		1.82		
		(4.77)		
Foreign-born illit. per 1000				3.50
				(10.4)
Log of time since last event in city	−.254***	−.261***	−.235***	−.238***
	(.064)	(.064)	(.060)	(.059)
Scale parameter	1.74***	1.74***	1.67***	1.67***
	(.223)	(.223)	(.223)	(.224)
Number of spells	1449	1449	1449	1449
Uncensored spells	50	50	46	46
Log likelihood	−237.64	−237.87	−233.91	−233.91

* $p < .10$,   ** $p < .05$,   *** $p < .01$.

growth of national labor unions and changes in immigration raised rates
of attacks on African-Americans but not on other groups. We suggested
that one explanation is that the rate of racial conflict was more sensitive
than are the rates of other forms of ethnic conflict to national waves of
competitive hostility, despite the fact that white immigrants were often
the source of that competition. Such differences are worth investigating
at the city level as well.

Table 9.5 compares estimates of models for the rate of black/white
conflict and the rate of ethnic conflict involving other groups during

1890–1914. Comparing first the effects in the odd-numbered columns that include the two segregation measures, percent African-American, illiteracy rate, and time dependence, we see virtually no differences in the magnitude and pattern of effects. Cities with highly segregated foreign-born had significantly lower rates of attacks on African-Americans and others, while larger cities had higher rates of attacks on either group. In column 1, the estimates for the effect of segregation over the quartile range tells us that the rate increases nearly forty percent from the third to the lowest quartile of segregation for the foreign-born. As might be expected, the size of the African-American population affects only the rate of antiblack events (column 2). However, size of the foreign-born population has no parallel effect on the rate of antiforeigner attacks.

Notice that illiteracy has no significant effect when targets of conflicts are analyzed separately. This absence of effects for illiteracy holds even when the illiteracy rate of the targeted population is examined, as in columns 2 (for black illiteracy rate) and 4 (for illiteracy rate of the foreign-born). That illiteracy rates have no effect on group-specific attacks is relevant to a number of popular arguments. Conventional theories of ethnocentrism and prejudice reviewed in Chapter 2 once held that cultural or even class-differences among newcomers and natives often account for initial levels of hate, distrust, and even attacks on culturally different groups. Using this argument, cities with high rates of black illiterates would have significantly higher rates of attacks on that group. But Table 9.5 casts doubt on this claim. The results suggest that one highly relevant measure of human capital—that of literacy—does not affect a group's probability of being attacked, once city size and occupational segregation are taken into account.

Fortunately our model of time dependence holds no matter which group is the victim of attack, although the effects are larger for attacks on African-Americans than attacks on other groups. This latter finding suggests that cycles of ethnic attacks spread antiblack hostility more rapidly than does diffusion across a variety of ethnic immigrant groups. Once again we are reminded of the potency of antiblack sentiment in American cities.

Conclusion

This chapter on the causes of ethnic collective action in American cities during 1877–1914 clarifies how economic competition (indicated by low isolation in occupations of foreign-born and native born in the first period, low isolation of foreign-born and nonwhites in the second period) also increased rates at the city level. Analysis of this early period of the effect of immigration show that mobility into and out of segregated occupations affects reactions by the majority (or native-born whites). This suggests that initial dispersion of ethnics releases a chain reaction, in response to ethnic competition for scarce jobs.

Taken as an indicator of the supply of low-skilled and low-wage labor, illiteracy has strong positive effects on the overall rate of ethnic collective action. That is, cities with higher rates of illiterates, no matter what their race or ethnicity is, experience higher rates of ethnic conflicts and protests. This is precisely what competition theory found for immigration and real wages at the national level: when the supply of low-wage labor increases at either the national or city level, ethnic conflict and protest rises in response to rising competition.

These results have several implications for existing theories of job segregation and ethnic conflict. Cultural division of labor theories specify that high levels of ethnic job segregation cause ethnic collective action. These data suggest an opposite process is actually at work: that declining segregation of foreign-born and nonwhites (in the latter period) raises rates of ethnic conflict and protest. Such findings are consistent with competition theory and split labor market formulations that hypothesized that the process of decreasing segregation of labor markets ignites ethnic conflicts and protests. The results are strikingly parallel to analysis of race riots in cities during the 1960s. In both periods, rates of ethnic turmoil peak in larger cities with higher proportions of minorities. Perhaps even more surprisingly, local rates of *both* ethnic conflicts and protests appear to be related to similar underlying patterns.

We also find support for theories suggesting that ethnic collective actions diffuse over time. The fact that the dependence of the rate on the time since the previous event is as strong at the city level as it is at the national level (as reported in Chapter 5) makes sense. This is because local unrest has a more immediate and dramatic impact on people's lives. Police harassment or arrests, the presence of barricades, violence, or public disruptions witnessed first-hand are far more likely to affect future behavior than newspaper reports or rumors from even nearby cities. We might expect that contagion effects differ more at the national level and local level in this period than in the recent one. By any estimate, communications networks were relatively underdeveloped in late nineteenth-century America, compared to instantaneous computer links that reduce the impact of geographical distance on information flows today. In both periods, however, diffusion processes are strong at the city and at the national level.

10

Ethnic Conflict and Dynamics of Ethnic Newspapers

(WITH ELIZABETH WEST)

This chapter shifts perspective and investigates a *consequence* of ethnic conflict. It examines the impact of ethnic conflict on rates of founding and failure of one type of ethnic organization, ethnic newspapers. Park's (1922) research on the immigrant press suggests that the fortunes of ethnic newspapers provide a historical picture of ethnic and racial solidarity in American society. According to Park, the existence of newspapers directed at linguistic groups indicates that such groups have the ability to mobilize financial resources, communicate and interpret news for their communities, and to link geographically-dispersed members of the ethnic community. The fact that some (but not all) European-American and African-American newspapers established before 1900 were still functioning nearly a century later (Wynar 1972) suggests that there may be a link between the vitality of ethnic institutions and their communities. Despite the apparent consensus on the importance of ethnic newspapers, few theories have attempted to explain what conditions encourage their founding or what factors support or inhibit their continued existence. This chapter focuses on how ethnic collective action influences the creation and failure of these key ethnic institutions.

The evidence presented in foregoing chapters suggests that ethnic identities become rallying points for conflict when competition for scarce resources intensifies. Competition theory further clarifies the mechanisms that link ethnic conflicts to the fates of ethnic organizations. Competition activates ethnic boundaries, which initially increases the salience of ethnic boundaries and their markers. Put differently, competition draws attention to variations in the relevance of specific boundaries. We believe that surges in ethnic competition also affect the chances of building and sustaining ethnic organizations. That is, we think that conflicts and attacks directed at ethnic communities foster reactive ethnic organizations. We also think that such attacks cushion these organizations from failure.

By an ethnic newspaper, we mean a newspaper that makes an explicit claim to serve an ethnic or racial population. Many ethnic newspapers were published in languages other than English. It may be helpful to give some examples of ethnic language newspapers in our data. The *Ameriska Domovina* is a Slovenian daily established in Cleveland in 1898; it still publishes news of national Slovenian organizations and communities. The *Tevynes Sargas*, a Lithuanian paper founded in 1896, was still publishing as late as 1972. The *Narod Polski*, a nationally-circulated paper for Polish-Catholics, was established in 1886 in Chicago and was still publishing by 1972. However, others, notably those attached to the Irish-American and African-American populations, were published in English.[1]   For instance, the *Irish American Times*, was published in Columbus, Ohio, from 1886 through 1888, and the *Queen City Bee*, identified as a "colored" (African-American) community newspaper, was published in Cincinnati, Ohio from 1903 to 1909.

Collective Action and Ethnic Organizations

As explained in Chapter 2, contemporary theories of collective action usually emphasize the role of *organizations* in facilitating mobilization and collective action. We draw upon several theoretical traditions to argue that the dynamics of social movements and their constituent organizations are intertwined. For instance, the resource mobilization tradition (outlined in Chapter 2) highlights the importance of organizations in the growth and success of social movements (Gamson 1975). Whereas early theorists treated collective action as a product of social disorganization and disintegration, modern studies in the resource mobilization tradition stress the importance of strong interaction networks and social ties.[2]   The focus of current theorizing has centered on the founding and disbanding rates of social movement organizations (McCarthy et al. 1988; Carroll and Huo 1988; Olzak 1989a). In their review of research on social movements, McAdam, McCarthy, and Zald (1988: 703) emphasize

---

[1] Not all Irish papers were in English; at least some Irish papers established before 1900 were published solely in Gaelic.

[2] For instance, recent research in this tradition has shown that participants in protest and conflict events are less likely to be alienated and socially isolated than embedded in a network of social relations (McAdam 1986). Existence of social movement organizations and characteristics such as their size, leadership and cohesion are claimed to be instrumental in securing the resources needed for collective action (Jenkins 1983; Jenkins and Eckert 1986; Zald and McCarthy 1987).

the view that organizations are key actors, concluding that, "the greater the density of social organization, the more likely that social movement activity will develop."

We suspect that prior ethnic collective action affects the life chances of social movement organizations as well. We argue that ethnic conflict strengthens ethnic organizations through its impact on the salience of ethnicity. Two subsets of this line of argument have been suggested in the research literature on ethnic relations. The "middleman minority" theory holds that discrimination and exclusion led ethnic groups such as Jews in Europe and Chinese in Malaysia to exploit the so-called "middleman" niche of commercial and financial activity between producers and consumers. Successful exploitation within the economic niche favored the persistence of the ethnic boundaries of those populations in middleman minority situations (Bonacich 1973). Portes and Bach (1985) proposed a similar argument. Their "ethnic resilience hypothesis" suggests that ethnic discrimination against immigrants resulted in their producing and maintaining separate ethnic institutions.

We think that a similar process of reactive ethnicity holds when ethnic conflict is directed against any ethnic boundary. However, we think the process may be more complicated than the middleman and ethnic resilience formulations originally proposed. Our claim is that ethnic conflict has two plausible consequences for the fate of ethnic organizations created by groups that are victims of ethnic conflict. The first argument hypothesizes a pure salience effect. This argument is that *ethnic conflict galvanizes ethnic communities, which precipitates the formation of formal organizations and improves the life-chances of existing ethnic organizations.* The salience argument leads us to expect that ethnic conflict intensifies ethnic solidarity, which in turn encourages foundings of ethnic organizations and maintains existing ones.[3]

The second part of the argument emphasizes the fact that repression also affects the fate of ethnic organizations. It suggests that at some very high level of attack, we expect that repression predominates, and ethnic organizations are suppressed.

Our ability to evaluate both parts of our argument requires that we measure solidarity apart from collective action. So for theoretical reasons we distinguish ethnic collective action from ethnic solidarity. Recall that in Chapter 1, *ethnic solidarity* is defined as the self-conscious identi-

---

[3]In pursuing this argument, we build on the claims of classical theorist Georg Simmel and others who argue that social conflict encourages group solidarity and cohesion for all groups (Simmel 1955 [1923]; Coser 1956).

fication by persons in an ethnic population of ethnic group membership and it includes maintenance of strong network ties and participation in ethnic institutions. *Ethnic collective action* is defined as public action of two or more persons that articulates a distinctly ethnic or racial grievance. Ethnic collective action includes both confrontations and civil rights protests. Here our focus is on the effect of ethnic conflicts, defined as collective actions in which two or more ethnic groups confront or attack one another.

Repression and the Fate of Ethnic Organizations. While some scholars have emphasized the social functions of conflict, others have emphasized that when massive attacks are mounted against ethnic/racial populations, repression effects predominate. For example, Jenkins and Eckert (1986) take the position that the relentless violence directed against African-Americans destroyed their existing institutions and suppressed the creation of new ones. This view has had its advocates in general theories of collective action as well. Both resource mobilization and rational choice theorists argue that repression takes its toll: as conflict increases, the costs of collective action rise, and the group's mobilization capacity is undermined (Tilly 1978).

Is it contradictory to argue that ethnic conflict both enhances and suppresses ethnic organizations? Perhaps not. Recently, collective action theorists suggest the possibility of a *nonmonotonic* relationship between collective action and repression (Snyder 1975; Tilly 1978). These theorists explain this relationship as a consequence of the costs and expected returns to collective action. In Tilly's (1978) scheme, relatively mild levels of repression (or a shift toward lower levels of repression) open new opportunities for challengers to act collectively to demand their rights and make claims against the state. In this "political process" view, small amounts of repression may be necessary to motivate activity and overcome apathy (Tilly 1978; McAdam 1982). But intense repression causes collective action to diminish or even disappear. As Tilly, Tilly, and Tilly (1975: 286) argue,

Under heavy repression, collective action subsides, collective violence subsides, and the effectiveness of those collective actions which do occur, and do generate violence, declines ... The maximum relative effectiveness of the high violence path probably falls between the extremes of repression and nonrepression, toward the repressive end of the range.

Others suggest that effects of repression may vary depending on the form of ethnic collective action under study. For instance, Olivier (1989) finds that low levels of police repression in South Africa increased the rate of black protest activity. High levels of police repression significantly decreased rates of black protest but significantly raised rates of collective violence involving black Africans.

A key insight from this literature is that the effect of attacks on collective action depends on the *level of conflict.* That is, a climate of everyday racial attacks is likely to affect ethnic organizations very differently when compared to situations where racial attacks are rare. Below we address the question of whether there might be similar curvilinear effects of repression on the founding and failure rates of ethnic organizations. Such a question can only be answered with longitudinal data on the life histories of political attacks and of ethnic organizations. Following Tilly, we propose a hypothesis that the *founding rates of ethnic newspapers rise at a decreasing rate at low levels of collective action, but then founding rates decline at peak levels of ethnic conflict.* This means that the first-order effect of level of conflict on the founding rate would be positive and the second-order effect would be negative. We also hypothesize that *the failure rate of ethnic newspapers declines at a decreasing rate at low levels of conflict and that failure rates of ethnic newspapers increase at peak levels of ethnic conflict.* This means that the first-order effect of level of conflict on the failure rate would be negative and the second-order effect would be positive.

Ethnic Newspaper Organizations and the Salience of Ethnicity. Variations in the salience of race or ethnicity in previous historical periods are difficult, if not impossible, to measure directly. Much research in the present period on the persistence of ethnic boundaries relies on individual responses to survey questions about group loyalties, willingness to participation in ethnic customs, marital endogamy rates, language usage, and other attitude measures of involvement in ethnic customs.[4] Of course, surveys of ethnic loyalties are not available for immigrants and racial groups in America from this distant historical period. So we rely on one indicator of the salience of racial and ethnic boundaries, the establishment of ethnic newspapers in urban America. At least one influential observer, Robert Park (1922: 5), claimed that the survival of ethnic newspapers and the vitality of ethnic communities were closely intertwined:

Our great cities, as we discover upon close examination, are mosaics of little language colonies, cultural enclaves, each maintaining its separate communal existence within the wider circle of the city's cosmopolitan life. Each one of these little communities is certain to have some sort of co-operative or mutual aid society, very likely a church, a school, possibly a theater, but almost in-

---

[4]Examples of studies using such data to measure group solidarity include Hechter 1978, Portes 1984, and Portes and Bach 1985.

variably a press. In the city of New York, at any rate, there is so far as can be learned, no language group so insignificant that it does not maintain a printing press and publish some sort of periodical: The Albanians, Armenians, Bulgarians, Chinese, Czechs, Croatians, Danes, Finns, French, Germans, Greeks, Italians, Japanese, Jews, Levantine Jews, Letts, Lithuanians, Magyars, Persians, Poles, Portuguese, Rumanians, Russians, Serbs, Slovaks, Slovenians, Spanish, the Swabians of Germany, the Swedes, Swiss, Syrians of New York City, all have a press.

Based upon Park's research, we assume that shifts in the salience of particular ethnic boundaries cause the establishment and disappearance of ethnic newspapers. That is, variations in the rate of the establishment and disappearance of ethnic newspapers for some ethnic population trace changes in levels of importance attached to that particular ethnic boundary. In order to illustrate the potential value of our approach, consider its bearing on the claims of some social scientists that, while differences between white ethnic groups have declined in importance in American society since 1900, the black/white racial boundary has continued to be salient (Farley and Allen 1987; Alba 1988). If density of ethnic newspapers does indeed trace the salience of ethnic boundaries, then Farley and Allen's claim would imply that the numbers of ethnic newspapers for at least some white ethnic populations would have declined while the number of black newspapers would have remained high during the period of interest. Figure 10.1 compares the numbers of immigrant, African-American, and Swedish-American newspapers in existence over the 1877–1914 period.

First, consider the density of immigrant and African-American papers. For immigrant papers, density ranged from 171 to 629; for black papers density varied from 9 to 117. Examination of the plot reveals some obvious differences between the white immigrant and African-American populations. The population of immigrant papers has a more serious problem of left censoring, since many were publishing by 1877. On the other hand, the population of African-American newspapers has a shape that is more typical of a "young" population of newspaper organizations (Carroll and Hannan 1989). Both populations show marked dips around 1893–94 and 1899–1900. However, they diverge markedly after the turn of the century; whereas the density of immigrant papers continued to rise steeply, the density of African-American newspapers actually declined by 1909.

When comparing the subset of Swedish papers to the trajectory of other two population of newspapers, however, another contrast emerges. Over the period of this study, Swedish newspapers sharply decline in number (from a peak of 73 in 1894 to 41 in 1914), while the overall set

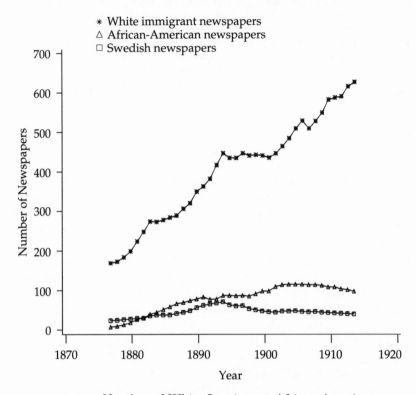

FIG. 10.1   Number of White Immigrant, African-American,
and Swedish Newspapers, 1877–1914

of immigrant newspapers does not decline during this period. Moreover, the number of African-American newspapers grows rapidly over this period, declining only by the end of our observation period. We believe that the continued vitality of the population of African-American and Immigrant newspapers over this period reflects the continuing strength of the racial and foreign-born boundary in America. In contrast, the great decline in the number of "Swedish-American" newspapers indicates the greatly reduced salience of this particular ethnic boundary.[5]

---

[5]Some readers suggest that it would have been interesting to analyze vital events in our newspaper populations for each ethnic group separately, e.g., Lithuanian-American, Irish-American, Polish-American, etc. Unfortunately, if we wish to analyze all the information available on ethnic newspapers that was collected, separate analysis by language or racial categories is not feasible. There were either too few organizations in the population (as is the case for Chinese newspapers) or there were

Institutional Politics and Ethnic Organizations. We also investigate whether institutional politics affected ethnic papers. Carroll's (1987) analysis of newspapers in Argentina and Ireland showed that political turmoil affected the vital rates of newspaper publications but that variables representing the normal political process did not. On the other hand, Snyder and Tilly's (1972) analysis of collective violence in France found that politics as usual had strong effects on the rate of one type of collective action—collective violence.[6] So it seems reasonable to include in models of vital rates an effect of a measure of anti-immigrant policies, specifically, passage of anti-immigrant laws. Presumably, passage of anti-immigrant legislation raised the salience of ethnic boundaries. Then the argument developed above holds that this would encourage the founding and depress the mortality of white immigrant newspapers. In particular, we hypothesize that *anti-immigrant legislation directed against ethnic and racial groups raises the founding rates and lowers the mortality rates of ethnic newspapers.*

The evidence presented thus far in this book suggests that violence against African-Americans was more sensitive to economic and political fluctuations. This may mean that attacks on African-Americans were instigated by different causal processes and therefore should be analyzed separately. It also suggests that African-American organizations emerged in more hostile environments than was the case for other ethnic language newspapers. Because the political and social environments faced by white immigrant and African-American organizations have been so different we analyze each population separately.

Previous Research on the Ecology of Newspapers Organizations

Newspapers and Political Turmoil. The ecology of newspaper industries has been the subject of a series of studies by Glenn Carroll and his associates. They have analyzed historical data on Argentina from the nineteenth century and on Ireland and seven SMSAs in the United States from the nineteenth and twentieth centuries. For present purposes, the most important set of findings concerns the relative importance of conventional measures of resources and of political turmoil for the founding rates and failure rates of newspapers.

Carroll and Huo (1986) estimated the effects of twelve "task" vari-

---

too few conflicts against the group (for example, attacks on Lithuanians). Nevertheless, the boundary distinction between African-American and white immigrant newspapers seems justified in this case.

[6]Political election years also raise strike rates (Snyder 1975).

ables (tangible inputs and outputs of the production process such as the wholesale price of newsprint and the cost of union wages) and found that fewer than half had any discernible impact on founding rates. To learn why these variables, which are commonly cited as important to the fate of an industry, performed so poorly in these models, Carroll and Huo estimated their effects on the circulation figures for several papers. In this setting these conventional "task" variables did have systematic impacts. These results suggest that, despite the fact that conventional explanations emphasize the relationship between "efficiency" and organizational longevity, performance is not a good predictor of exit from the population.

Newspapers and the Political Environment. Carroll and Huo (1986) and Carroll (1987) turned toward the political environment in search of a better explanation of foundings and mortalities of newspaper organizations. They distinguished two dimensions of political environments as they affect organizational populations: *institutional politics* and *political turmoil.* Institutional politics are defined as anticipated political events such as elections and regime changes. Political turmoil includes collective action and other extra-parliamentary actions that are politically directed. They found that political turmoil affected rates of founding and mortality but institutional politics did not.[7]

It might seem that political turmoil simply increases the carrying capacity of the environment by creating more "news." Carroll and Huo (1986) and Carroll (1987) suggest an alternative interpretation. They argue that the connection between political turmoil and the founding of newspapers reflects the emergence of new or newly-identified social groups. That is, political challenges create new opportunities in the polity, as new (or relabeled) sources of support, membership, and resources become available (Tilly 1978). Support for this explanation comes from the fact that Carroll and Huo found that political turmoil was associated with the formation of all types of newspapers (for example, religious, occupational, and ethnic)—not just political newspapers.

We also investigate whether institutional politics affected the founding and failure rates of ethnic papers. We think it likely that, holding the number of foreign-born in the population constant, mobilization of sentiment against immigrants also encouraged the passage of laws that sought to restrict and eventually stop immigration from Europe.[8] We hypothesize that *passage of anti-immigrant legislation directed against*

---

[7]Others such as Delacroix and Carroll 1983, Carroll and Delacroix 1982, and Carroll and Hannan 1989 report similar results.

[8]Since there were only a few anti-immigrant laws passed over this period, and we

ethnic and racial groups lowers the founding rates and raises the mortality rates of immigrant newspapers.

Density Dependence. Based on recent research in organizational ecology, we include the effects of ethnic conflict in models of founding rates and mortality rates that also specify the effects of several other processes now known to affect these rates. We include a specification of the effects of *density*, defined as the number of newspapers in the population. The model assumes that rates of founding and mortality of an organizational population are functions of competition (C) and legitimation (L) (Hannan 1986, 1989; Hannan and Freeman 1987, 1988; Carroll and Hannan 1989; Hannan and Carroll 1991). The theory assumes that the founding rate is proportional to legitimation and inversely proportional to competition. Legitimation and competition in turn are specified to be functions of density.[9]

Prior Foundings and Failures. In their analysis of Argentine and Irish newspapers, Carroll and Delacroix (1982), Delacroix and Carroll (1983), and Carroll and Hannan (1989) found that the number of foundings and failures of newspapers in the prior year affected vital rates in the year following. Their explanation for these results is that peak periods of founding and failures signal market conditions for newspaper owners entering and leaving the industry. Based on this research, we add a similar specification to our analysis, to see if prior foundings and prior failures affect the rate, net of the effects of conflict and population density.

Additional Factors. We also consider the effects of two kinds of environmental resources. Variation in *size of the ethnic/racial population* ought to be the major determinant of the environmental "carrying capacity" of the immigrant newspaper population, because it is a fundamental resource indicating rising demand for foreign language newspapers. Growth in the size of the foreign-born population and black population ought to increase founding rates and decrease mortality rates of immigrant and African-American newspapers respectively. The inclusion of population size in our models also allows us to examine the possibility

---

measure it as a dummy variable, it makes little sense to include measures of non-monotonic effects for this conflict variable in the same way that we did for conflicts.

[9]The theory holds that density (N) increases legitimation at a decreasing rate and that density increases competition within populations at an increasing rate. This argument implies a *nonmonotonic relationship* (an inverted U-shaped relationship) between density and the founding rate. In particular, the theory hypothesizes a positive first-order and negative second-order effect of density on the founding rate. The theory holds that the mortality rate is a mirror image of the founding rate (insofar as density dependence is concerned). For further information on this research, see Hannan and Freeman 1988, 1989, and Hannan 1986, 1989.

that the rising foreign-born population drives both the rate of ethnic conflict and the rate of foundings of ethnic newspapers. Thus our analysis investigates one source of spuriousness directly. In particular, we analyze whether there is an effect of ethnic (or racial) conflict on the founding and failure rates of white immigrant (or African-American) newspapers, net of the fact that the size of the foreign-born population (or African-American population) is increasing during this period.[10]

More general economic effects are also likely to affect the growth of newspaper organizations. Unfavorable economic conditions, measured by *depressions*, ought to have a negative effect on the founding rate of ethnic newspapers and a positive effect on their mortality rate. Based on past research, we suspect that the "liability of newness" affects the mortality of organizations, including newspapers. To examine this possibility we include the effect of aging in our mortality analyses (using a Gompertz specification of age dependence) (Hannan and Freeman 1989).

Design and Methods
Previous analyses of models of the organizational ecology of newspaper populations have analyzed effects at both the national and local levels (Carroll and Hannan 1989). What unit of analysis is the appropriate one to use here? Carroll and Huo (1986) analyzed newspaper populations at the metropolitan level because this geographical boundary was their market boundary. This has not been as true for white immigrant newspapers. Such papers often served as network communication centers for a nation-wide linguistic community. Daily or weekly issues were often widely dispersed to immigrant communities across the country by mail, railroad, and steamboat. Historical evidence suggests that the same holds true for black newspapers. For instance, Tuttle (1970) claims that, in the South, violence often accompanied the arrival of the weekly shipment of *The Chicago Defender*. Consider, for example, Tuttle's (1970: 26) description of what happened in the small town of Longview, Texas, during the summer of 1919:

A Saturday morning event in Longview's black district, as in black sections in towns across the South, was the arrival on the train of the weekly *Chicago Defender*. That July 5 issue of the newspaper was of special interest, for it had a story about Longview ... Jones, who was also the local *Defender*

---

[10]Size of the foreign-born and African-American population are of course only two possible measures of demand characteristics that could be used. Unfortunately, in historical data of this kind, information on specific economic indicators of demand for ethnic newspapers is not readily available for this period. Nevertheless, we share the view of previous newspaper industry analysts that potential readership is the most important indicator of demand (Carroll 1987).

agent, drove his automobile to the downtown business district the following Thursday, July 10. But when he returned to the car, he encountered three white men who brusquely demanded that he come with them ... Another of the men pulled a wrench out of his coat and struck Jones a heavy blow on the head. Other blows followed. Jones fell to the pavement, struggled to get up, but fell again.

Racial events reported in this African-American paper were apparently relevant to some residents living hundreds of miles away from its place of publication.   There is also evidence that this was not an isolated incident. Rudwick (1964) reports that the *Chicago Defender* was banned from time to time in many southern communities. He states that the *Defender* was criticized by local politicians for inflaming racial tensions in many northern cities as well.   Such claims included the accusation that the *Defender* spread false rumors and fears among blacks during race riots in Detroit and Springfield, Illinois.

One solution to the unit of analysis problem is to leave open the question of which level of analysis is most appropriate and to conduct analyses at both the national and local levels.   This strategy allows us to compare system-level and city-level processes of competition and conflict. We first analyze foundings and failures of all non-German ethnic newspapers in 77 largest cities of the United States (in 1880).[11] We then analyze the founding and failure rates *within* the two largest cities in the US during this period: New York and Chicago.[12]

Data on foundings and mortality of newspapers were collected from two newspaper directories: Rowell's *American Newspaper Directory,* and Ayer's *American Newspaper Directory Annual.* We define year of founding as the establishment year as recorded in one of these directories. For the small number of cases where this date was missing, we coded the first year that the paper was listed in one of these annuals as the establishment date.   Similarly, the year of its last appearance in one

---

[11] German papers were excluded from the national-level analysis, since the majority were founded much earlier than 1877 and many changed their names and affiliation in the period just prior to World War I, as they were under suspicion of loyalty. They are included in the population of Chicago papers, since Germans constituted a large proportion of the ethnic community there.

[12] It would have been interesting to analyze the effects of newspaper founding and failure using city-year spells for 77 cities. However, aside from New York and Chicago, the yearly counts of foundings and failures at the city level would be too thin. It is equally unfortunate that African-American newspapers were published in only a few cities during this period, preventing a comprehensive city-level analysis. This means that analysis in Chicago and New York is necessarily limited to white immigrant papers for this period. The data on conflicts are also too sparse to warrant analysis of conflicts at the city level, so our measure of ethnic conflict is an aggregate count of attacks that occurred in any one of 77 cities.

of these annual directories was coded as the year that the newspaper organization disbanded. Some of these newspapers were still publishing at the end of 1914; their histories are treated as right-censored.

Methods of Analysis. Because the date of each newspaper founding is known only to the year, we estimate effects of covariates on the rate within the framework of Poisson regression. That is, we form regression models for the (annual) count of foundings of ethnic newspapers, denoted here by y_t. The regression model represents the rate, λ_t, as a function of observed covariates. To ensure that λ_t can only take non-negative values, it is parameterized as a log-linear function of the covariates:

$$\lambda_t = \exp\left(\mathbf{x}_t' \beta\right). \tag{10.1}$$

This regression model assumes that each observed count is a realization of a Poisson process whose rate is given by (10.1). In other words, the conditional probability function at time t is given by

$$\Pr(Y_t = y_t \mid \lambda_t) = \frac{\lambda_t^{y_t} e^{-\lambda_t}}{y_t!}, \tag{10.2}$$

where λ_t is the mean and the variance of the distribution of the dependent variable, i.e.,

$$E(Y_t) = \mathrm{Var}(Y_t) = \lambda_t.$$

The Poisson assumption that the expected value of Y_t is equal to its variance is often not justified (Cameron and Trivedi 1986). In order to test this assumption we also estimated the founding rates using negative binomial regression, which allows for the possibility that the variance of the dependent variable is greater than its mean. However, these models did not fit significantly better than the Poisson models, so we report only the latter in our tables.[13]

To analyze the mortality rate, the data set was reorganized into a discrete-time "event-history" of the life span of each newspaper. In order to accommodate time-variation in covariates, we analyze newspaper-year spells. Each newspaper's lifespan is broken into yearly segments and associated with appropriate levels of all covariates for that year. So the dependent variable in our analysis is a binary variable that tells for each newspaper (in each year of its existence) whether the newspaper was still in existence at the end of the year. This variable is zero for all but the last year observed for each newspaper. For newspapers whose histories are censored on the right, it is also zero for the final year of observation.

---

[13]In estimating standard errors in the Poisson and negative binomial regressions we used White's (1980) heteroskedastic-consistent covariance matrix estimator. This procedure has an advantage over the inverse Hessian method in that it allows for the presence of heteroskedasticity in the data.

We analyze these data using a logit model proposed by Cox (1972). Our presentation follows Lawless (1982: 372–74) and Freeman and Hannan (1989). Let

$$P_i(\mathbf{x}) = \Pr(\text{a newspaper survives past age } a_i \mid \mathbf{x}), \qquad (10.3)$$

and

$$p_i(\mathbf{x}) = \frac{P_i(\mathbf{x})}{P_{i-1}(\mathbf{x})} = \Pr \left(\text{a newspaper survives past } \right.$$
$$\left. \text{age } a_i \mid \text{ survival past age } a_{i-1}, \mathbf{x} \right) \qquad (10.4)$$

Finally, let P_i denote a baseline survival probability with

$$P_i(\mathbf{x}) = P_i^{\exp(\mathbf{x}'\beta)}. \qquad (10.5)$$

That is, the covariates, $\mathbf{x}$, shift the baseline survival probability.

The logit model uses as the dependent variable the log-odds of failing in the interval between ages a_{i-1} and a_i:

$$\log \left(\frac{1 - p_i(\mathbf{x})}{p_i(\mathbf{x})} \right) = \log \left(\frac{1 - p_i}{p_i} \right) + \mathbf{x}'\beta. \qquad (10.6)$$

In other words, the log-odds of failing for any particular newspaper equals the baseline odds of failing plus a linear function of the covariates.

Independent Variables. We include several environmental covariates expected to influence ethnic organizations during this period, including a measure of economic well-being, and an indicator of the demand for foreign-language newspapers, the size of the foreign-born population (in the country or in the city of New York or Chicago, respectively), and the size of the African-American community.[14] The foreign-born population measures were interpolated yearly from U.S. Historical Statistics (1975), and from the U.S. Census data on the number of foreign-born in Chicago and New York.[15]

---

[14]We also estimated models that included the net immigration flow, to examine an alternative hypothesis that the immigrant population (as a measure of the size of the pool of new readers) would drive the rate of ethnic language newspapers more directly than would the size of the foreign-born population (which would include many who have assimilated linguistically). The result of this analysis was that the immigration variable increases the founding rate and decreases the failure rate. Furthermore, replacing the size of the foreign-born population with immigration did not change any other effects in the model substantially. This might have been expected, since the change in the number of foreign-born in the country in adjacent years is a function of immigration flows.

[15]Of course, these exploratory indicators are not exhaustive. Specifically, we might well have argued to include economic indicators such as growth in the GNP, or unemployment rates in our analysis. Unfortunately, very little systematic information on these indicators is available for the entire 1877–1914 period analyzed. Furthermore, we investigated but found no evidence that there were any systematic effects of other

The analysis of founding and failure rates of ethnic newspapers includes measures of racial and ethnic conflict. In this chapter we consider the yearly counts of conflicts as independent variables. They are the number of attacks on white immigrants and the number of attacks on African-Americans (both are measured only at the national level).[16]

We think that these yearly counts distinguished by target improve over past measures of similar concepts of "political turmoil" that relied on dummy variables indicating the presence of unrest during that year (e.g., Carroll and Huo 1986).

Recall that we have distinguished two different effects of the levels of ethnic conflict. The first is a "salience hypothesis" which proposes that conflict increases the founding rate but decreases the failure rate. The second effect of conflict we labeled a "repression hypothesis, " in which massive amounts of conflict depress the founding rate and elevate the mortality rate of ethnic newspapers during peak periods of attack. Our modeling strategy is to examine whether the nonmonotonic specification significantly improves over a model that specifies that conflict has only monotonic effects on the rate.

To examine the hypothesis that ethnic conflict has a nonmonotonic effect, we specify and estimate a model that is similar to the one developed for testing nonmonotonic effects of density (see Hannan and Freeman 1989: 131–35). That is, we assume that the founding and mortality rates depend upon the count of ethnic/racial attacks (A) as follows:

$$\lambda_t = \exp\left(\theta A + \delta A^2\right). \tag{10.7}$$

The nonmonotonic hypothesis for founding rates is that the first- order effect (θ) is positive and the second-order effect (δ) is negative. Note that exactly the opposite signs in each case are expected for the effects of conflict on the mortality rate.

Results

Founding Rates in the System of Cities. We first examine the aggregate results for immigrant and African-American newspapers in 77 cities taken as a system, then analyze ethnic newspapers in two cities,

---

commonly used economic indicators from this period, such as capital investment, price index, inflation estimates, and wage rates.

[16]It would have been ideal to compare effects of attacks on African-Americans and attacks on European immigrants on each group's newspaper populations, however, there were too few black newspapers established in any city to perform any effective analysis at the city level for black newspapers. So necessarily, our comparisons of results at the city level are limited to foundings and failures for white immigrant papers only.

New York and Chicago. The results for founding rates of immigrant newspapers in the 77 cities appear in the first and second columns and for African-American newspapers in columns 3 and 4 of Table 10.1.

Tables 10.1 through 10.4 report a likelihood ratio, sometimes known as G-squared or Deviance. It can be used to compare the goodness-of-fit of nested models. If the null hypothesis is true, the difference between likelihood ratios has a chi-square distribution with degrees of freedom equal to the number of constraints that have been freed. For example, to perform a likelihood ratio test between the models in column 1 and column 2 of Table 10.1, compare the numbers 29.9 to 29.4. The difference is .5 with 1 degree of freedom, which is not significant. Thus the specification in model (2) for nonmonotonic effects of attacks does not improve the fit significantly over that seen in model (1). In the analysis of African-American newspapers, the same type of comparison of the G-square statistics suggests that the nonmonotonic specification in column 4 does not improve significantly over that in column 3. So, the G-square statistics tell us to focus on the monotonic specifications found in columns 1 and 3.

This means that for white immigrant papers, the results in column 1 suggest that ethnic attacks have a significant monotonic effect on the founding rate. How big is this effect? The estimates in column 1 suggest that the founding rate of immigrant papers was about 20% higher in the year following the one when antiforeigner violence was at its peak of 11 events, when compared to the year after a year without any ethnic attacks. As we noted, the results in column 2, which add the second-order effect of attacks, are not significantly better than the model which specifies only a first-order effect of attacks, in column 1. We interpret these results as support for the salience hypothesis.

Now turn to the African-American newspaper results. In comparing the relevant G-square statistics, we find that the results in column 4 that specify a nonmonotonic effect of attacks on blacks do not improve over the monotonic specification in column 3. Apparently the effect of conflict on African-American newspapers is negative and monotonic. The repressive effect of racial conflict on the founding rate of African-American newspapers was a powerful one. The estimates in column 3 in Table 10.1 imply that the founding rate in years following a year that had 13 antiblack attacks (the observed maximum) was about 40% lower than in those following a year with no recorded attacks on African-Americans. If repression had doubled, so that 26 attacks on blacks had occurred, the estimates imply that the founding rate would be about 96% lower (when compared to years with no attacks). These results suggest that hostile

TABLE 10.1

Poisson Regression Estimates of the Founding Rates of Immigrant
and African-American Newspapers in 77 Cities, 1877–1914

(Heteroskedastic Consistent Standard Errors in Parentheses)

	Immigrant Newspapers		Black Newspapers	
	(1)	(2)	(3)	(4)
Constant	.188	.535	−13.3**	−13.1***
	(1.32)	(1.45)	(5.94)	(5.20)
Number of Attacks	.019**	.047*	−.042**	.046
on Ethnic Group	(.008)	(.035)	(.019)	(.053)
Attacks on Group Squared		−.284		−.948**
(in hundreds)		(.312)		(.457)
Anti-Immigrant Legislation	−.180***	−.196***		
	(.064)	(.059)		
Foreign-Born Population	.235***	.208**		
(in millions)	(.073)	(.086)		
African-American Population			2.53**	2.48**
(in millions)			(1.17)	(1.03)
Depression Year	.173***	.193***	.086	.087
	(.047)	(.060)	(.118)	(.112)
Log Density	.465**	.429**	1.17***	1.13***
	(.239)	(.246)	(.155)	(.136)
Density Squared	−.573***	−.496**	.039	.014
(in thousands)	(.181)	(.224)	(.037)	(.037)
Prior Foundings	.004	.003	−.025**	−.020*
	(.003)	(.004)	(.013)	(.012)
Prior Failures	−.008***	−.009***	.008	.005
	(.003)	(.003)	(.014)	(.015)
Time Trend			−3.65***	−3.49***
			(1.24)	(1.07)
Number of Observations	37	37	37	37
Likelihood Ratio	29.9	29.4	23.3	21.1

$^*p < .10,$ $^{**}p < .05,$ $^{***}p < 01.$

actions against blacks had potent effects on African-American newspaper organizations during this period.

So conflict suppressed foundings in the African-American community, while it encouraged founding of ethnic organizations in the white immigrant community. The opposing effects of conflict on white and black newspaper populations make sense when we take results from previous research on racial violence into account. Racial violence peaked during this period, while anti-immigrant activity subsided (Olzak 1989a). As hostility to white ethnics dissipated, the importance of nationality boundaries for white immigrants lessened. At the same time, the gap in occupational and income attainment between whites and blacks was widening. One explanation for this downturn in fortunes for the African-American community is that discrimination, prejudice, and attacks against blacks rose during this period (Lieberson 1980). In this view, the proliferation of attacks on blacks undermined the stock of resources (including organizational ones) that might have helped African-Americans economically. If this explanation is accurate, we would expect that the founding rate of black newspapers would have been highly sensitive to outbreaks of racial violence during this period, in ways that are consistent with our results.

There is some evidence in Table 10.1 that laws restricting white immigrants had a negative effect on ethnic community organizations. We reasoned that the passage of anti-immigrant legislation indicates the success of the anti-immigrant movement in America, signalling a less favorable climate for immigrants and their organizations. As the negative and significant coefficients in columns 1 and 2 suggest, this reasoning finds considerable support. The estimated effect in column 1, $-.186$, means that the founding rate was 16.5% lower in years when these laws were implemented than in other years.

Control Variables. As we expected, size of the ethnic group has a significant and positive effect on the rate of founding of white ethnic newspapers and of African-American newspapers. That is, larger numbers of foreign-born in the population provided the resources and stimulated the demand for ethnic language newspapers. The same holds true for African-American population size and the creation of newspapers in that community. But note also that the effects of conflicts, density, and depressions are net of the effects of population size. Thus rising demand measured by size of the ethnic population apparently does raise the founding of ethnic newspaper organization. But net of this effect, the effects of ethnic turmoil remain, and so cannot be interpreted as a spurious by-product of rising ethnic diversity in these cities.

The effects of prior foundings and failures differs across models. While prior failures significantly depress the founding rate for white immigrant papers, the level of prior foundings has no effect. Curiously, the effect of prior foundings is just significant, but it is negative for African-American newspapers. In contrast, the effect of high numbers of previous foundings is in the expected positive direction for white immigrant papers (but it is not significant). One possibility is that previously high levels of foundings might have depleted resources in African-American communities compared to white immigrant communities, where more capital and other resources were evidently available for establishing new organizations.

Economic depressions, indicating a less favorable business climate, were expected to suppress founding rates of both types of newspapers. But periods of depression *increased* the founding rate in each population, and this effect is significant for white immigrant papers. The failure to find a strong negative effect for founding rates for the population of African-American newspapers is especially surprising since we might have expected that African-American communities existed much closer to a financial margin of profitability than more prosperous ethnic communities. Perhaps these results mean that ethnic organizations provide a buffer for white immigrants in uncertain economic periods (Bodnar, Simon and Weber 1982).

Are the effects of density and density-squared on the founding rate of immigrant and African-American newspapers the same? According to the estimates in columns 1 through 4, the effect of density is positive and significant for all four columns. This implies that as the populations of newspaper organizations grew, the founding rates increased. However, adding the second-order effect of density improves the fit significantly only for white immigrant papers, which suggests that when the population of immigrant papers approached its carrying capacity, competition effects of density predominate, slowing the founding rate. We found no evidence of nonmonotonic effects of density for African-American newspapers. We suspect this may be due to the fact that the population of African-American newspapers was relatively young, and thus may not have reached its peak density during our observation period.[17]

Hannan and Freeman (1989) interpret the pattern of effects found for white immigrant papers as support for arguments that legitimation and competition are a function of density. We agree with this interpretation. Apparently, despite their unique characteristics and functions, white ethnic newspaper organizations react to the density of their populations in ways that are similar to other organizational forms.

To rule out an alternative hypothesis that the effects of density and conflict are simply the result of the passage of time, in all models we compared equations that included a time trend variable. We report models that include the effect of time only in cases where the time trend variable was statistically significant. This was true in the case

---

[17]Although the coefficients for the effects of density appear quite different in magnitude when the two newspaper populations are compared, keep in mind that the number of black newspapers was much smaller than the number of white immigrant papers.

TABLE 10.2

Poisson Regression Estimates of the Founding Rates
of Immigrant Newspapers in New York and Chicago, 1877–1914

(Heteroskedastic Consistent Standard Errors in Parentheses)

	New York Newspapers		Chicago Newspapers	
	(1)	(2)	(3)	(4)
Constant	−12.6***	−13.7***	.477	−2.88
	(4.79)	(4.74)	(3.32)	(2.63)
Number of Attacks	.052*	−.053	.071***	−.023
on Ethnic Group	(.034)	(.068)	(.015)	(.050)
Attacks on Group Squared		1.20**		1.02**
(in hundreds)		(.649)		(.461)
Anti-Immigrant Legislation	−.092	.022	−.151	−.087
	(.277)	(.295)	(.205)	(.203)
Foreign-Born Population	3.43***	3.38***	.220	.405
(in millions)	(.717)	(.679)	(.370)	(.370)
Depression Year	.170	.072	.239**	.311***
	(.137)	(.147)	(.111)	(.110)
Log Density	3.97***	4.24***	.408	1.23**
	(1.26)	(1.24)	(.767)	(.601)
Density Squared	−.290***	−.288***	−.048*	−.089***
(in thousands)	(.070)	(.065)	(.033)	(.026)
Prior Foundings	.013	.016	.016	.014
	(.018)	(.017)	(.018)	(.014)
Prior Failures	−.008	−.004	.024*	.025*
	(.009)	(.010)	(.017)	(.016)
Time Trend	−1.26***	−1.30***		
	(.329)	(.312)		
Number of Observations	37	37	37	37
Likelihood Ratio	55.1	52.2	30.2	27.4

$^{*}p < .10$, $^{**}p < .05$, $^{***}p < .01$.

of African-American papers, as can be seen in columns 3 and 4, which implies that the founding rate is correlated with the passage of time during this period. It is important to note, however, that attacks on blacks, depressions, and newspaper population densities all affect the rate significantly, net of the effect of time, and including this measure of time does not change any of the substantive results.

Founding Rates of Immigrant Papers in Chicago and New York. To examine whether these aggregate results also hold at the city level, we analyzed the founding rates of immigrant papers for two of the country's largest cities, New York City and Chicago. These results strongly parallel those from the aggregated analyses. For white immigrant papers, there is strong support for a monotonic effect of racial conflict which is positive and significant. This means that the founding rate of newspapers read by immigrants in New York and Chicago was greatly increased during surges of anti-immigrant attacks that occurred all over the country.[18]

Other similarities and differences between Tables 10.1 and 10.2 appear. The size of the foreign-born population raises the founding rate of immigrant papers in New York significantly, but not in Chicago. Depression years raise the founding rate of immigrant papers in Chicago, but not in New York. Nevertheless, we find that density dependence affects the population of ethnic newspapers at the city level and this is consistent with research on a wide variety of other types of organizations. Our results suggest that there are strong nonmonotonic effects of density in the predicted direction for all coefficients of density of newspaper organizations.

In sum, the analysis of founding rates suggests that populations of ethnic newspapers were affected both by the mobilization processes of ethnic conflict and by the organizational processes of competition and legitimation. The size of the foreign-born population and economic depressions also affected the founding rate of white immigrant newspapers. For African-American papers, racial violence sharply curtailed the founding rate, suggesting that repression effects were dominant in this community. In contrast, analysis of immigrant papers suggests that the salience effect of conflicts raised the founding rates of ethnic newspapers.

Mortality Rates of Immigrant and African-American Newspapers.
Should we expect effects on mortality to be mirror images of those found in the analysis of founding rates? Our answer is a qualified one. We examine the hypothesis from population ecology theory that the density of newspapers should affect the mortality rate in the opposite direction from its effects on founding rates. So we expect that depressions slow

---

[18]In a series of other models not reported, we investigated the effect of regular, institutionalized political processes on the founding rates (in addition to the effects of ethnic turmoil). Specifications included dummy variables for regular election years, and for the percentage of votes obtained by a challenging third party in national elections. Neither election years, proportion of votes for third parties, nor a measure of Populist support had an effect on the founding rates of immigrant or African-American papers. So our findings are consistent with Carroll's (1987) findings for the Irish and Argentinean newspaper industries. In all three populations political turmoil had a greater influence on founding rates than did the institutionalized political process.

the founding rate but raise the mortality rate of immigrant and African-American newspapers.

However, we also expect some important differences. The most important of these is due to the fact that the population "at risk" of founding and failure is conceptually and operationally different. Indeed, it would be difficult, if not impossible, to identify exactly what characteristics makes a potential publisher of ethnic newspapers actually publish, or group of news writers successfully establish an ethnic newspaper. Founding rates are conceptualized as a counting process for the population, in which organizations enter the population at different times. In contrast, the failure rate is, in part, a function of individual organizational characteristics, including the number of years that an organization has been in existence. Since we have information on the establishment dates, we can examine the "liability of newness" hypothesis, which predicts that younger newspapers have a higher mortality rate. Aside from the additional measures of age of organization, our analyses of mortality parallel those presented in Tables 10.1 and 10.2. We proceed in the same way, first reporting mortality results for immigrant and African-American papers, then discussing mortality results for immigrant papers in New York and Chicago.

How does our hypothesis of nonmonotonic effects of conflict fare with respect to the mortality rate? Recall we argue that conflicts will affect the mortality rate of ethnic newspapers because they become highly visible symbols of an ethnic community. To examine this hypothesis, we compare the G-square statistics for the monotonic and nonmonotonic models of ethnic attacks in each ethnic population (Column 1 vs. Column 2 and Column 3 vs. Column 4). The comparison of the G-square statistics suggests that our results support the claim that the effect of attacks on the mortality rate of white immigrant newspapers depends nonmonotonically on the level of attacks. The same result does not hold for the mortality of African-American newspapers. The parameter estimates in column 2 in Table 10.3 indicate that the failure rate of white immigrant papers declines as the number of attacks rises, but at a diminishing rate. As the number of observed attacks rises from zero to its peak of 11 events, the rate declines by 83%. Eventually, the rising numbers of attacks causes the rate of failure of white immigrant papers to increase. Thus our hypothesis about the effects of repression and salience appears to hold in Model 2. However, because the point at which the relationship between attacks and the mortality rate is beyond the observed maximum number of attacks on immigrants, the results should be interpreted cautiously.

Other sources of hostility against immigrants also appear to have

TABLE 10.3

Logistic Regression Estimates of the Failure Rates of Immigrant
and African-American Newspapers in 77 Cities, 1877–1914

(Asymptotic Standard Errors in Parentheses)

	Immigrant Newspapers		Black Newspapers	
	(1)	(2)	(3)	(4)
Constant	.452	−1.07	−6.21**	−6.87***
	(1.97)	(2.00)	(2.56)	(2.55)
Number of Attacks on Ethnic Group	−.021	−.163***	−.024	.087
	(.016)	(.048)	(.031)	(.075)
Attacks on Group Squared (inhundreds)		.015***		−1.10
		(.005)		(.704)
Anti-Immigrant Legislation	−.165	−.085		
	(.105)	(.108)		
Foreign-Born Population (in millions)	−.180**	−.068		
	(.092)	(.099)		
African-American Population (in millions)			.002	.130
			(.250)	(.270)
Age of the Newspaper	−.041***	−.041***	−.053***	−.053***
	(.004)	(.004)	(.011)	(.011)
Depression Year	−.091	−.198**	.404***	.405***
	(.078)	(.086)	(.147)	(.147)
Log Density	−.470	−.313	.898	.830
	(.344)	(.344)	(.555)	(.554)
Density Squared (in thousands)	.003	−.001	−.041	−.075
	(.003)	(.003)	(.072)	(.075)
Prior Foundings	.017***	.024***	.026	.032
	(.005)	(.005)	(.027)	(.028)
Prior Failures	.012***	.018***	.011	.010
	(.004)	(.004)	(.022)	(.022)
Number of Observations	16262	16262	3273	3273
Likelihood Ratio	1342.4	1332.5	584.5	581.9

*p < .10,   **p < .05,   ***p < .01.

affected the survival of white immigrant newspapers. Passage of anti-
immigrant legislation decreased the mortality rate of immigrant newspapers (but not significantly so). Taken together these results suggest that
the longevity of immigrant newspaper organizations is actually enhanced
during periods characterized by moderate levels of antiforeigner sentiment and behavior.

In Table 10.3 we see more evidence that the pattern of results for
African-American newspapers diverges from the results for white immigrant newspapers. When mortality rates are compared, it appears that

African-American newspapers were less sensitive to yearly fluctuations in the climate of hostility and collective action than were white immigrant newspapers.[19] White immigrant newspapers were more resilient when white immigrants were victims of attacks by the majority population. In contrast, the mortality rate of African-American newspapers was more sensitive to depressions, which appear to affect mortality rates of black newspapers significantly (as seen in column 3 and column 4).

Control Variables. A liability of newness hypothesis suggests that young newspapers face a particularly hazardous environment, while older ones have developed a clientele, reputation, and organizational routines which encourage their longevity (Hannan and Freeman 1989).[20] The effect of age is consistent with this interpretation: the failure rate declines rather spectacularly with age.

Table 10.3 also presents the results for the effects of density of newspapers on the failure rates of ethnic newspapers. Looking across columns 1–4 we can see that the effect of density dependent legitimation and competition is not significant for either white immigrant or black newspapers. Although these results run counter to population ecology arguments, it is important to note the fact that we have only partial histories for both organizational populations. Because we end our observations in 1914, we believe we observe only the beginning of the processes. Historical reports suggest that both newspaper populations continued to grow after 1914, thus our observations may end before newspaper densities reached their peaks.

It appears, then, that face-to-face confrontations affected rates of founding and mortality more than other factors did and that this effect is stronger for the mortality rate of white immigrant newspapers than for newspapers in the African-American community. Nevertheless, black newspapers had a higher overall rate of mortality, net of the covariates, as seen by a comparison of the difference in the constants in columns 3 and 4, compared to the constants in columns 1 and 2.

---

[19]We also investigated whether institutional politics affected mortality of African-American newspapers. In related analyses (not shown here), we found that neither election years, presidential election years, nor a count of the votes for third parties in national elections had a significant effect on the failure probability of African-American newspapers.

[20]In this data set 49 papers are recorded as starting and finishing in the same year. It is possible that some ethnic newspapers that failed after only a couple of months of publishing were not recorded in our data source that was published yearly. So our results on the liability of newness may actually *understate* the vulnerability of newly established papers. Nevertheless, based upon past research, we believe age is key control variable, so we control for these effects using a Gompertz model in columns 1–4.

TABLE 10.4

Logistic Regression Estimates of the Failure Rates of
Immigrant Newspapers in New York and Chicago, 1877–1914

(Asymptotic Standard Errors in Parentheses)

| | New York Newspapers | | Chicago Newspapers | |
	(1)	(2)	(3)	(4)
Constant	2.84	1.78	−29.7**	−32.3***
	(3.86)	(3.88)	(11.7)	(12.2)
Number of Attacks	−.067**	−.223***	−.057	−.133
on Ethnic Group	(.032)	(.086)	(.042)	(.107)
Attacks on Group Squared		1.87**		.009
(in hundreds)		(.937)		(.011)
Anti-Immigrant Legislation	.260	.406*	.183	.234
	(.211)	(.225)	(.256)	(.264)
Foreign-Born Population	−3.27***	−3.37***	−2.23**	−2.18**
(in millions)	(.551)	(.548)	(.971)	(.975)
Age of the Newspaper	−.029***	−.029***	−.049***	−.049***
	(.007)	(.007)	(.009)	(.009)
Depression Year	−.079	−.190	.009	−.021
	(.142)	(.153)	(.187)	(.191)
Log Density	−1.31	−1.06	6.66**	7.29**
	(.953)	(.957)	(2.79)	(2.91)
Density Squared	.388***	.389***	−.192**	−.217**
(in thousands)	(.079)	(.078)	(.095)	(.101)
Prior Foundings	−.042**	−.035*	−.024	−.021
	(.019)	(.019)	(.024)	(.025)
Prior Failures	.023	.029*	−.033	−.033
	(.015)	(.015)	(.037)	(.037)
Number of Observations	3703	3703	3160	3160
Likelihood Ratio	747.9	744.0	568.6	568.0

$^*p < .10,$ $^{**}p < .05,$ $^{***}p < .01.$

Mortality of Ethnic Newspapers in New York and Chicago. Table
10.4 examines whether the impact of ethnic conflict was localized as well
as national in scope. Table 10.4 reports our analyses of the mortality
rates of New York ethnic newspapers (in columns 1 and 2) and Chicago
ethnic newspapers (in columns 3 and 4) in models that are parallel to
those in columns 1 and 2 in the previous table. By comparing the two
pairs of models, we can answer the question of whether nonmonotonic
effects of attacks affect the mortality rate in these two cities.

If we compare the G-square statistics for the monotonic and nonmonotonic specifications for the effect of attacks on immigrants on the

mortality rates, we can see that the nonmonotonic specification is a significant improvement for New York City but not for Chicago. In New York, the nonmonotonic specification for the effect of attacks on white immigrants fares much better than the monotonic specification for the effect of attacks (a G-square of 747.9 compared to a G-square of 744.0, with 1 degree of freedom). So for New York, we focus on the results in column 2. On the other hand, for Chicago, the nonmonotonic specification does not improve over the simpler monotonic specification for attacks, and so we discuss the results in column 3 for Chicago.

For New York immigrant newspapers, the number of yearly attacks on immigrants has the greatest negative impact on the mortality rate in the *middle* of the observed range. As the number of attacks on white immigrants rose from 0 to 6 attacks, the failure rate of immigrant newspapers is decreased by 50%. But the estimates suggest that when the number of attacks rises above 6 per annum, this effect decreases the mortality rate but at a diminishing rate. Moreover, the effect of ethnic attacks changes sign and becomes positive at 12 attacks per year. So, at very high rates of ethnic attack, a repression effect predominates. Thus the estimates in column 2 suggest that if 15 attacks had occurred in a year, the mortality rate would have more than doubled. At an annual rate of 16 attacks, the mortality rate would have tripled.

In Chicago, adding the second-order effect of attacks is not significant. In this city, ethnic attacks also appear to buffer ethnic newspapers from disbanding, but this effect is not statistically significant. Nor is there any evidence that a nonmonotonic effect of attacks is significant, however, both coefficients are in the predicted direction.

The size of the foreign-born population and the newspaper's age have the same effects as they did in the national-level analysis. Both decrease the mortality rate. While economic depressions decreased the mortality rates when all immigrant newspapers were analyzed together, depressions evidently did not affect the mortality rate of immigrant papers in these two cities. Such results suggest that the local environment may condition the way ethnic organizations were able to respond to fluctuations in the national economy.

We find somewhat different patterns for the effect of density at the city level from the effect on the mortality rate at the aggregate level. For New York, the effect of density of white immigrant papers in columns 1 and 2 has the expected sign, and in column 1 this effect is significant. As the theory suggests, small numbers of papers slow the disbanding rate of newspaper organizations, but when there is a high density of ethnic papers, competition predominates, increasing the death rate of papers. Column 4 for Chicago reveals a complete reversal of this pattern. That is, in both columns 3 and 4, the second-order effect of density is negative and significant, suggesting that large numbers of ethnic newspapers in Chicago produced a favorable climate for them, aside from the effects of prior foundings and failures and other economic and political covariates included in the model.

Discussion

We return to our key claim that ethnic conflict has both positive and negative effects on ethnic organizations that we labeled "salience" and "repression." How did our hypothesis fare? For the creation of ethnic newspapers, the evidence is straightforward. As we originally suspected, the consequences of ethnic conflict are vastly different for white immigrant and African-American communities. Whereas conflict against white immigrants encourages the founding of ethnic organizations, conflict against blacks significantly lowers the rate of creation of newspaper organizations for African-Americans. When the founding rate models that include a nonmonotonic effect of attacks are compared to models that specify a monotonic effect, all suggest that a monotonic specification is warranted. The salience effect predominates in the analysis of the white immigrant press and the repression effect predominates in the analysis of African-American papers. In nearly all cases, the monotonic effect of conflict is significant and in the direction expected. For white immigrant papers, then, there is strong support for the hypothesized effect of salience. For the establishment of African-American papers, the effect of conflict is also monotonic, but the effect is significantly negative, indicating that repression against black organizations was in this case successful.

Stepping back from the details, we can observe that the findings support historians' claims that hostilities against white immigrants had different consequences for that community when compared to attacks against African-Americans. Not only was the frequency of conflict against African-Americans higher, conflict apparently *suppressed* the creation of African-American newspapers significantly. For white papers, just the opposite is true.

The relationship between conflict and organizational longevity is even more complex. Whether the newspaper data are analyzed at the system or city level, the effect of *small amounts* of conflict on the mortality rate of white immigrant papers is *always negative and significant*. But in the analysis of the failure rate of white immigrant papers analyzed at the system level and analyzed for New York City, the results suggest that at higher levels of attacks, repression will in fact increase the mortality rate. In this city, relatively infrequent numbers of attacks were more beneficial to the survival of immigrant papers than either periods experiencing no attacks or periods with very high numbers of attacks on white immigrants. Only at very high numbers of ethnic attacks did our results present evidence that repression increased the mortality rate of white immigrant papers. For African-American newspapers, however, the effect of attacks against their organizations was nearly always detrimental, but it was not always significantly so. Evidently, the main effect of racial violence is to curtail the creation of black newspapers, rather than to affect their mortality.

As we noted in the beginning of this chapter, most research on collective action and social movements emphasizes the role that organizations play in facilitating collective action. In this chapter we have found support for the opposite causal process—that ethnic conflict also encourages ethnic organizations to form in some settings. Our results suggest that both salience and repression influenced whether or not an ethnic group's press would survive in a climate of hostility.

These results have several important implications for the resource mobilization theory of collective action. Resource mobilization theory holds that an important determinant of collective action in a system is the level of prior economic and organizational resources available to contending groups (McCarthy and Zald 1977; Tilly 1978). Changes in the levels of resources appear to stimulate a variety of collective actions (Jenkins 1983). The results presented here provide evidence that collective action affect organizations as well. Especially for the black community, massive attacks short-circuited the establishment of a key institution, the African-American press. In contrast, attacks on white immigrants not only encouraged the creation of immigrant newspapers, but it significantly slowed their dissolution rate.

One can imagine that differences in the direction of effects of racial and ethnic conflicts in different ethnic communities sent important signals to other organizations, including banks, other businesses, loan networks, and other organizations that could benefit minority communities. Such differences in organizational responses to repression could have had significant impacts on perceptions of community power and viability of institutions within the African-American community as well. Nevertheless, we acknowledge that these claims about the consequences of ethnic organizational demographics are highly speculative. Our results present only a first step in untangling the complicated process by which repression and conflict affect ethnic solidarity. But we think that by comparing white immigrant and African-American newspaper organizations, these results begin to contribute to our understanding of the fact that ethnic and racial community resources sharply diverged during this period. Our analysis suggests that the consequences of ethnic violence depend upon a group's resource environment and their ability to muster an organizational defense against future attacks.

Conclusions

It was Robert Park who first suggested that tracing the natural histories of ethnic newspapers might provide some insights into the organizational structure of immigrant communities. Our analysis suggests that examination of the history of this organizational population produced additional information about the role of ethnic and racial conflict in the United States. That is, our results suggest that the target and frequency of ethnic attacks shaped the organizational landscape of ethnic institutions in later decades. We believe these results shed light on some of the questions about the long-term experience of ethnic and racial minorities. Our results indicate that perhaps as a result of hostility and attacks, white immigrants created and sustained ethnic organizations. For the establishment of African-American newspapers, however, the effect of repression significantly decreases this rate.

The finding that attacks on white immigrants stimulate rather than deter new immigrant organizations suggests that the causal relationship between repression and extinction of ethnic organizations is not a straightforward one. Contrary to arguments that posit the decline of ethnic organizations during periods of repression and hostility, our analysis found that white ethnic newspapers may have thrived under conditions of repression and attack. We think that this is an important step toward understanding why ethnic boundaries persist in the modern world, and why ethnic organizations are often resilient to change and dissolution.

11

Summary and Conclusions

At the outset we noted that outbursts of ethnic violence in America seem to come in clusters. Despite considerable consensus that ethnic violence occurred with regularity in America,[1] few social scientists or historians have offered a unifying theoretical framework that attempts to account for the conditions responsible for these patterns of ethnic violence. Rarer still are empirical attempts that compare events with different targets.

This book attempts to address the gaps in our understanding of American racial and ethnic conflict with an application of ecological theories of niche overlap and competition. Here we have applied ideas about niche overlap to human communities and suggest that ethnic conflict can be analyzed usefully as a feature of attempts at competitive exclusion. The theoretical claim is that intensification of ethnic competition generates collective actions by dominant ethnic groups that are designed to maintain their dominance and control. The key argument is that *competition intensifies the salience of ethnic boundaries and promotes spontaneous forms of ethnic collective action.* A related argument considers the reverse causal process, the possibility that the occurrence of ethnic collective actions also raises the salience of ethnic boundaries.

This competition argument has implications for the timing of ethnic conflict as well as for the conditions that cause conflict. Our hypothesis is that *ethnic conflict surges when barriers to ethnic group contact and competition begin to break down.* The critical examination of this hypothesis here involves investigating whether occupational desegregation of minority groups affected the rate of ethnic collective action in American cities. To test these ideas about niche overlap and ethnic conflict, I analyzed event-history data on 262 ethnic and racial conflicts

---

[1]For examples of this consensus see Park 1950, Higham 1955, Saxton 1971, Woodward 1974, Shapiro 1988, and Rabinowitz 1980.

and protests that occurred in 77 (largest population) American cities from 1877 through 1914.

This final chapter examines the broader implications of the results. In particular, I focus on the ramifications of these results for related theories of race relations and collective violence. This chapter also explores the ways the results reported here might aid our understanding of contemporary ethnic/racial unrest. I speculate that the finding that low levels of occupational segregation cause higher rates of ethnic conflict is particularly relevant for the modern period, which has been characterized by upward mobility of ethnic minorities in many countries. In particular, the last section of this chapter suggests that desegregation also affects rates of racial unrest in contemporary America as it apparently did one hundred years ago.

Implications of the Results

A key question guiding sociological inquiries of race relations in the United States is: do increases in ethnic and racial inequality increase rates of ethnic violence? To address this question adequately, some benchmarks regarding levels of segregation and inequality among ethnic groups are needed. Our analysis supported other research in finding a substantial racial gap in opportunity and resources from 1877 through 1914. Research by sociologists and historians has indicated that as early as 1900, European-Americans were moving out of low-paid and segregated occupations and African-Americans were becoming more segregated at the bottom rungs of the socio-economic ladder.[2] However, the results reported in this book suggest that white immigrants gained an economic edge over blacks decades earlier than has been previously supposed. Our analysis shows that between 1870 and 1880, white immigrants held more diverse jobs in cities where the black community was also becoming more numerous. Such findings suggest that a racial job queue was in place in America as early as 1880. According to these results, the existence of a racial job queue benefitted white immigrants at the expense of blacks even before the largest wave of migration of blacks to the North had taken place.

Furthermore, an increase in job segregation was not the only misfortune experienced by blacks during this period. At the same time that a racial gap in opportunities widened, violence against African-Americans increased sharply relative to the rate of violence against nonblack groups. Not surprisingly, the climate of racial violence also affected the growth

---

[2] For examples, see Thernstrom 1973, Blassingame 1973, Bodnar et al. 1982, and Lieberson 1980.

of organizations in the black community. The peak in racial repression evidently affected the founding rate of black newspapers adversely. Such attacks were evidently far more effective in suppressing black organizations than were similar (but less virulent) attacks on white immigrants during the same period. In fact, we find that attacks on white ethnic communities encouraged the creation of one type of immigrant organization, significantly driving the founding rates of immigrant papers upward.

Competition and Conflict Against Different Targets. The results of the preceding chapters force us to confront an uncomfortable conclusion—despite the fact that many ethnic groups pose threats of economic competition to the established power structure, more violence was directed against African-Americans than against other groups. Such violence obviously had devastating consequences for the black community. As many scholars of African-American history have pointed out, racial hostilities against blacks were both relentless and effective in repressing blacks during this period. Moreover, peaks in counts of attacks differ for different ethnic targets. Lynching of blacks and urban violence against African-Americans rose over the period of this study while violence against Asian- and European-American immigrants evidently subsided after 1910. Casual observations of these time trends might have led us to conclude that the *causes* of attacks on blacks and white immigrants diverge as well.

But our analysis suggests that such a conclusion is simplistic. The first stage of our analysis considered events from cities considered as a system, and examined the effects of macro-level processes of immigration, economic contraction, and growth of the labor movement. At the national level, there are substantial similarities in the patterns of effects across targets. When results of the effects of competition on rates of ethnic/racial conflict are examined in detail, it becomes clear that competition is responsible for raising rates of ethnic conflict involving all groups. Indicators of changes in the strength of competition have especially potent effects. For instance, the analysis of the effects of immigration and business failures indicates that competition intensified when the number of newcomers rose and economic opportunities declined.

When attacks on African-Americans, Chinese-Americans, and others are analyzed separately, several more complications emerge. It appears that somewhat different aspects of competition intensified the rate of attack on each group. When the rates are considered separately for the three groups, attacks on African-Americans and Chinese targets seem more sensitive to fluctuations in wages of common laborers and to the business failure rates than were attacks on white immigrants. In contrast, attacks on white immigrants were more sensitive to fluctuations in immigration flows, as might be expected. Nevertheless, when all three groups are compared, attacks on European- and African-Americans share strikingly similar causes (while attacks on Chinese-Americans do not).

During this period, the labor movement organized strikes, sometimes in response to competition from foreign or black workers. Additionally, many observers noted that labor unrest often coincided with racial strife. Such patterns suggest that labor unrest might have been causally linked to ethnic turmoil during this period. We next investigated whether the volume of *labor strikes* affected the rate of ethnic and racial conflicts. Several arguments drawn from the work of labor historians and sociologists suggest that black strikebreakers were often recruited to sites of labor dispute during periods of intense labor mobilization. Racial tensions and conflict flared under such conditions. But we reasoned that the relationship between labor unrest and racial conflict may be spurious. Both forms of collective action may have resulted from the growth of labor organizations, which encouraged parallel forms of unrest.

We argued that the growth of the union movement and the rising supply of low-wage labor increased levels of ethnic competition in urban labor markets, which in turn raised rates of ethnic conflict. The findings support this latter argument. The results show that models that included two measures of the growth of labor unions eliminated all of the supposed effect of strikes on the rate. They also show that the founding rate of national labor unions and the number of unions in existence significantly raised the rate of conflicts and violent conflicts against all groups. Furthermore, the effect of the growth of labor union organizations is strongest for antiblack conflicts.

We next compared forms of violence against one racial target: African-Americans. This analysis investigated similarities in the causes of rural lynching and urban violence against African-Americans. Until recently, competition theories of ethnic and race relations had focused on economic processes. This book broadens the scope of competition theory to include *political competition*. We speculated that political challenges and economic competition could have independent effects on regional and temporal variations in lynchings and in urban violence against blacks. The hypothesis was that rates of racial violence rose with political competition (in challenges to white supremacy in the South), net of the effects of immigration, urbanization of blacks, and economic contractions. Event-history analyses of urban racial violence and time-series analyses of lynchings show that economic slumps, particularly those that affected the least skilled workers, increased rates of both lynching and urban racial violence, as did rising competition from immigration. Lynching also appears to have been sensitive to factors affecting the southern region directly. In particular, lynching was affected by Populist challenges to one-party rule as well as by the changing fortunes of the cotton economy.

We also examined the effect of *local competition* on rates of upward mobility for immigrants. We first examined whether there was evidence for local ethnic/racial job queues for the period 1870–80, a period prior to the one analyzed by Lieberson (1980). If a job queue was operating, then a growing proportion of black workers in a city would gradually enable white immigrant workers to move out of segregated jobs and experience upward mobility. In order to test this claim, we analyzed changes in levels of occupational segregation of the foreign born. The results support the hypothesis. Foreign-born workers in cities with initially large and growing numbers of blacks experienced less occupational segregation, while those in cities with growing numbers of foreigners experienced higher levels of occupational segregation. Interestingly enough, the amount of illiteracy of immigrants in a city appeared irrelevant to this process.

Conventional theories of race relations once assumed that concentration of poverty, illiteracy, and other indicators of inequality among ethnic groups caused ethnic and racial turmoil (Gordon 1964; Hechter 1975). This book focuses on one particular part of this argument—that the degree of ethnic job segregation affects ethnic conflict. So in direct contrast to models emphasizing that *segregation* of ethnic and racial populations causes ethnic conflict, this book claims that *desegregation* causes ethnic conflict.

The theories emphasizing ethnic segregation as a cause of ethnic unrest often specify that conflict is a function of extreme inequalities in opportunity or occupational attainment. In such arguments, extreme levels of ethnic segregation also imply disadvantage and inequality.[3] Such gaps in attainment purportedly fuel ethnic antagonism and give rise to higher levels of racial and ethnic unrest. A testable implication of this perspective is that effacement of ethnic and racial differences diminishes conflict between ethnic groups. The converse should also hold. According to the cultural division of labor perspective, ethnic segregation increases rates of ethnic conflict.

In contrast, the theory advanced here holds that *low levels* of eth-

---

[3]See, for example, Hechter 1975: 19–43.

nic and racial inequality will produce a high rate of ethnic and racial conflict. We explored the effects of *occupational desegregation in cities* on rates of conflicts and protests. We analyzed effects on these rates of variations among cities in ethnic/racial competition, literacy, and occupational segregation on these rates. Competition initiated by desegregation of African-and European-Americans in occupations in urban settings significantly increased the rate of conflict. The results suggest that dispersion of the foreign-born from segregated occupations raised rates of ethnic conflicts against all groups, especially during 1890–1914. As expected from previous research on race riots, large cities and cities with higher proportions of nonwhites had higher rates of interracial conflict. Cities with higher illiteracy rates experienced higher rates of both conflict and protest.

The results from analysis at the local level have implications for existing theories of job segregation and ethnic conflict. Conventional segregation theories specify that high levels of segregation cause ethnic conflict. The results reported in this book suggest just the opposite is true. In fact, the finding is that declining and low levels of segregation of the foreign-born raised rates of both conflict and protest significantly. Taken together, the occupational segregation and conflict analysis of cities clarify the process. Occupational segregation initially reinforces ethnic boundaries, yet it appears that the breakdown of segregation sparks conflict between ethnic groups.

Diffusion and the Salience of Ethnic Boundaries. To answer the question of whether ethnic violence diffuses over time, we explored the nature of *time dependence* on the rate of ethnic conflict and protest. Models of time dependence have implications for social science theories that hold that collective action comes in waves (or cycles of protest). A way to test this claim is by examining the timing of events over some long period. Because event-history methods exploit all the potentially available information about the timing and sequencing of events, we were able to examine a model that specifies that diffusion affects the rate of ethnic collective action. To test the diffusion theories, we examined several different specifications of time dependence. One model specified that a month's count of events would significantly raise the rate. Another model specified that diffusion only occurs within distinct *forms* of collective action, so that the effect of the previous conflict would raise rates of conflict but not protest. Nearly all of these models suggested that recency had the expected effect. We found evidence that a powerful and general diffusion process appears to affect both the rates of conflict and protest, in that the rate of collective action declines as the duration since the previous event grows large. In both the national- and city-level analyses, highly significant effects were also found using a Weibull model, even when both of the alternative specifications of diffusion were also included in the model. Estimates of Weibull models imply that the rate of collective action declines with the passage of time since the previous event. Specifically, our results suggest that the rate of conflict and protest is significantly higher immediately after an event has just occurred in a city or in the country as a whole, than when three or more months have passed without any ethnic collective action.

The introductory chapters argued that diffusion raises the rate of subsequent ethnic/racial actions through its effect on *the salience of ethnic boundaries.* That is, immediately after an event has occurred, ordinary confrontations between members of different ethnic or racial populations take on a new and more threatening interpretation. Just after a racial event happens, race and ethnic membership become relevant where they were not before, and urban confrontations of all kinds increasingly come to be seen as racially motivated by the press, by local authorities, and by residents.

According to this view, recent ethnic events magnify the salience of ethnic identity. But the consequence of rising salience of ethnicity is not limited to individual perceptions. It also apparently influences violent behavior toward ethnic groups. So the diffusion results reported here offer one way to understand the historical divergence in the trends of violence mobilized against different ethnic groups. If diffusion affects the rate, then even small increases in violence against African-Americans (or any other group) cause the rate of violence against this group to spiral. At the same time, negative time dependence implies that a small decline in anti-immigrant violence diminishes the subsequent rate of attacks on white immigrants. Models that include estimates of effects of time dependence fit the historical data extremely well: violence against European- and Asian-Americans all but disappeared by 1914, yet violence against African-Americans has remained relatively high.

When viewed from a historical perspective, differences in these two trajectories of violent attacks suggest a social movement explanation for those ethnic boundaries that declined in importance as well. This explanation is that the passage of anti-immigrant laws undercut the anti-immigrant movement. The success of the anti-immigrant movement was its undoing, as the flow of immigrants from Asia and South, Central, and Eastern Europe was controlled by immigration restrictions and other related labor legislation (Garis 1927). As a result, the frequency in attacks declined and the boundaries around specific white ethnic nationalities declined in importance. So it is possible that many other linguistic or religious boundaries that were salient in the late nineteenth century *could have* remained strong, but they did not. For example, scholars report that differences in a wide number of socioeconomic and behavioral indicators among categories of white immigrants have all but disappeared in recent decades (Lieberson and Waters 1988; Alba 1988).

An explanation consistent with these facts is that the diffusion of ethnic violence affected *which* ethnic boundary became predominant. The rate of attacks on whites and the rate of attacks on African-Americans are mirror images of each other: recent violence against African-Americans causes sharp inclines in the rate while the recent absence of violence against European-Americans diminishes the rate. The effect of negative time dependence on both rates is symmetric. The point is that both trends were caused by the same process. Diffusion processes also explain why the black/white color boundary became the dominant one in the early twentieth century and has remained so (Farley and Allen 1989).

Generality of Competition Processes. Processes of immigration, economic contraction, and growth of the labor movement raised the rate of protests and conflict involving *all* ethnic and racial minorities. In order to understand why competition from white immigrants led to violence against *any* racial or ethnic target, we need to move away from the particular empirical findings and return to general competition theory arguments. Chapters 1 and 2 pointed out that it is not always the case that the groups commanding the lowest wages experience higher rates of attack. Rather, the version of competition theory developed here argues that the breakdown of a rigid system of discrimination and the racial queue sparks ethnic collective action. In this view, repression against the least powerful minorities is most likely to occur when competition among all groups intensifies. So it is not periods of extreme racial separation that generate peaks of violence, but rather periods when conditions are just beginning to improve (for some but not all minorities). More generally, as formerly disadvantaged groups begin to achieve a higher standard of living, they begin to compete with those just above them in the status and job hierarchy. Competition intensifies as a result, causing dominant groups to attempt to regain their superiority and exclude others.

I have also suggested that it may not be necessary that competition involve face-to-face competition at a worksite or specific neighborhood. The theoretical point here is that labor market competition among blacks, white immigrants, and native-born whites drove the rates of both kinds of collective action. Models with identical specifications showed strikingly similar patterns: *Competition similarly affected the rate of at-*

tacks against African-, Asian-, and European-Americans. Even more startling is the finding from the city-level analysis of 1890–1914 that competition affected protest and conflict similarly, even though the two types of collective action typically have distinct goals and grievances. And, despite the fact that southern cities were more likely to experience racial unrest, competition affected rates of lynching and racial violence in northern and southern cities similarly. Finally, there were parallel effects of competition at the national and city levels of analysis in that economic decline and rising ethnic diversity contributed to the rates.

The Calculus of Collective Violence. We can now address the implications of the results for several other leading perspectives that attempt to explain temporal variation in collective violence in general. These strategies follow the lead of Gamson, Tilly, and many others who hold that violence is best analyzed as a strategy of last resort, used only after other legal means have been exploited. Consistent with this view, rational choice theorists would claim (all else being equal) that costs of collective action increase greatly when violence is used in power struggles. Selective use of political repression and disenfranchisement of powerless groups are often attractive alternatives to public violence.[4]

Resource mobilization and rational choice theorists have suggested that, for dominant groups, the costs of social control increase with violence (Tilly 1978). For instance, compare the cost of policies to limit immigration and the costs of excluding blacks who were already highly incorporated into the domestic labor force. As Lieberson and others have suggested, it was too late to exclude the large numbers of African-American workers in the labor force after the Civil War. Moreover, if split labor market theories are correct, employers did not want to exclude sources of cheap and highly controllable labor during a period of peak industrialization and labor organizing (Wilson 1978). As historians have documented, many employers who benefitted from a low-wage labor force needed the so-called reserve army that blacks sometimes represented. The political and economic costs to excluding blacks from the developing industrial labor force in the North was too high a price for most employers.

---

[4] Recall from Chapter 2 the point that competition theory does not insist that conflict is an inevitable outcome of competition. In the language of competition theorists such as Bonacich and Barth, creation of rigid caste systems and institutionalization of racial exclusionary laws are also effective at restricting levels of competition without having to resort to violence (Barth 1969; Bonacich 1973). It may turn out that ethnic violence is the least preferable one in most situations, a solution of last resort. More empirical research that conceptualizes racial segregation and violence as types of "competing risks" would be extremely useful.

But this does not mean that white workers welcomed blacks into their community. The fact the white employers recruited blacks while white workers resisted their employment and settlement meant that actions to prevent black migration were likely to be mobilized locally, whereas the response to limit white immigration was national in scope (Higham 1955). Such exclusionary movements were greatly facilitated by the organizational growth of national labor unions (see Chapter 6). In contrast, social movements to limit immigration of Asians began on local levels (in California) but moved quickly to the national and congressional arena (Garis 1927), where they met with spectacular success (Saxton 1971; Nee and Nee 1986). Social movements organized against blacks include local white Citizens' Councils and posse groups, but it is revealing that these organizations were mostly local in character. In contrast, exclusionary movements against European- and Asian-Americans were mostly national in scope.

The results reported in this book suggest that there is a powerful causal dynamic between exclusion and repression. Based on these results, we suspect there are important empirical thresholds of exclusion and breakdown of exclusionary barriers that spark this competitive dynamic. Even small movements away from complete occupational segregation of ethnic minorities trigger ethnic competition and efforts to constrain it. Competition for jobs during periods when ethnic diversity is rising encourages dominant groups to use organizations to restrain open competition. These solutions include passing rules restricting the rights of access to valued resources as well as violence. In the United States, they sometimes involved reviving old systems of *Apartheid*, such as Jim Crow laws and disenfranchisement strategies (Woodward 1974).

Whether such systems are successful is debatable. As Enloe (1980) pointed out, modern states often solve problems of ethnic diversity and competition by expanding police and military powers of repression, both of which are costly. If the events that took place during the 1980s and 1990s in Eastern Europe and the Soviet Union hold more generally, then solutions that involve ethnic repression are also highly unstable. If institution of a rigid cultural division of labor (as in South African *Apartheid*) can be viewed as a temporary solution to exclude competitors, then the potential for racial and ethnic competition in any multiethnic social system is rarely close to zero. Another relevant and recent example of this point is provided by the crumbling of one of the most repressive racialist systems in recent world history. As events in South Africa have shown, the once remote disintegration of *Apartheid* may actually occur (Olivier 1990).

Rising competition encourages dominant groups of all kinds to attempt to pass exclusionary laws, enact immigration quotas, restrict labor force competition, in the form of quotas, union rules, seniority rules, and other means commonly employed by professions, workers, and ethnic groups to restrict entry to valued occupations. If attempts at imposing exclusionary rules are successful, there may be no further need to resort to violence or terrorism. Such an explanation fits the fact that while attacks on Asian-Americans were numerous prior to 1882, they dropped to nearly zero after that date. If we accept the passage of the Chinese Exclusion Act in 1882 as a benchmark of success of the anti-Asian movement in America, then the subsequent decline in hostility against Asians becomes understandable. According to this reasoning, the political success of the anti-Asian movement reduced the motivation, rationale, energy, and organizational momentum that had previously mobilized attacks on Asian-Americans. Seen in this light, the Immigration Act of 1924 was the culmination of an enormously successful and more general antiforeigner campaign (Bennett 1988). Passage of laws that successfully restricted immigration thus dissipated fears of foreigners and nativism in America.

Movements to restrict mobility of blacks geographically were far less successful. Some mostly-white communities did erect local barriers to blacks (and many remain). But they were distinctly local in scope. Even Jim Crow segregation laws that separated public facilities into so-called "equal" ones were instituted piecemeal, first in response to Republican party threats organized during the 1890s by poor whites and newly franchised blacks (Woodward 1974). The movement to disenfranchise blacks in the South was also distinctly state-based and thus local in character. The point is that it was much harder to mobilize national antiblack campaigns than it was to focus local movements in the South, where most blacks lived. One reason for the difference in magnitude of response to blacks compared to white immigrants is because legal measures of repression against Asian and European-Americans were so successful, more violent means were rendered unnecessary. The very success of anti-Asian repression undercut violent attacks on Asian-Americans in later decades. In the South, particularly, repression of blacks may have initially reduced competitive tensions but they did not remove blacks from the South entirely.

It is thus revealing that lynching violence peaked in the late nineteenth in the South, when blacks became newly empowered politically (Chalmers 1965; Jackson 1967; Rabinowitz 1980). For those northern communities that were mostly white, acts or threats of violence against blacks peaked in 1900 to 1910. The preceding arguments suggest that racial attacks on blacks became a common strategy for repressing blacks at the end of the nineteenth century. Many observers have suggested that rural lynchings and violence against blacks are best analyzed as an instrument of social control of blacks in the South (James 1988; Beck and Tolnay 1990). But attacks on blacks in the urban North were also more numerous than attacks on other groups.

The asymmetry in the magnitude of organizational resources controlled by dominant versus subordinate groups provides a clue to understanding why blacks were disproportionately victims of violence. Previously we found that the growth of the labor movement spurred racial violence based on economic threats. In the case of lynching, we find that political threats from Populist party organizations were also key causes of racial violence. According to our analysis, the brief flurry of success of the Populist movement during the mid-1890s significantly raised rates of lynching in the United States. Apparently, political and economic competition which threatens the dominant group incites racial violence and this violence escalates with organizational strength.

Ethnic Organizations and the Salience of Ethnic Boundaries. Variation in the salience of ethnic conflicts also plays a role in determining the fate of one type of ethnic organization—ethnic newspapers. Our results show that conflict and repression shape the dynamics of populations of ethnic newspapers. Conflict appears to stimulate rather than deter new organizations, but this effect holds only for white immigrant newspapers. For the creation of white newspapers, we found evidence that a strong nonmonotonic effect of racial conflict was at work. This meant that the founding rate of white immigrant papers was encouraged during periods of ethnic attack while the founding rate of African-American papers was discouraged during periods of racial attack. These results suggest to us that the causal relationship between suppression and extinction of ethnic boundaries is complex.

One complication has been suggested by resource mobilization theory: an important determinant of collective action in a system is the level of economic and organizational resources available to contending groups. Changes in levels of resources available to contending groups appear to stimulate a variety of collective actions. Our analysis of one type of ethnic organization—ethnic newspapers—shows that the opposite causal process also holds. That is, ethnic conflicts also encourage ethnic organizations in some settings. Perhaps as a result of hostility and attacks, white immigrant communities created and sustained ethnic organizations that consequently deterred further attacks of hostility against newcomers. To examine this claim with evidence, we ask whether ethnic conflict causes victimized ethnic communities to build solidary organizations, in defense of their communities under attack. Not only did white ethnic papers survive antiforeigner attacks, they evidently *thrived* during periods of massive antiforeigner attacks. However, the effect of hostility on establishment of African-American newspapers depressed the creation of black newspapers no matter what level of violence had occurred previously. In our view, these results suggest that factors that raise the salience of ethnic boundaries provide fertile environments for white but not black organizations.

This discussion suggests that the causal relationship between suppression and extinction of ethnic boundaries is not a straightforward one. We think that responding to the complexity of this relationship represents an important step toward understanding why some ethnic boundaries persist in the modern world. For immigrants, organizations flourish in environments of turmoil. White immigrant newspapers provided foundations for enclave communities founded by immigrants and supported by a dense network of information and institutions. Yet the very survival of ethnic institutions provided networks and jobs, and undoubtedly contributed to the fact that, during the decades that follow this study, immigrants began to disperse geographically (Lieberson 1980; Massey and Denton 1989). The result is that white ethnics assimilated and became upwardly mobile as the number of white foreign-language newspapers declined (Wynar 1972).

There appeared to be a different dynamic of organization building and repression that affected the black community. Attacks on African-American communities undercut key resources for those communities. The result was a stagnation of growth in organizational resources in African-American communities. The beginning of the racial gap in organizational and financial resources can be traced to this historical period. Moreover, the gap remains a relevant force in determining contemporary racial inequality. Such persistence of inequality reinforces the black/white color line to this day.

Suggestions for Future Theory and Research

Earlier theories of ethnic collective action emphasized the importance of ethnic/racial segregation and repression for understanding the persistence of ethnic boundaries and ethnic politics. This book suggests a more complicated relationship between segregation and conflict. While extreme levels of ethnic segregation in occupations may reinforce ethnic solidarity, it does not appear to foster ethnic conflict. Rather, extreme levels of segregation are best analyzed as outcomes of competition. According to this view, extreme segregation reduces levels of contact and competition, thus lowering the rate of conflict among groups. Instead, ethnic *desegregation* tends to produce conflicts that generate attempts at repression and resegregation.

In discussing results of the analysis of ethnic newspapers, we noted that attempts at repression can sometimes facilitate the creation of ethnic organizations and intensify ethnic solidarity. Conflict can thereby transform ethnic/racial organizations into social movements that protest oppression. Which social movements predominate—those advocating civil rights or those calling for repression of minorities—(and for how long) presumably depends upon changing sets of power relations and organizational resources.

Is there a common sequence of events underlying the relationship between desegregation and conflict? Do initial announcements of changes in policies about segregation of public facilities and schools activate racial tensions, or does racial conflict against desegregation grow slowly over time? These questions have contemporary relevance in the United States and in other settings. It seems natural to consider how modern civil rights legislation has shaped race relations as well. Because the primary theoretical focus of this volume has been political and economic competition, this study has left unexplored the active role of legislation and government agencies. It seems plausible that the actions of powerful and legitimate authorities, such as the local government, police, the state militia, and other organizations affect the rate of contemporary ethnic and racial violence.

One path to explore would be to ask whether timing of state actions independently influences racial unrest. Does the speed with which the state responds—by repression, by changing laws and policies, and by enforcement of civil rights' protections—affect the rate of ethnic violence? The empirical literature on the impact of recent school desegregation and busing in the United State suggests that *initial* processes of racial desegregation had the largest impact on race relations, while subsequent desegregation policies had much smaller effects (Taylor 1986; Useem 1980). This research has also considered unintended consequences of desegregation policies. The consensus holds that districts that used busing to achieve racial balance came to have significantly higher levels of racial segregation than they did previously. Few of these studies have examined the impact of the antibusing movement and antibusing collective actions on changes in the level of segregation.

If *initial* processes of racial desegregation activate competitive exclusion and conflict, the next step would be to investigate the independent effects of *the speed* of government response, apart from the effects of changes in the level of desegregation. Based on this discussion of levels and rates of desegregation, I suggest three questions that might stimulate debate on issues of desegregation, government policy, and racial conflict in the contemporary period.

1. *Does the level of racial desegregation affect the rate of racial unrest?* Many observers have noted that racial conflict exploded following the implementation of busing policies in American cities such as Boston during the mid-1970s. Perhaps initial movement away from complete segregation has an especially powerful effect on racial unrest. That is, one hypothesis is that the most powerful effects of desegregation on racial conflict will occur with initial movement away from the state of complete segregation. Regions with less segregation should experience less unrest, according to this hypothesis.

2. *Does the speed of desegregation affect the rate of racial conflict?* I also speculate that the speed of integration influences racial unrest (which is independent of the shift away from total segregation). Rapid and initial changes in segregation laws ought to produce more unrest than slow and incremental decreases in segregation in housing and school settings. This is because adjustments and adaptations are slow to catch up to rapid social change; organizational inertia makes traditional behaviors and norms extremely hard to change.

3. *Do shifts in state policies and laws regarding racial populations affect the rate of racial unrest?* This question links local desegregation practices considered in this book with macro-political processes. The key issue is whether actions of national governments regarding race relations affect racial unrest directly, apart from their impact on segregation levels. It seems reasonable to suspect that political actions of states and their agents also influence the rate of racial unrest.

Conclusion: Is Racial Violence a Constant or Varying Feature?

This book began with the observation that, although ethnic and racial violence is often claimed to be a relentless and characteristic feature of American life, sporadic peaks in ethnic turmoil and racial terrorism are equally apparent. At the same time, the results reported here show that particular forms of racial violence, such as lynching, eventually subsided. In other cases, antiforeigner and nativist activity seemed to shift to alternative victims or to the use of different tactics, moving from violence to lobbying of union leaders. Just how fundamental is ethnic and racial conflict in American society? Can these seemingly conflicting observations be explained? One way to understand these apparently contradictory historical themes is by providing some theoretical underpinnings to models of ethnic and racial unrest that specifically address the causes of these cycles of protest and conflict.

The explanations offered and tested in this book were drawn from competition theory. The core argument is that breakdown of racially and ethnically ordered systems unleash forces of competitive exclusion against the least powerful targets in the system. To the extent these least powerful groups are also identifiable ethnic or racial minorities, the rate of attacks against them surges dramatically. Competition theory informs us about which societal conditions are likely to unleash racial terrorism and conflict *and* which groups are most likely to fall victim to it.

The overriding and disturbing evidence in this book suggests that African-Americans were consistently victimized by whites when competition levels rose. The results suggest this is true even when labor force competition was mainly from white immigrants. While it is true that Asians and European-Americans fell victim to racial conflicts, the number and scale of nonblack violent events falls as violence against blacks rises by 1900.

Our dual focus on the timing of events and forces of competition helps clarify why the distinctly *sociological* mechanism of competition drove rates of violence against African-Americans upward. That is, ethnic violence is not necessarily directed against recently arrived white immigrants, rather, it is organized when competition levels rise and are directed toward those who are least able to retaliate. These patterns are still with us today. There is considerable evidence that the differentials in rates of racial and ethnic attacks and in the chances for organizational survival were mutually reinforcing. Such divergent opportunity structures simultaneously closed to blacks and opened to white immigrants for decades afterwards. Whether or not competition remains a potent cause of racial unrest in the future remains an open research question.

Appendices

A

Occupational Categories in 1870 and 1880 Censuses

AGRICULTURE
    Agricultural laborers
    Farmers and planters
    Gardeners, nurserymen, and vine-growers

PROFESSIONAL AND PERSONAL SERVICES
    Barbers and hairdressers
    Boarding and lodging-house keepers
    Clergymen
    Clerks and copyists (not specified)
    Dentists
    Domestic servants
    Hotel and restaurant keepers and employees
    Journalists
    Laborers
    Launderers and laundresses
    Lawyers
    Livery-stable keepers and hostlers
    Musicians and teachers of music
    Officials and employees (civil) of government
    Physicians and surgeons
    Teachers

TRADE AND TRANSPORTATION
     Trade
    Clerks, salesmen, and accountants in stores
    Commercial travelers, hucksters, and peddlers
    In banking and brokerage of money and stocks

Insurance

Saloon keepers and bartenders

Traders and dealers

Transportation

Draymen, hackmen, teamsters, etc.

Officials and employees of express companies

Officials and employees of railroad companies

Officials and employees of street railroad companies

Officials and employees of telegraph companies

Sailors, steamboatmen, stewardesses, canalmen, pilots, and watermen

MANUFACTURING, MINING, AND MECHANICAL INDUSTRIES

Apprentices to trades

Bakers

Blacksmiths

Bookbinders and finishers

Boot and shoe makers

Brewers and maltsters

Brick and stone masons, marble and stone cutters

Brick and tile makers

Cabinet makers and upholsterers

Carpenters and joiners

Carriage, car, and wagon makers

Cigar makers and tobacco workers

Coopers

Cotton-, woolen-, and silk-mill operatives

Employees in manufacturing establishments (not specified)

Engineers and firemen

Fishermen and oystermen

Gold and silver works and jewelers

Harness, saddle, and truck makers

Iron and steel workers

Leather curriers, dressers, finishers, and tanners

Lumbermen, raftsmen, and woodchoppers

Machinists

Manufacturing officials of manufacturing companies

Mill and factory operatives (not specified)

Millers

Miners
Painters and varnishers
Paper-mill operatives
Plumbers and gasfitters
Printers
Saw-mill operatives
Ship carpenters, caulkers, riggers, and smiths
Tailors, dressmakers, and milliners
Tinners
Wheelwrights

NOTE: Agricultural occupations were omitted from the calculation of the occupational segregation index for cities due to the fact that extremely small numbers (often 0) were so engaged in 1870 and 1880 (in Chapters 8 and 9) and even fewer were so engaged by 1890.

B

Design of the Ethnic Collective Action Project

This appendix describes the design of the research that produced the data analyzed in the foregoing chapters. It provides a detailed account of the methods used to code data on events.

The design described here permits analysis at three levels: the national level of urban America, the city level, and the ethnic population level. The national-level analysis tests arguments about the effects of ethnic competition and tight labor markets on the rates of urban ethnic collective action. The data are aggregated from information gathered on the cities listed in Table B.1. Core analyses at the city level use city differences in ethnic population size, rates of migration and immigration, measures of ethnic job segregation and measures of ethnic enclave organization as independent variables. The third level of analysis is the ethnic population in a city. The arguments to be tested at this level pertain to the effects on the rate of ethnic collective action of (a) ethnic immigration and the rate of influx into a city, (b) ethnic segregation (and dispersion) from ethnic occupations, and (c) the presence of ethnic enclaves. Data gathered from relevant U.S. censuses and from ethnic newspapers in sample cities were used to calculate appropriate indicators in this analysis. Arguments about ethnic populations more and less segregated into occupations will be compared across ethnic groups, and across cities.

This project has collected information on all ethnic collective events occurring between January 1, 1877 and December 31, 1914 in the 77 largest cities in the United States. This set of cities represents the largest cities (in terms of population) during this period for which information on ethnicity and labor force composition can be obtained.

The original research design called for collecting information on ethnic events in the largest 80 cities in the United States in 1880 (see Table

TABLE B.1
Set of Cities Studied

01 Albany N.Y.	41 Nashville Tenn.
02 Allegheny Penn.[a]	42 Newark N.J.
03 Atlanta Ga.	43 New Bedford Mass.
04 Baltimore Md.	44 New Haven Conn.
05 Boston Mass.	45 New Orleans Louis.
06 Bridgeport Conn.	46 New York N.Y.[b]
07 Buffalo N.Y.	47 Manhattan N.Y.
08 Cambridge Mass.	48 Brooklyn N.Y.
09 Camden N.J.	49 Queens N.Y.
10 Charleston S.C.	50 Staten Island N.Y.
11 Chicago Ill.	51 Oakland Calif.
12 Cincinnati Ohio	52 Omaha Neb.
13 Cleveland Ohio	53 Paterson N.J.
14 Columbus Ohio	54 Peoria Ill.
15 Dayton Ohio	55 Philadelphia Penn.
16 Denver Colo.	56 Pittsburgh Penn.[a]
17 Des Moines Iowa	57 Portland Oreg.
18 Detroit Mich.	58 Providence R.I.
19 Duluth Minn.	59 Reading Penn.
20 Elizabeth N.J.	60 Richmond Va.
21 Erie Penn.	61 Rochester N.Y.
22 Evansville Ind.	62 St Joseph Misso.
23 Fall River Mass.	63 St Louis Misso.
24 Grand Rapids Mich.	64 St Paul Minn.
25 Harrisburg Penn.	65 Salt Lake City Utah
26 Hartford Conn.	66 San Francisco Calif.
27 Hoboken N.J.	67 San Antonio Tex.
28 Indianapolis Ind.	68 Sacramento Calif.
29 Jersey City N.J.	69 Scranton Penn.
30 Kansas City Kans.	70 Seattle Wash.
31 Kansas City Misso.	71 Somerville Mass.
32 Lawrence Mass.	72 Springfield Mass.
33 Los Angeles Calif.	73 Syracuse N.Y.
34 Louisville Kent.	74 Trenton N.J.
35 Lowell Mass.	75 Troy N.Y.
36 Lynn Mass.	76 Utica N.Y.
37 Manchester N.H.	77 Washington D.C.
38 Memphis Tenn.	78 Wilkes-Barre Penn.
39 Milwaukee Wisc.	79 Wilmington Del.
40 Minneapolis Minn.	80 Worcester Mass.

[a]In 1907, the separate cities of Allegheny and Pittsburgh were merged.
[b]In the city-level analyses, New York City included Manhattan, Queens, Staten Island. Brooklyn was analyzed separately since it constituted a distinct administrative unit over most of this period.

B.1 for initial list of cities). However, the (currently named) boroughs (that were once separate units) of Manhattan, Staten Island, Queens, and the Bronx could not be separated in the data for the entire period. Fortunately, information on labor force participation, racial composition, and events can be distinguished for one of these boroughs, that of Brooklyn. So the city unit of New York actually includes all currently existing boroughs minus that of Brooklyn. We found that we could distinguish events occurring in Kansas City, Missouri from Kansas City, Kansas, so a new city was added to our original list, resulting in a total of 78 cities. However, we merged data on Allegheny and Pittsburgh in most city and national-level analyses because these Allegheny was merged into Pittsburgh in 1907. That brings the final total of city units to 77 cities for which administrative boundaries are stable from 1877–1914.

The number of cities in the city-level analyses depends also on the independent variables used. For the city-level analysis over the earliest period, 1877–89, the number of cities for which information exists is 50. For the period 1890–1914, data are available for 77 cities.

The method of analysis is event-history analysis. This approach uses information on the timing and duration of and between events, as Chapter 4 has described. The actual analyses associates "waiting times," or durations between events at the chosen level of analysis with levels of covariates (for example, change in national immigration) at that level (and perhaps also higher levels). Because of the heavy reliance on event-history analysis, the coding procedures described below pay special attention to the timing and sequencing of events in cities. Other event characteristics of interest include the ethnicity of the groups involved, the instigator (and target) of the collective action, the duration of the event, whether violence is present, whether the event involves formal organizations, numbers of participants, and links (if any) between events.

These characteristics describe the *dependent variable*—events of ethnic collective events occurring in eighty American cities during 1877–1914. This appendix explains the detailed processes for locating information on such ethnic collective events and for gathering and coding the data describing each event.

Definition of an Event. An ethnic collective event is defined as a contentious gathering that has an ethnic character. A contentious gathering is an occasion in which several people come together outside the government or other legitimated channel to make a claim affecting those outside the group taking action (Tilly 1978). A contentious gathering has an ethnic character if those taking action identify themselves as members of an ethnic group, make ethnic claims, or dispute claims made by other ethnic groups.

This project collects information on two types of contentious gatherings involving ethnic groups: conflicts and protests. An ethnic conflict is one in which members of two or more ethnic groups confront each other. An ethnic protest is a contentious gathering in which members of an ethnic population make a claim or articulate a grievance in order to affect public policy or to increase public awareness of the claim or grievance. The distinction between conflicts and protests is elaborated further below.

Thus we collect information on events that are (a) collective, (b) contentious, (c) ethnic, and (d) public. We also add the restriction that (e) the event not be an instance of some recurring organized activity. Therefore we do not include such events as a regularly scheduled meeting of the Black Republican Caucus or a Saint Patrick's Day parade within the scope of ethnic collective events. We also exclude such occurrences as fund-raising events by an established organization like the B'nai B'rith, regularly held meetings, routine lobbying of the government, cultural events and festivals, and action focused on conditions outside the United States (for example, Irish-American fund-raising for anti-British actions in Ireland).

The kinds of events that do fall within the scope of this definition of ethnic collective events include nonroutine civil rights marches, cross-burnings by the Ku Klux Klan, strikes that have ethnic goals rather than (or in addition to) economic goals, ethnic riots, and demonstrations using ethnic symbols and espousing ethnic goals. The events are (1) a white-instigated attack on Blacks in New Orleans (June 1889), (2) and inter-ethnic conflict between Italians and Irish in New York (March 1884), (3) a protest meeting held by Blacks in Philadelphia (May 1886), (4) an event of three days' duration that involved demonstrations against Chinese employment in San Francisco (February 1880), and (5) a protest meeting held by French Canadians in Worcester (March 1883).

Contentious events with an ethnic character can be characterized by the *target or audience* of the actions and the *articulated objectives* or purposes of the actions. Above, we distinguished conflicts and protests. In the case of ethnic protests, it makes sense to focus on the audience of the claims and demands. In many cases, the intended audience is not present for protests. In the case of ethnic conflicts, the contentious gathering usually involves direct confrontation between members of two or more ethnic groups. In the case of ethnic vandalism, however, the ethnic target is generally distinguished symbolically. Thus it makes sense to focus on the target of the conflict, distinguishing protagonist from target whenever possible. In some cases, ethnic conflicts may be instigated to affect some audience in addition to affecting the target group, but this is usually a secondary objective of the action. Therefore, in characterizing protests we identify the audience and the articulated goals and objectives and in characterizing conflicts we identify the targets and objectives. An *ethnic conflict event* is a contentious gathering in which (a) members of one ethnic group (b) confront or attack members of one or more ethnic groups and (c) articulate some ethnic claim or grievance. The last condition excludes from consideration events such as a routine bar fight between members of two ethnic groups.

An *ethnic protest event* is a contentious gathering in which (a) members of an ethnic group (b) state a claim or grievance (c) in order to affect the behavior of some audience such as public officials or the public-at-large. Recall that the definition of contentious gathering excludes regular public actions of ethnic organizations and private meetings.

As subsequent sections make clear, we collect information on numerous dimensions of collective events, including type of event; ethnic identity of protagonist(s), target(s), audience(s); number of participants; date of onset and duration of the event; occurrence of violence; and a full chronology of the event (the sequence of main actions within the event).

Source of Data
The primary source of the ethnic collective events to be used in this analysis is the *New York Times* (*NYT* for short). Events are coded directly from the newspaper account onto a "Narrative Form" (see next section). The information on this narrative sheet is then transferred according to detailed coding rules described below to produce machine-readable files.

We begin with the Index to the *NYT* as an initial source of potential events. The "News" section of the Index is reviewed for each year and the coder compiles a master list of possible events. This list consists of the date and location of the article and the brief heading from the Index. For this time period (1877–1914) the Index is not extensively classified, so the entire Index must be scanned. In addition, a number of key words are checked systematically. These include phrases such as "riot," "gathering," "mass meeting," "protest," the names of the sample cities, and ethnic labels as in "Chinese riot," "Negro convention," "Irish and Italian disturbances."

After this master list is compiled for each year, a coder checks each item in the microfilm copy of the relevant daily edition(s) of the *NYT*. All coding is done from the daily newspaper accounts.

The coder must answer two questions in order to determine whether to include an event. First, did the event actually occur in a city in the sample? This must be verified from the newspaper account since the location of the event and the dateline of the article may differ. Second, does the action meet our criteria of ethnic character? Unless the article specifies which ethnic groups are involved and an ethnic goal, claim or statement, the event is not coded. If the coder can answer both these questions in the affirmative, she/he completes a Narrative Form for the event. One form is filled out for each event. The coding unit is the event—not the article. The reports about an event may not appear in a single article. In this case, the coder follows the event through successive articles, perhaps over several daily editions, in order to assemble all available information and to determine the duration of the action. As a second verification that the entire event has been captured, the coder checks the newspapers of a few days before and a few days after the entry on the master list for any additional reports.

Reports of events have also been cross-checked with accounts in histories of the set of cities insofar as possible. Such checks are useful to learn whether the *NYT* tends to miss certain kinds of events as well as to develop a comprehensive census of events over the period.

Coding Procedures: The Narrative Form
The coder completes all parts of the narrative form unless otherwise noted. The items recorded are as follows.

Title of Article. The coder prints the main title of the article as given in the newspaper account.

Publication Data. This consists of the complete date of the article in numerals and the page number and column location.

Ethnic Group(s) Involved. The coder lists the ethnic groups participating in the event or targeted by the action, using the Ethnic Group Code (Table B.2).

Type of Event. A brief description of the type of event being recorded is entered here. For example, "majority against minority ethnic group."

City. The name of the city in which the event occurred.

Start Date. The date when the event began, entered in numerals. A newspaper account usually gives the date the action began specifically. In the few instances in which it does not, we calculate the starting point from other information. For example, if the only report of a convention is one for the last day, it is common to find a phrase like "on this third day of the Negro convention" from which the first day can be computed.

End Date. The date when the event ended, entered in numerals. A crucial requirement of the event history methodology is that the boundaries delimiting each event are clear. In general, we consider an action as one event if some of the participants or leaders are present; the goal

TABLE B.2
Ethnic Group Codes

01 African-American (Black, Negro)	28 Korean
02 Albanian	29 Latin American (excl. Cuban,
03 American Indian	Mexican, Puerto Rican)
04 Anglo-Canadian (excl. French)	30 Lithuanian
05 Arabic (incl. Lebanese)	31 Mexican-American
06 Armenian	32 Montenegrin
07 Basque	33 Moravian (Czech)
08 Bohemian (incl. Herzegovinian)	34 Norwegian
09 Bulgarian	35 Pacific Islands (incl. Filipino)
10 Caribbean (incl. Cuban,	36 Polish
Puerto Rican)	37 Portuguese
11 Chinese	38 Rumanian
12 Croatian (Yugoslavian)	39 Serbian (Yugoslavian)
(incl. Dalmatian)	40 Silesian (Czech/Polish)
13 Danish	41 Slovakian
14 Dutch (incl. Flemish)	42 Slovenian (Yugoslavian)
15 East Indian (incl. Pakistani)	43 Spanish (Spain)
16 English	44 Swedish
17 Estonian	45 Swiss
18 Finnish	46 Turkish
19 French	47 Ukrainian
20 French Canadian	48 Welsh
21 German (excl. Jewish-German)	49 West Indian
22 Greek	50 Yankee (Undifferentiated Whites)
23 Hebrew (Jewish)	51 Russian (excl. Estonian,
24 Hungarian (Magyar),	Jewish-Russian,
Austro-Hungarian	Lithuanian, Ukrainian)
25 Irish	52 Undifferentiated Foreign-born
26 Italian	53 Undifferentiated Scandinavian
27 Japanese	

or issue is the same; the type of activity is similar *and* the pause between actions is no longer than twenty-four hours. In San Francisco in 1880, for instance, large groups of unemployed white working men met at a place called the Sand Lots for most of three days to protest the employment of Chinese. We code this as one continuous event lasting three days. During the same period, the various leaders of this protest movement held small meetings on different evenings. Each of these gatherings is coded as a "meeting" and considered a separate event since the locations and personnel differ. They also are distinguished from the spontaneous gatherings at the Sand Lots (*NYT* Feb. 26–28, 1880).

Duration of Event in Decimal Days. Length of the event in decimal days. One day equals any twenty-four hour period. Thus if an event starts in the evening of one day and lasts until the evening of the next day, the duration is one day. Only rarely do newspapers accounts give specific information on the time of day an event starts or ends, or on the number of hours it lasts. A number of key words have been used to estimate the length of the event when the duration time is not reported. From these key words the duration is coded in decimal days; one day (one 24-hour period) is coded 1.00. If the account says the event lasted several hours or this length can reasonably be assumed, duration is coded as .25. The following examples from the *NYT* illustrate the typical information and our coding decisions:

- "Public meeting held on the night of June 9" (*NYT* June 10, 1877). Estimate of duration: .25 days.
- "Crowds smashing Chinese houses beginning about 7pm ... A few attacks continued into the early morning" (*NYT* July 27, 1877). Estimate of duration: .50 days.
- "Convention ... met today at 12 o'clock, had a morning and an evening session the next day and adjourned at 9 o'clock" (*NYT* December 14, 1883). Estimate of duration: 1.50 days.
- "For the last week a wholesale eviction has been going on" (starting May 1, 1880) (*NYT* May 6, 1880). Estimate of duration: 5.00 days.

Number of Participants. The actual number of people involved in the event. If the account gives different numbers for different ethnic groups, the coder records the total number. Officials, for example the police, are not counted as participants in ethnic collective events if they are present in their official capacity. Accounts sometimes give the number of participants explicitly in a phrase like "A convention of colored men ... to the number of 400" (*NYT* December 13, 1883) or "3000 Americans assembled" (*NYT* May 5, 1888). If no number is reported in the article, "no number specified" is recorded.

Coder's Estimate of Number of Participants. This is an estimate of size provided by the coder and based on phrases in the account. Keyword phrases such as "mass meeting," "crowd," "large gathering" indicate the size of the event. The following keywords are used: small group (1), medium size group (2), large meeting (3), mob or hundreds of persons (4), thousands (5).

Sequence of Events. The coder summarizes what happened in the event. This summary includes the number of participants or the phrases describing the size of the event, who took part, what they did, and any useful quotations that illustrate the intent and important aspects of the event.

Ethnic Symbols or Goals Mentioned. A list or brief sentence record-ing any specific symbols, epithets, or organizational labels used by par-ticipants in the event.

Use of Violence. The coder enters "yes" or "no" depending on whether any violence or threat of violence was present in the event. If "yes," the coder completes items 1, 2 and 3. If "no," the coder proceeds to the item on target of activity.

1. Repressive forces used. Coder enters "yes" or "no." If "yes," the coder indicates what government agent was involved, for example, the police.
2. Levels or categories of violence. Coder enters the types of violence present—threats, fights, property damage, instruments used, and so forth.
3. Number killed or injured. Coder enters the number of people in-jured and/or the number of people killed, if any. If no one was injured or killed, the coder enters "none."

Target of Activity. The coder enters a phrase describing the target of the ethnic action. This may be an ethnic group, a government official or agency, or a business.

Presumed Origins. The coder makes a brief note of the general ba-sis for the activity. For instance, newspaper articles indicating "long-standing racial animosity in the area" would be reported in this section. Other ethnic events are noted if they are specified as causes of the present conflict or protest. If the article does not contain any information on the origins, the coder enters "none indicated."

Previous Spell of Ethnic Activity Mentioned. This is completed with a brief description of a previous event (for example, "last week there was a similar disturbance"). If no information is given on any previous activity, the coder enters "none mentioned."

Precipitating Act. This refers to an actual occurrence that presum-ably led to the event in question. The precipitating act is not necessarily an ethnic event itself but it may be. An example is a black man being arrested by the police and a protest (if it is based upon claims of racial discrimination) being held that day by the black community. The arrest by the police is the precipitating act; the protest is the first ethnic col-lective action coded. If there is no precipitating act listed in the article, the coder enters "none mentioned." If a precipitating act also meets our criteria for an *ethnic* event, we check to see if it has been coded.

Outcomes. An outcome is a judicial decision, an arrest, a conviction, a change in the law, an action taken by a business, etc. Because the *NYT* was published daily, events unfold chronologically so that proximate outcomes may be more likely than ultimate outcomes to be reported within the time span covering an event. Another way to state this is that follow-ups to any specific event are difficult to find. If no information becomes available on outcomes after checking the Index and the microfilms for that year, the coder leaves this section blank.

Presence of Formal Organization(s). A common hypothesis of the research mobilization theories of social movements is that the presence of organizations leads to further collective action (see Chapter 3). In this section of the narrative, the coder indicates if a formal organization was mentioned as present in the newspaper report. The coder also notes the name of any organization present according to which ethnic group was organized.

The coder marks on the narrative whether the organization mentioned is a new or old (already existing) organization. With this information, we can distinguished ethnic collective events which mark the creation of new organizations from those in which a previously formed organization plays a part.

Detailed Codes for Ethnic Collective Events
This section includes rules for coding only the ethnic collective events for computer analysis.

CITY. City in which event occurred, coded from two-digit code from city list (Table B.1).

ID. Five digit code unique to an event. The leading two digits tell the city in which the event occurred; the three trailing digits tell the order of the event in the city. So, for example, 05003 indicates the third event in city 05 (Boston).

ST. Year in which event occurred, coded as the last three digits, thus 1880 is recorded as 880.

STDY. The day of the year, in calendar days, coded as the date on which the event began (taking care to check dateline and story to see if there is 1 day lag in reporting as there usually is). January 1, 1880 has STDY = 001, first day of the year, February 14 = 045, and December 31 = 365. February 29 is coded the same as February 28th unless there is a need (to code duration, several events occurring around February 28–29th, etc.) to take the gap into account. If events occur on both February 28 and February 29 in the same city in the same year, the last digit is changed to reflect ordering (for example, STDY = 059 for February 28, STDY = 060 for February 29th in same city, same year). This holds only if there is a gap in activity over the two days, indicating that two unique events occurred February 28 and 29th (in a leap year). Example:

If there is activity on February 27, none on February 28 and activity again on February 29, then code February 29 as March 1 to show the gap of February 28.

TOTDUR. Duration—the length of event entered as a five-digit code with two decimal places, indicating the number of days or decimal part of a day which the event lasts. Any one 24-hour period = 1 day, coded 001.00. Counted as one event if the same grievance, target, personnel and goals are present and the action is more or less continuous with gap(s) of less than or equal to 24 hours. Counted event as a new event with a separate duration if there is a gap in action of more than 24 hours. Examples: Riot against Chinese begins Feb. 11, 1880 at about noon, lasts into the evening and continues on into the night. Riot continues with only minor pauses until the evening of Feb. 12, 1880. Duration coded as 1.25 decimal days (noon to noon plus 1/4 day). Protest by Irish begins after work, stops at about midnight, begins again the next morning and continues until that evening when the action stops. Duration coded as 1.00 decimal days (evening of one day until evening of the next day).

NITE. Constancy:
  0. Action is more or less continuous but with some gaps (for example, late night hours). Gaps are less than 24 hours.
  1. Action is relentless lasting well into or throughout the night with few letups. Examples: The riot against the Chinese described above would be coded 1. The protest by the Irish would be coded 0.

EVNT. Type of Event:
  01. Ethnic conflict meeting by members of the dominant ethnic group (for example, Yankees, undifferentiated whites) acting against one or more minority ethnic groups in a meeting with some organizational structure. This may include a name or label such as the "Anti-Chinese League." The meeting is not open to the general public; it can be "behind closed doors."
  02. Minority ethnic group is the target of ethnic conflict by the majority ethnic group or by other ethnic group(s).
  03. Ethnic group engaged in ethnic protest that is spontaneous and confrontational, not institutional (for example, a civil rights demonstration).
  04. Ethnic group (or groups) engaged in ethnic conflict with other ethnic group (or groups).
  05. Two or more minority ethnic groups engaged together in ethnic conflict against majority group.

06. Two or more ethnic populations are the target of ethnic conflict by the majority ethnic group (for example, an antiforeign-born demonstration).

07. Generalized ethnic conflict, undifferentiated riot, or melee of an indeterminate number of groups with an indication of the ethnic character of the riot.

08. Ethnic protest meeting: An ethnic group gathers to make an ethnic claim in a setting with some organizational structure. The people meeting do so as delegates, officers or representatives of organizations to voice a grievance for the ethnic group as a whole.

09. Ethnic group is engaged in ethnic protest that is spontaneous in order to make a claim of an ethnic or racial grievance directly to a Federal, state or local government office, agency or official. Excluded are "petitions" or "editorials" by one or more persons without accompanying collective actions. Included are grievances or protests against police or others officials by minority group.

ENDEV. Type of Event at End of Action: Coded as 0 if situation returns to inactive state. Otherwise an event code for the subsequent event is recorded.

NGRPS. Total Number of Ethnic Groups Involved: Example: If a group of whites (undifferentiated) holds a demonstration protesting Chinese employment the number of groups = 2 (the whites who are acting and the Chinese who are targeted).

GRP1. Ethnic Group Code—Group 1: Two digit code form Ethnic Group Code (Table B.2) for first group involved in event.

GRP2. Ethnic Group Code—Group 2: Two digit code from Ethnic Group Code list for second group involved in event. Coded 00 if no second group present.

GRP3. Ethnic Group Code—Group 3: Two digit code from Ethnic Group Code list for third group involved in event. Coded 00 if no third group present.

GRP4. Ethnic Group Code—Group 4: Two digit code from Ethnic Group Code list for fourth group involved in event. Coded 00 if no fourth group present.

GRP5. Ethnic Group Code—Group 5: Two digit code from Ethnic Group Code list for fifth group involved in event. Coded 00 if no fifth group present.

INT1. Ethnic Group Code—Initiator 1: Two digit code from Ethnic

Group Code list for first group initiating event. Coded 00 if no initiator known.

INT2.   Ethnic Group Code—Initiator 2: Two digit code from Ethnic Group Code list for second group initiating event. Coded 00 if no second initiator known.

NPART. Number of Participants: Actual number of participants as stated in report. Coded 99999 if no number given in newspaper account.

SIZE.   Coder Estimate of Group Size: Single digit code assigned based on keywords in report. (Coded 9 if no information provided and no estimate of size was made):

1. 5–9 participants. Typical keywords: "A committee of wealthy colored people" (*NYT* June 27, 1877); "Placards are being posted" (*NYT* March 9, 1880)

2. 10–99 participants. Typical keywords: "Convention met...attendance was small" (*NYT* August 1, 1877); "A party of ruffians" (*NYT* March 24, 1884)

3. 100–499 participants. Typical keywords: "A mass meeting" (*NYT* August 12, 1881); "Chickering Hall was well filled" (*NYT* February 13, 1883)

4. 500–999 participants. Typical keywords: "A largely attended meeting" (*NYT* December 12, 1885); "Several hundred people" (*NYT* October 19, 1887)

5. 1000 plus participants. Typical keywords: Crowd of "more than a thousand angry negroes" (*NYT* May 25, 1902)

THRT. Threat of Violence: This is coded 1 inclusively with all other violence variables. So if PROP, PERS, TAKE, WEAP, GUN, or KILL is coded as 1, THRT will also be coded 1.

0. No menacing behavior reported.

1. Menacing behavior reported.

PROP. Property Damage:

0. No damage reported.

1. Some damage to property reported.

PERS. Personal Injury:

0. No one reported to be injured.

1. Report of injury.

TAKE. Takeover of Spaces, Persons or Buildings:

0. No.

1. Yes.

WEAP. Use of Blunt Weapons (for example, rocks, clubs):

   0. No.

   1. Yes.

GUN. Use of Lethal Weapons (for example, knife, gun, lynching rope)

   0. No.

   1. Yes.

KILL. Number of Persons Killed: Number of deaths as mentioned in report. Coded 000 if no deaths mentioned.

ORG1. Level of Organizational Structure for Ethnic Group #1: (In most cases this is the instigator)

   0. No organizational structures involved, or none mentioned in report. This means that no proper organizational name (for example, Pipe Fitters' Union, Ebenezer Methodist Church, Anti-Exclusion League) is mentioned in report.

   1. Some minimal organization(s) present for Group 1. That is, there is some leadership hierarchy, membership roles (i.e., church members, union members). Clear evidence that, although an organization or organizational members were present, there is no one identifiable organization that is the primary instigator.

   2. One or more organizations was listed by proper name. There is some indication that onlookers joined in. That is, there is some overlap between organizations mentioned and the participants in the event, but not all Group 1 participants are members of the organization(s).

   3. There is a named organization or convention with Group 1 participants also almost certain to be members of one or more organizations. There is a high degree of overlap between Group 1 participants and some organizational membership such that few other participants or outside agitators are mentioned besides those from known organization(s).

   9. Does not apply: no such ethnic group in event.

ORG2. Level of Organizational Structure present for Ethnic Group #2: Uses codes 0, 1, 2, 3, 9, as above.

ORG3. Level of Organizational Structure present for Ethnic Group #3: Uses codes 0, 1, 2, 3, 9 as above.

ORG4. Level of Organizational Structure present for Ethnic Group #4: Uses codes 0, 1, 2, 3, 9 as above.

ORG5. Level of Organizational Structure present for Ethnic Group #5: Uses codes 0, 1, 2, 3, 9 as above.

HIST1. Organizational History for Ethnic Group #1: If more than 1 organization present, major or primary organization behind the event is considered.

 0. None mentioned.

 1. New organization formed, delegates or convention cited.

 2. Renamed organization, new formation of formerly existing organization.

 3. Existence of older, formerly established (if only for 1 day) organization. Organizational existence taken for granted in report.

 9. Does not apply.

HIST2. Organizational History for Ethnic Group #2: Uses codes 0, 1, 2, 3, 9 as above.

AUD. Outside Audience of Action:

 0. Audience unspecified or considered public at large.

 1. Specific other ethnic group mentioned as audience.

 2. Specific organization or part of organizational hierarchy mentioned as audience (but not just an ethnic group; not government or school board).

 3. Government agency, official, department, school board.

REACT. What type of action is event currently being coded in response to?

 0. Rural event. Real event but occurred in rural area, small town or fringe area—outside of a city.

 1. Event in a city, but not in a city on list.

 2. Response to some action(s) but not an identifiable "event." For example, generalized bad feelings, anti-Chinese atmosphere, ill-treatment of blacks in South, fight between black and white grocery store owners or other similar two-person action.

 3. Precipitating event also coded—these are two-stage events.

 9. Not in response to any specific or known action(s).

OVER5. Are there more than 5 events linked to the event being coded?

 0. No.

 1. Yes.

References

Aalen, O. O. 1978. "Nonparametric Inference for a Family of Counting Processes." *Annals of Statistics* 6: 701–26.

Alba, R. D. 1988. *Ethnicity and Race in the U.S.A.* New York: Routledge, Chapman & Hall, Inc.

Aldrich, H., and R. Waldinger. 1990. "Ethnicity and Entrepreneurship." *Annual Review of Sociology* 16: 111–35.

Aldrich, H., J. Cater, T. Jones, D. McEvoy, and P. Velleman, 1985. "The Protected Market Hypothesis." *Social Forces* 63: 996–1009.

Allardt, E. 1979. *Implications of the Ethnic Revival in Modern Industrial Society: A Comparative Study of the Linguistic Minorities in Western Europe.* Helsinki: Commentationes Scientatium Socialium.

Amburgey, T. L. 1986. "Multivariate Point Process Models in Social Research." *Social Science Research* 15: 190–207.

Amburgey, T. L. , and G. R. Carroll. 1984. "Time Series Models for Event Counts." *Social Science Research* 13: 38–54.

American Federation of Labor. 1896–1940. *The American Federationist.* Washington, D.C.

Aminzade, R. 1984. "Capitalist Industrialization and Patterns of Industrial Protest: A Comparative Urban Study of Nineteenth-Century France." *American Sociological Review* 49: 437–53.

Archdeacon, T. J. 1983. *Becoming American: An Ethnic History.* New York: Free Press.

Ashenfelter, O., and G. E. Johnson. 1969. "Bargaining Theory, Trade Unions, and Industrial Strike Activity." *American Economic Review* 59: 34–49.

Ayer, N. W. Various years. *American Newspaper Directory Annual.* Philadelphia: Ayer Press.

Banton, M. 1983. *Racial and Ethnic Competition.* New York: Cambridge University Press.

Barth, F. 1956. "Ecologic Relationships of Ethnic Groups in Swat, North Pakistan," *American Anthropologist* 58: 1079–89.

Barth, F. (editor) 1969. *Ethnic Groups and Boundaries.* Boston: Little, Brown.

Barton, J. 1975. *Peasants and Strangers: Italians, Roumanians, and Slovaks in an American City, 1890–1950.* Cambridge, Mass.: Harvard University Press.

Becker, G. S. 1973. *A Theory of Discrimination.* Chicago: University of Chicago Press.

Bell, W. 1954. "A Probability Model of the Measurement of Ecological Segregation." *Social Forces* 32: 357–64.

Bennett, D. H. 1988. *The Party of Fear: From Nativist Movements to the New Right in American History.* Chapel Hill: University of North Carolina Press.

Beck, E. M. , and S. E. Tolnay. 1990. "The Killing Fields of the Deep South: The Market for Cotton and the Lynching of Blacks, 1882–1930." *American Sociological Review* 55: 526–39.

Berk, R. A. 1983. "An Introduction to Sample Selection Bias in Sociological Data." *American Sociological Review* 48: 386–99.

Berk, R. A., and H. Aldrich. 1972. "Patterns of Vandalism During Civil Disorders as an Indicator of Selection of Targets." *American Sociological Review* 37: 533–47.

Blalock, H. M., Jr. 1957. "Percent Non-White and Discrimination in the South." *American Sociological Review* 22: 677–82.

Blalock, H. M., Jr. 1967. *Toward a Theory of Minority-Group Relations.* New York: Wiley.

Blassingame, J. W. 1973. *Black New Orleans, 1860–1880.* Chicago: University of Chicago Press.

Blau, P. M., and J. Schwartz. 1984. *Crosscutting Social Circles.* New York: Academic Press.

Blauner, R. 1971. *Racial Oppression in America.* New York: Harper and Row.

Blossfeld, H. P., A. Hamerle, and K. U. Mayer. 1988. *Event History Analysis: Statistical Theory and Application in Economics and the Social Sciences.* Hillsdale, N.J.: Erlbaum.

Bodnar, J., R. Simon, and M. P. Weber. 1982. *Lives of Their Own: Blacks, Italians and Poles in Pittsburgh, 1900–1960.* Urbana, Ill.: University of Illinois Press.

Bonacich, E. 1972. "A Theory of Ethnic Antagonism: The Split Labor Market." *American Sociological Review* 37: 547–59.

Bonacich, E. 1973. "A Theory of Middleman Minorities." *American Sociological Review* 38: 583–94.

Bonacich, E. 1976. "Advanced Capitalism and Black/White Relations." *American Sociological Review* 41: 31–51.

Bonacich, E., and J. Modell. 1981. *The Economic Basis of Ethnic Solidarity: Small Business in the Japanese American Community.* Berkeley and Los Angeles: University of California Press.

Bornschier, V., and C. Chase-Dunn. 1985. *Transnational Corporations and Underdevelopment*. New York: Praeger.

Boskin, J. 1976. *Urban Racial Violence in the Twentieth Century*. Beverly Hills: Glencoe Press.

Boswell, T. 1986. "A Split Labor Market Analysis of Discrimination Against Chinese Immigrants, 1850–1882." *American Sociological Review* 51: 352–71.

Botz, G. 1976. *Gerwalt in der Politik. Attentate, Zussamenstoße, Putschversuche, Unruhen in Österreich 1918 bis 1934*. Munich: Wilhelm-Fink.

Breton, R. 1964. "Institutional Completeness of Ethnic Communities and the Personal Relations of Immigrants." *American Journal of Sociology* 84: 293–318.

Britt, D. W., and O. Galle. 1974. "Structural Antecedents of the Shape of Strikes: A Comparative Analysis." *American Sociological Review* 39: 642–51.

Brody, D. 1960. *Steelworkers in America*. Cambridge, Mass.: Harvard University Press.

Bruce, R. V. 1959. *1877: Year of Violence*. Indianapolis: Bobbs-Merrill.

Bürklin, W. P. 1987. "Governing Left Parties Frustrating the Radical Nonestablishment Left: The Rise and Inevitable Decline of the Greens." *European Sociological Review* 3: 109–26.

Burstein, P. 1985. *Discrimination, Jobs, and Politics: The Struggle for Equal Employment Opportunity in the United States Since the New Deal*. Chicago: University of Chicago Press.

Cafferty, P., B. R. Chiswick, A. M. Greeley, and T. Sullivan 1983. *The Dilemma of American Immigration: Beyond the Golden Door*. New Brunswick, N.J.: Transaction Press.

Cameron, A. C., and P. K. Trivedi. 1986. "Econometric Models Based on Count Data: Comparisons and Applications of Some Estimators and Tests." *Journal of Applied Econometrics* 1: 29–53.

Carroll, G. R. 1987. *Publish and Perish: The Organizational Ecology of Newspaper Industries*. Greenwich, Conn.: JAI Press.

Carroll, G. R., and J. Delacroix. 1982. "Organizational Mortality in the Newspaper Industries of Argentina and Ireland: An Ecological Approach," *Administrative Science Quarterly* 27: 169–98.

Carroll, G. R., and M. T. Hannan. 1989. "Density Dependence in the Evolution of Newspaper Populations," *American Sociological Review* 54: 524–41.

Carroll, G. R., and Y. P. Huo. 1986. "Organizational Task and Institutional Environments in Ecological Perspective: Findings From the Local Newspaper Industry." *American Journal of Sociology* 91: 838–73.

Carroll, G. R., and Y. P. Huo. 1988. "Organizational and Electoral Paradoxes of the Knights of Labor." Pp. 175–94 in *Ecological Models of Organizations*, edited by G. R. Carroll. Cambridge, Mass.: Ballinger.

Chalmers, D. M. 1965. *Hooded Americanism: The First Century of the Ku Klux Klan, 1865–1965*. Garden City, N.Y.: Doubleday.

Chermesh, R. 1982. "Press Criteria for Strike Reporting: Counting or Selective Presentation." *Social Science Research* 11: 88–101.

Chirot, D., and C. Ragin. 1975. "The Market, Tradition and Peasant Rebellion: The Case of Romania in 1907." *American Sociological Review* 40: 428–44.

Coleman, J. S. 1981. *Longitudinal Data Analysis.* New York: Basic.

Coleman, J. S., S. D. Kelly, and J. A. Moore. 1982. "Achievement and Segregation in Secondary Schools." *Sociology of Education* 55: 162–82.

Commons, J. R. 1918. *History of Labor in the United States*, Volume II. New York: Macmillan.

Corbin, D. A. 1981. *Life, Work, and Rebellion in the Coal Fields: The Southern West Virginia Miners, 1880–1922.* Urbana: University of Illinois Press.

Corzine, J., J. Creech, and L. Huff-Corzine. 1983. "Black Concentration and Lynchings in the South: Testing Blalock's Power-threat Hypothesis." *Social Forces* 61: 774–96.

Corzine, J., L. Huff-Corzine, and J. C. Creech. 1988. "The Tenant Labor Market and Lynching in the South: A Test of the Split Labor Market Theory." *Sociological Inquiry* 58: 261–78.

Coser, L. 1956. *The Functions of Social Conflict.* New York: The Free Press.

Cox, D. R. 1972. "Regression Models and Lifetables." *Journal of the Royal Statistical Society* 34 Series B: 187–220.

Cox, D. R. 1975. "Partial Likelihood." *Biometrika* 62: 269–76.

Cox, D. R., and V. Isham. 1980. *Point Processes.* London: Chapman and Hall.

Cox, D. R., and D. Oakes. 1984. *Analysis of Survival Data.* London: Chapman and Hall.

Danzger, M. H. 1975. "Validating Conflict Data." *American Sociological Review* 40: 570–84.

David, P., and P. Solar. 1977. "A Bicentenary Contribution to the History of the Cost of Living in America." *Research in Economic History* 2: 1–80.

Davis, M. 1980. "Why the U.S. Working Class is Different." *New Left Review* (Oct): 5–44.

Delacroix, J., and G. R. Carroll. 1983. "Organizational Foundings: An Ecological Study of the Newspaper Industries of Argentina and Ireland," *Administrative Science Quarterly* 28: 274–91.

Delacroix, J., and C. Ragin. 1981. "Structural Blockage: A Cross-National Study of Economic Dependency, State Efficacy, and Underdevelopment." *American Journal of Sociology* 86: 1311–47.

Della Porta, D., and S. Tarrow. 1986. "Unwanted Children: Political Violence and the Cycle of Protest in Italy, 1966–1973." *European Journal of Political Research* 14: 607–32.

Deutsch, K. 1966. *Nationalism and Social Communication.* Cambridge, Mass.: MIT Press.

Dinnerstein, L., and F. C. Jaher. 1970. *The Aliens.* New York: Meredith.

Doreian, P. 1981. "Estimating Linear Models with Spatially Distributed

Data." Pp. 359–88 in *Sociological Methodology*, edited by S. Leinhardt. San Francisco: Jossey-Bass.

Easterlin, R. A., D. Ward, W. S. Bernard, and R. Ueda. 1982. *Immigration: Dimensions of Ethnicity.* Cambridge, Mass.: Harvard University Press.

Edwards, P. K. 1981. *Strikes in the United States, 1881–1974.* New York: St. Martin's Press.

Ehrlich, R. 1974. "Immigrant Strikebreaking Activity: A Sampling of Opinion Expressed in the National Labor Tribune." *Industrial and Labor Relations Review* 28: 529–42.

Eisinger, P. K. 1973. "The Conditions of Protest Behavior in American Cities." *American Political Science Review* 67: 11–28.

Eisenstadt, S. N., and S. Rokkan (editors) 1973. *Building States and Nations*, vol. 2. Beverly Hills, Calif.: Sage.

Enloe, C. 1980. *Ethnic Soldiers.* Athens, Georgia: University of Georgia Press.

Farley, R. J. 1977. "Residential Segregation in Urbanized Areas of the United States in 1970." *Demography* 14: 497–518.

Farley, R. J. 1984. *Blacks and Whites: Narrowing the Gap?* Cambridge, Mass.: Harvard University Press.

Farley, R. J., and W. R. Allen. 1989. *The Color Line and the Quality of Life in America.* New York: Oxford Press.

Feierabend, I. K., and R. L. Feierabend. 1966. "Aggressive Behavior Within Polities, 1948–1962." *Journal of Conflict Resolution* 10: 249–71.

Feierabend, I. K., R. L. Feierabend, and T. R. Gurr (editors) 1972. *Anger, Violence, Politics: Theories and Research.* Englewood Cliffs, N.J.: Prentice Hall.

Fink, L. (editor) 1977. *Labor Unions.* Westport, Conn.: Greenwood Press.

Fink, L. 1983. *Workingman's Democracy.* Urbana, Ill.: University of Illinois Press.

Fligstein, N. 1981. *Going North: Migration of Blacks and Whites From the South, 1900–1950.* New York: Academic Press.

Foner, P. 1947. *History of the Labor Movement in the United States*, vol. 1. New York: International Publishers.

Foner, P. 1964. *The Policies and Practices of the American Federation of Labor 1900–1909.* New York: International Publishers.

Foner, P. 1982. *Organized Labor & the Black Worker: 1619–1981.* New York: International Publishers.

Flanigan, W. H., and E. Fogelman. 1970. "Patterns of Political Violence in Comparative Perspective." *Comparative Politics* 3: 1–20.

Franzosi, R. 1987. "The Press as a Source of Socio-Historical Data: Issues in the Methodology of Data Collection from Newspapers." *Historical Methods* 20: 5–16.

Franzosi, R. 1989. "From Words to Numbers: A Generalized and Linguistics-Based Coding Procedure for Collecting Textual Data." In *Sociological Methodology 1989*, edited by C. Clogg. San Francisco: Jossey-Bass.

Freeman, J., and M. T. Hannan. 1989. "Technical Change, Inertia, and Organizational Failure." Technical Report 89-5, Department of Sociology, Cornell University. Ithaca, N.Y. (Presented at the meetings of the European Group on Organizational Studies, Berlin, July 1989).

Galtung, J. 1986. "The Green Movement: A Socio-Historical Exploration." *International Sociology* 1: 75–90.

Gamson, W. A. 1975. *The Strategy of Social Protest*. Homewood, Ill.: Dorsey Press.

Garis, R. L. 1927. *Immigration Restriction: A Study of the Opposition to and Regulation of Immigration into the United States*. New York: MacMillan.

Gause, G. F. 1934. *The Struggle for Existence*. Baltimore: Williams and Wilkins.

Gellner, E. 1969. *Thought and Change*. Chicago: University of Chicago Press.

Gellner, E. 1983. *Nations and Nationalism*. Ithaca, N.Y.: Cornell University Press.

Glazer, N., and D. P. Moynihan (editors) 1975. *Ethnicity: Theory and Experience*. Cambridge, Mass.: Harvard University Press.

Goldstone, J. A. 1980. "The Weakness of Organization: A New Look at Gamson's 'The Strategy of Social Protest.' " *American Journal of Sociology* 85: 1017–60.

Goldstone, J. A. 1986. "State Breakdown in the English Revolution: A New Synthesis." *American Journal of Sociology* 92: 257–322.

Gompers, S. 1925. *Seventy Years of Life and Labor*. Edited by Nick Salvatore. Ithaca, N.Y.: Industrial Labor Relations Press [1984].

Goodwyn, L. 1978. *The Populist Movement: A Short History of the Agrarian Revolt in America*. New York: Oxford University Press.

Gordon, D. M., R. Edwards, and M. Reich. 1982. *Segmented Work, Divided Workers*. New York: Cambridge University Press.

Gordon, M. 1964. *Assimilation in American Life*. New York: Oxford University Press.

Griffin, J. I. 1939. *Strikes: A Study in Quantitative Economics*. New York: Columbia University Press.

Griffin, L. J., M. E. Wallace, and B. A. Rubin. 1986. "Capitalistic Resistance to the Organization of Labor Before the New Deal: Why? How? Success?" *American Sociological Review* 51: 147–67.

Grimshaw, A. D. 1969. *Racial Violence in the United States*. Chicago: Aldine Publishing.

Guest, A., and J. Weed. 1976. "Ethnic Residential Segregation: Patterns of Change." *American Journal of Sociology* 81: 1088–111.

Gurr, T. R. 1970. *Why Men Rebel*. Princeton, N.J.: Princeton University Press.

Gurr, T. R. 1972. "The Calculus of Civil Conflict." *Journal of Social Issues: Special Issue on Collective Violence and Civil Conflict* 28: 27–47.

Gutman, H. G., and D. H. Bell (editors). 1987. *The New England Working Class and the New Labor History*. Urbana, Ill.: University of Illinois Press.

Hahn, S. 1983. *The Roots of Southern Populism*. New York: Oxford University Press.

Hamblin, R., R. B. Jacobsen, and J. L. L. Miller. 1973. *A Mathematical Theory of Social Change.* New York: Wiley.

Hannan, M. T. 1979. "The Dynamics of Ethnic Boundaries in Modern States." Pp. 253–75 in *National Development and the World System.* Edited by J. Meyer and M. T. Hannan. Chicago: University of Chicago Press.

Hannan, M. T. 1986. "A Model of Competitive and Institutional Processes in Organizational Ecology." *Technical Report* 86-13. Department of Sociology, Cornell University, Ithaca, New York.

Hannan, M. T. 1989a "Macrosociological Applications of Event-History Analysis: State Transitions and Event Recurrences." *Quantity and Quality* 23: 351–83.

Hannan, M. T. 1989b. "Competitive and Institutional Processes in Organizational Ecology." Pp. 388–402 in *Sociological Theories in Progress: New Formulations*, edited by Joseph Berger, Morris Zelditch, Jr., and Bo Andersen. Newbury Park, Calif.: Sage.

Hannan, M. T., and G. R. Carroll. 1981. "Dynamics of Formal Political Structure." *American Sociological Review* 46: 19–35.

Hannan, M. T., and G. R. Carroll. 1991. *Dynamics of Organizational Populations.* New York: Oxford University Press.

Hannan, M. T., and J. Freeman. 1987. "The Ecology of Organizational Founding: American Labor Unions, 1836–1985." *American Journal of Sociology* 92: 1210–13.

Hannan, M. T., and J. Freeman. 1988. "The Ecology of Organizational Mortality: American Labor Unions, 1836–1985." *American Journal of Sociology* 94: 25–52.

Hannan, M. T., and J. Freeman. 1989. *Organizational Ecology.* Cambridge, Mass.: Harvard University Press.

Hannan, M. T., and N. B. Tuma. 1979. "Methods for Temporal Analysis." *Annual Review of Sociology* 5: 303–28.

Hannan, M. T., and A. A. Young. 1977. "Estimation of Panel Models: Results on Pooling Cross Sections and Time Series." Pp. 52–83 in *Sociological Methodology 1977*, edited by D. Heise. San Francisco: Jossey-Bass.

Hanushek, E. A., and J. E. Jackson. 1977. *Statistical Methods for Social Scientists.* New York: Academic Press.

Hareven, T. 1982. *Family Time and Industrial Time.* Cambridge, Mass.: Harvard University Press.

Hawley, A. H. 1945. "Dispersion Versus Segregation: Apropos of a Solution of Race Problems. *Papers of The Michigan Academy of Science, Arts and Letters.* Ann Arbor, Mich.: University of Michigan Press.

Hawley, A. H. 1950. *Human Ecology.* New York: Ronald Press.

Heckman, J. J. 1979. "Sample Selection Bias as Specification Error." *Econometrica* 45: 153–61.

Hechter, M. 1975. *Internal Colonialism.* Berkeley, Calif.: University of California Press.

Hechter, M. 1978. "Group Formation and the Cultural Division of Labor." *American Journal of Sociology* 84: 293–318.

Hechter, M. 1984. "A Theory of Group Solidarity." Pp. 16–57 in *The Microfoundations of Macrosociology*, edited by M. Hechter. Philadelphia: Temple University Press.

Hechter, M. 1987. *Principles of Group Solidarity*. Berkeley, Calif.: University of California Press.

Hechter, M., D. Friedman, and M. Appelbaum. 1982. "A Theory of Ethnic Collective Action." *International Migration Review* 16: 412–34.

Hechter, M., and M. Levi. 1979. "The Comparative Analysis of Ethno-Regional Movements." *Ethnic and Racial Studies* 2: 26–74.

Hepworth, J. T., and S. G. West. 1988. "Lynching and the Economy: A Time-Series Reanalysis of Hovland and Sears." *Journal of Personality and Social Psychology*. 55: 239–47.

Hershberg, T. (editor). 1981. *Philadelphia: Work, Space, Family, and Group Experience*. New York: Oxford University Press.

Hibbs, D. A., Jr. 1973. *Mass Political Violence*. New York: Wiley.

Hibbs, D. A. 1976. "Industrial Conflict in Advanced Industrial Societies." *American Political Science Review* 70: 1033–58.

Hibbs, D. A. 1978. "On the Political Economy of Long-Run Trends in Strike Activity." *British Journal of Political Science* 8: 153–75.

Higgs, R. 1977. *Competition and Coercion: Blacks in the American Economy, 1865–1914*. New York: Cambridge University Press.

Higham, J. 1955. *Strangers in the Land: Patterns of American Nativism: 1860–1925*. New Brunswick, N.J.: Rutgers University Press.

Hirschman, C. 1983. "America's Melting Pot Reconsidered." *Annual Review of Sociology* 9: 397–423.

Hofstader, R. 1955. *The Age of Reform*. New York: Knopf.

Horn, N., and C. Tilly 1986. "Catalogs of Contention in Britain, 1758–1834." New School for Social Research Working Paper Series, No. 32. New York.

Horowitz, D. L. 1985. *Ethnic Groups in Conflict*. Berkeley, Calif.: University of California Press.

Hovland, C. I., and R. Sears. 1940. "Minor Studies of Aggression: Correlation of Lynchings with Economic Indices." *Journal of Psychology* (Winter): 301–10.

Huntington, S. P. 1968. *Political Order in Changing Societies*. New Haven: Yale University Press.

Hutchinson, G. E. 1957. "Homage to Santa Rosalia, or Why Are There So Many Kinds of Animals." *American Naturalist* 93: 145–59.

Ichioka, Y. 1988. *The Issei: The World of the First Generation of Japanese Immigrants, 1885–1924*. New York: Free Press.

Inglehart, R. 1977. *The Silent Revolution: Changing Values and Political Styles Among Western Publics*. Princeton, N.J.: Princeton University Press.

Inverarity, J. 1976. "Populism and Lynching in Louisiana, 1889–1896: A Test of Erikson's Theory of the Relationship Between Boundary Crises and Justice." *American Sociological Review* 41: 262–80.

Jackson, K. T. 1967. *The Ku Klux Klan in the Cities, 1915–1930*. New York: Oxford University Press.

James, D. R. 1988. "The Transformation of the Southern Racial State: Class and Race Determinants of Local-State Structures." *American Sociological Review* 53: 191–208.

Jeffries, V., R. H. Turner, and R. T. Morris. 1971. "The Public Perception of the Watts Riot as Social Protest." *American Sociological Review* 36: 443–51.

Jenkins, J. C. 1982. "Why Do Peasants Rebel? Structural and Historical Theories of Modern Peasant Rebellions." *American Journal of Sociology* 88: 487–515.

Jenkins, J. C. 1983. "Resource Mobilization Theory and the Study of Social Movements." *Annual Review of Sociology* 9: 527–53.

Jenkins, J. C., and C. M. Eckert. 1986. "Channeling Black Insurgency: Elite Patronage and Professional Social Movement Organizations in the Development of the Black Movement." *American Sociological Review* 51: 812–29.

Jenkins, J. C., and A. Kposowa. 1990. "Explaining Military Corps D'Etat: Black Africa, 1957–1984." *American Sociological Review* 55: 861–75.

Jenkins, J. C., and C. Perrow. 1977. "Insurgency of the Powerless: Farm Workers Movements (1946–1972)." *American Sociological Review* 42: 249–68.

Johnson, C. 1966. *Revolutionary Change*. Boston: Little, Brown.

Johnson, P. B., D. O. Sears, and J. B. McConahay. 1971. "Black Invisibility, the Press, and the Los Angeles Riot." *American Journal of Sociology* 76: 698–721.

Judge, G. C., W. E. Griffiths, R. C. Hill, H. Lutkepohl, and T. Chao Lee. 1985. *The Theory and Practice of Econometrics*. Second edition. New York: Wiley.

Kalbfleisch, J. D., and R. L. Prentice. 1980. *The Statistical Analysis of Failure Time Data*. New York: Wiley.

Kaufman, B. 1982. "The Determinants of Strikes in the United States, 1900–1977." *Industrial and Labor Relations Review* 35: 473–90.

Keely, C. B. 1979. *U.S. Immigration: A Policy Analysis*. New York: Population Council.

Kelly, W. R., and L. Isaac. 1984. "The Rise and Fall of Urban Racial Violence in the U.S.: 1948–1979." *Research in Social Movements, Conflict, and Change* 7: 203–33.

Kielbowicz, R. B., and C. Schere. 1986. "The Role of the Press in the Dynamics of Social Movements." *Research in Social Movements, Conflicts and Change* 9: 71–96.

Klandermans, B. 1984. "Mobilization and Participation: Social Psychological Expansions of Resource Mobilization Theory." *American Sociological Review* 49: 583–600.

Kousser, J. M. 1974. *The Shaping of Southern Politics: Suffrage Restriction and the Establishment of the One-Party South.* New Haven, Conn.: Yale University Press.

Kriesi, H. 1988. "Local Mobilization for the Peoples' Petition of the Dutch Peace Movement," Pp. 41–82 in *From Structure to Action: Comparing Movement Participation Across Cultures,* edited by B. Klandermans, H. Kriesi, and S. Tarrow. Greenwich, Conn.: JAI Press.

Ladner, R. A., B. J. Schwartz, S. J. Roker, and L. S. Titterand. 1981. "The Miami Riots of 1980: Antecedent Conditions, Community Responses and Participant Characteristics." *Research in Social Movements, Conflicts and Change* 4: 171–214.

Lawless, J. F. 1982. *Statistical Models and Methods for Lifetime Data.* New York: Wiley.

Lauwagie, B. 1979. "Ethnic Boundaries in Modern States: Romano-Lil Revisited." *American Journal of Sociology.* 85: 310–37.

Levins, R. 1968. *Evolution in Changing Environments.* Princeton, N.J.: Princeton University Press.

Leifer, E. 1981. "Competing Models of Political Mobilization: The Role of Ethnic Ties." *American Journal of Sociology* 87: 23–47.

Lieberson, S. 1961. "A Societal Theory of Race Relations." *American Sociological Review* 26: 902–08.

Lieberson, S. 1969. "Measuring Population Diversity." *American Sociological Review* 34: 850–62.

Lieberson, S. 1979. "An Asymmetrical Approach to Segregation," Pp. 61–82 in *Ethnic Segregation in Cities.* Edited by C. Peach, V. Robinson, and S. Smith. London: Croom Helm.

Lieberson, S. 1980. *A Piece of the Pie: Blacks and White Immigrants Since 1880.* Berkeley, Calif.: University of California Press.

Lieberson S., and D. Carter. 1982. "Temporal Changes and Urban Differences in Residential Segregation: A Reconsideration." *American Journal of Sociology* 88: 296–310.

Lieberson, S., and A. R. Silverman. 1965. "The Precipitants and Underlying Conditions of Race Riots." *American Sociological Review* 30: 887–98.

Lieberson, S., and M. Waters. 1988. *From Many Strands.* New York: Russell Sage Foundation.

Liebman, R., J. R. Sutton, and R. Wuthnow. 1988. "Exploring the Social Sources of Denominationalism: Schisms in American Protestant Denominations, 1890–1980." *American Sociological Review* 53: 343–52. .

Light, I. 1972. *Ethnic Enterprises in America.* Berkeley, Calif.: University of California Press.

Light, I., and E. Bonacich. 1989. *Ethnic Entrepreneurs.* Berkeley: University of California Press.

Lincoln, J. R. 1978. "Community Structure and Industrial Conflict: An Analysis of Strike Activity in SMSAs." *American Sociological Review* 43: 199–220.

Linz, J. 1973. "Early State Building and Late Peripheral Nationalisms: The

Case of Spain." Pp. 32–116 in *Building States and Nations*, vol. 2, edited by S. N. Eisenstadt and S. Rokkan. Beverly Hills, Calif.: Sage.

Lipset, S. M., and S. Rokkan. 1967. "Cleavage Structures, Party Systems, and Voter Alignments." Pp. 1–62 in *Party Systems and Voter Alignments*, edited by S. M. Lipset and S. Rokkan. New York: The Free Press.

Lodhi A. Q., and C. Tilly. 1973. "Urbanization, Criminality and Collective Violence in Nineteenth Century France." *American Journal of Sociology* 79: 296–318.

Loewen, J. W. 1988. *The Mississippi Chinese: Between Black and White*. Second edition. Prospect Heights, Ill.: Waveland Press.

Lowi, T. 1971. *The Politics of Disorder*. New York: Basic Books.

Markoff, J. 1985. "The Social Geography of Rural Revolt at the Beginning of the French Revolution." *American Sociological Review* 50: 761–81.

Markoff, J. 1986. "Literacy and Revolt: Some Empirical Notes on 1789 in France." *American Journal of Sociology* 92: 323–49.

Markoff, J. 1988. "Peasant Grievances and Peasant Insurrection: France in 1789." Presented at the annual meetings of the American Sociological Association, Atlanta.

Markoff, J., and G. Shapiro. 1973. "The Linkage of Data Describing Overlapping Geographical Units." *Historical Methods Newsletter* 7: 34–45.

Marwell, G., and P. Oliver. 1984. "Collective Action Theory and Social Movements Research." *Research in Social Movements, Conflicts and Change* 7: 1–27.

Marx, G. T., and J. T. Wood. 1975. "Strands of Theory and Research in Collective Behavior." *Annual Review of Sociology* 1: 363–428.

Massey, D. 1978. "On the Measurement of Segregation as a Random Variable." *American Sociological Review* 43: 587–90.

Massey, D., and L. Blakeslee. 1983. "An Ecological Perspective on Assimilation and Stratification." Presented at the annual meetings of the American Sociological Association, Detroit.

Massey, D., and N. Denton. 1989. "Hypersegregation in U.S. Metropolitan Areas: Black and Hispanic Segregation Along Five Dimensions." *Demography* 26: 373–92.

McAdam, D. 1982. *Political Process and the Development of Black Insurgency*. Chicago: University of Chicago Press.

McAdam, D. 1983. "Tactical Innovation and the Pace of Insurgency." *American Sociological Review* 48: 735–54.

McAdam, D. 1986. "Recruitment to High-Risk Activism: The Case of Freedom Summer." *American Journal of Sociology* 92: 64–90.

McAdam, D., J. D. McCarthy, and M. Zald. 1988. "Social Movements." Pp. 695–738 in *Handbook of Sociology*, edited by N. J. Smelser. Newbury Park, Calif.: Sage.

McCarthy, J. D. 1987. "Pro-life and Pro-choice Mobilization: Infrastructure Deficits and New Technologies," Pp. 49–66 in *Social Movements in an Organizational Society*, edited by M. Zald and J. D. McCarthy. New Brunswick, N.J.: Transaction Books.

McCarthy, J. D., M. Wolfson, D. P. Baker, and E. Mosakowski. 1988. "The Founding of Social Movement Organizations: Local Citizens' Groups Opposing Drunken Driving." Pp. 71–84 in *Ecological Models of Organizations*, edited by G. R. Carroll. Cambridge, Mass.: Ballinger.

McCarthy, J. D., and M. Zald. 1977. "Resource Mobilization and Social Movements: A Partial Theory." *American Journal of Sociology* 82: 1212–41.

McPhail, C. 1971. "Civil Disorder Participation: A Critical Examination of Recent Research." *American Sociological Review* 36: 1058–73.

McPhail, C., and R. Wohlstein. 1983. "Individual and Collective Behaviors Within Gatherings, Demonstrations, and Riots. *Annual Review of Sociology* 9: 579–610.

McPherson, M. J. 1983. "An Ecology of Affiliation," *American Sociological Review* 48: 519–35.

Melucci, A. 1988. "Getting Involved: Identity and Mobilization in Social Movements." In *From Structure to Action: Comparing Movement Participation Across Cultures*, edited by B. Klandermans, H. Kreisi, and S. Tarrow. Greenwich, Conn.: JAI Press.

Meyer, J. W., and M. T. Hannan (editors) 1979. *National Development and the World System*. Chicago: University of Chicago Press.

Mink, G. 1986. *Old Labor and New Immigrants in American Political Development*. Ithaca, N.Y.: Cornell University Press.

Mintz, A. 1946. "A Re-examination of Correlations Between Lynchings and Economic Indicators." *Journal of Abnormal and Social Psychology* 41: 154–60.

Montgomery, D. 1979. *Worker's Control in America*. New York: Cambridge University Press.

Morgan, W. R., and T. N. Clark. 1973. "The Causes of Racial Disorders: A Grievance-Level Explanation." *American Sociological Review* 38: 611–24.

Morris, A. D. 1981. "Black Southern Student Sit-In Movement: An Analysis of Internal Organization." *American Sociological Review* 46: 744–67.

Morris, A. D. 1984. *The Origins of the Civil-Rights Movement: Black Communities Organizing for Change*. New York: Free Press.

Muller, E. N. 1985. "Income Inequality, Regime Repressiveness, and Political Violence." *American Sociological Review* 50: 47–61.

Nagel, B. 1986. "Gypsies in the United States and Great Britain: Ethnic Boundaries and Political Mobilization." Pp. 69–90 in S. Olzak and J. Nagel (eds.) *Competitive Ethnic Relations*. New York: Academic Press.

Nagel, J. 1986. "The Political Construction of Ethnicity." Pp. 93–112 in S. Olzak and J. Nagel (eds.) *Competitive Ethnic Relations*. New York: Academic Press.

Nagel, J., and S. Olzak. 1982. "Ethnic Mobilization in New and Old States: An Extension of the Competition Model." *Social Problems* 30: 127–43.

Nee, V., and B. de Bary Nee. 1986. *Longtime Californ': A Documentary Study of an American Chinatown*. Second edition. Stanford: Stanford Press.

Nelson, W. 1972. "Theory and Application of Hazard Plotting for Censored Data." *Technometrics* 14: 945–65.

Nielsen, F. 1980. "The Flemish Movement in Belgium After World War II: A Dynamic Analysis." *American Sociological Review* 45: 76–94.

Nielsen, F. 1985. "Ethnic Solidarity in Modern Societies." *American Sociological Review* 50: 133–45.

Obershall, A. 1978. "The Decline of the 1960s Social Movements." *Research in Social Movements, Conflicts and Change* 1: 257–89.

Oliver, M. L., and J. H. Johnson, Jr. 1984. "Inter-ethnic Conflict in an Urban Ghetto." *Research in Social Movements, Conflict and Change* 6: 57–94.

Oliver, P. 1984. "If You Don't Do It Nobody Else Will: Active and Token Contributors to Local Collective Action." *American Sociological Review* 49: 601–10.

Oliver, P., and G. Marwell. 1988. "The Paradox of Group Size in Collective Action: A Theory of Critical Mass. II." *American Sociological Review* 53: 1–8.

Oliver, P. E., G. Marwell, and R. Prahl. 1988. "Social Networks and Collective Action: A Theory of the Critical Mass." *American Journal of Sociology* 94: 502–34.

Oliver, P., G. Marwell, and R. Teixera. 1985. "A Theory of Critical Mass, I: Interdependence, Group Heterogeneity, and the Production of Collective Goods." *American Journal of Sociology* 91: 522–56.

Olivier, J. 1989. "Collective Violence in South Africa: A Study of Ethnic Collective Action in the Pretoria-Witwatersrand-Vaal Triangle Area, 1970–1984." Unpublished Ph.D. Dissertation. Cornell University, Ithaca, New York.

Olivier, J. 1990. "Causes of Ethnic Collective Action in the Pretoria-Witwatersrand-Vaal Triangle, 1970 to 1984." *South African Sociological Review* 2: 89–108.

Olson, M. 1965. *The Logic of Collective Action.* Cambridge, Mass.: Harvard University Press.

Olzak, S. 1982. "Ethnic Mobilization in Quebec." *Ethnic and Racial Studies* 5: 253–75.

Olzak, S. 1983. "Contemporary Ethnic Mobilization." *Annual Review of Sociology* 9: 355–74.

Olzak, S. 1986. "A Competition Model of Ethnic Collective Action in American Cities, 1877–1889." Pp. 29–46 in *Competitive Ethnic Relations*, edited by S. Olzak and J. Nagel. Orlando, Fla.: Academic Press.

Olzak, S. 1987. "Causes of Ethnic Protest and Conflict in Urban America, 1877–1889." *Social Science Research* 16: 185–210.

Olzak, S. 1988. "Were the Causes of Racial Conflicts and Lynchings in Late 19th and Early 20th Century America the Same?" Presented at the annual meetings of the American Sociological Association, Atlanta.

Olzak, S. 1989a. "Labor Unrest, Immigration, and Ethnic Conflict: Urban America 1880–1915." *American Journal of Sociology* 94: 1303–33.

Olzak, S. 1989b. "Analysis of Events in Studies of Collective Action." *Annual Review of Sociology* 15: 119–41.

Olzak, S. 1989c. "The Changing Job Queue: Causes of Shifts in Ethnic Job Segregation in American Cities, 1870–1880." *Social Forces* 63: 996–1009.

Olzak, S., and D. DiGregorio. 1985. "Ethnic Collective Action Project Manual." Technical Report #85-1, Department of Sociology, Cornell University, Ithaca N.Y.

Olzak, S., and J. Nagel (editors) 1986. *Competitive Ethnic Relations*. Orlando, Fla.: Academic Press.

Olzak, S., and E. West 1987. "Ethnic Conflict and Protest and the New Immigration in the United States, 1965–1985: Research Design and Codebook." Technical Report 86-19, Department of Sociology, Cornell University, Ithaca N.Y.

Olzak, S., and E. West. 1989. "Ethnic Conflicts and the New Immigrants, 1965–1985." Presented at the annual meeting of the American Sociological Association, San Francisco.

Olzak, S., and E. West. 1991. "Ethnic Conflict and the Rise and Fall of Ethnic Newspapers." *American Sociological Review* 56: 458–74.

Opp, K. D. 1988. "Grievances and Participation in Social Movements." *American Sociological Review* 53: 853–64.

Padilla, F. 1986. "Latino Ethnicity in the City of Chicago." Pp. 153–71 in S. Olzak and J. Nagel (eds.) *Competitive Ethnic Relations*. New York: Academic Press.

Paige, J. M. 1971. "Political Orientation and Riot Participation." *American Sociological Review* 36: 810–20.

Paige, J. M. 1975. *Agrarian Revolution*. New York: Free Press.

Park, R. E. 1922. *The Immigrant Press and Its Control*. New York: Harper and Brothers.

Park, R. E. 1949. *Race and Culture*. Glencoe, Ill.: Free Press.

Park, R. E., and E. W. Burgess. 1921. *Introduction to the Science of Sociology*. Chicago: University of Chicago Press.

Pettigrew, T. F. 1958. "Personality and Sociocultural Factors in Intergroup Attitudes: A Cross-National Comparison." *Journal of Conflict Resolution* 2: 29–42.

Pettigrew, T. F. 1969. "Racially Separate or Together." *Social Forces* 25: 43–69.

Portes, A. 1981. "Models of Structural Incorporation and Present Theories of Immigration." Pp. 279–97 in *Global Trends in Migration*, edited by M. M. Kritz, C. B. Keely, and S. M. Tomasi. New York: CMS Press.

Portes, A. 1984. "The Rise of Ethnicity: Determinants of Ethnic Perception Among Cuban Exiles in Miami." *American Sociological Review* 49: 383–97.

Portes, A., and R. Bach. 1985. *Latin Journey: Cuban and Mexican Immigrants in the United States*. Berkeley, Calif.: University of California Press.

Portes, A., and L. Jensen. 1987. "What's An Ethnic Enclave? The Case for Conceptual Clarity." *American Sociological Review* 52: 768–71

Powderly, T. V. 1884. "Record of the Proceedings of the Eighth Regular Session of the General Assembly, September 1-10, 1884," in the *Terence Vincent Powderly Papers Proceedings: General Assembly, 1878–1902*. Catherwood Library Collection, School of Industrial Relations, Cornell University, Ithaca, N.Y.

Powderly, T. V. 1889. *Thirty Years of Labor*. Columbus, Ohio: Excelsior Publishing House.

Rabinowitz, H. N. 1980. *Race Relations in the Urban South*. Urbana: University of Illinois Press.

Ragin, C. 1977. "Class, Status and 'Reactive' Ethnic Cleavages: The Social Bases of Political Regionalism." *American Sociological Review* 42: 438–50.

Ragin, C. 1979. "Ethnic Political Mobilization: The Welsh Case." *American Sociological Review* 44: 619–35.

Ragin, C. 1986. "The Impact of Celtic Nationalism on Class Politics in Scotland and Wales." Pp. 199–219 in S. Olzak and J. Nagel (eds.) *Competitive Ethnic Relations*. New York: Academic Press.

Ragin, C. 1987. *The Comparative Method*. Berkeley, Calif.: University of California Press.

Rasler, K. 1986. "War, Accommodation, and Violence in the United States, 1890–1970." *American Political Science Review* 80: 921–43.

Reed, J. S. 1972. "Percent Black and Lynching: A Test of Blalock's Theory." *Social Forces* 50: 356–60.

Reich, M. 1981. *Racial Inequality*. Princeton, N.J.: Princeton University Press.

Rokkan, S. 1970. *Citizens, Elections, and Parties*. Chicago: Rand McNally.

Rosenthal, N., M. Fingrutd, M. Ethier, R. Karant, and D. McDonald. 1985. "Social Movements and Network Analysis: A Case Study of Nineteenth-Century Women's Reform in New York State." *American Journal of Sociology* 90: 1022–54.

Ross, S. J. 1985. *Workers on the Edge: Work, Leisure and Politics in Industrializing Cincinnati, 1788-1890*. New York: Columbia University Press.

Rowell, G. P., and Company. Various years. *Rowell's American Newspaper Directory*. New York: George P. Rowell and Company.

Rubin, B. 1986. "Class Struggle American Style: Unions, Strikes and Wages." *American Sociological Review* 51: 618–33.

Rudwick, E. 1964. *Race Riot at East St. Louis, July 2, 1917*. Urbana, Ill.: University of Illinois Press.

Rule, J., and C. Tilly. 1965. *Measuring Political Upheaval*. Princeton, N.J.: Center of International Studies.

Rule, J., and C. Tilly. 1972. "1830 and the Un-natural History of Revolution." *Journal of Social Issues* 28: 49–76.

Salert, B., and J. Sprague. 1980. *The Dynamics of Riots*. Ann Arbor: Inter-University Consortium for Political and Social Research.

Sanders, J., and V. Nee. 1987. "Limits of Ethnic Solidarity in the Enclave Economy." *American Sociological Review* 52: 745–67.

SAS Institute Inc. 1985. *SAS Users' Guide*, Version 5 Edition. Cary, N.C.: SAS Institute.

Saxton, A. 1971. *The Indispensable Enemy: Labor and the Anti-Chinese Movement in California*. Berkeley, Calif.: University of California Press.

Schelling, T. 1973. *Micromotives and Macrobehavior*. Philadelphia: University of Pennsylvania Press.

Schlesinger, A. M., Jr. (editor). 1983. *The Almanac of American History*. Greenwich, Conn.: Bison.

Schwartz, M. 1976. *Radical Protest and Social Structure*. New York: Academic Press.

See, K. O. 1986. "For God and Crown: Class, Ethnicity, and Protestant Politics in Northern Ireland." Pp. 221–45 in *Competitive Ethnic Relations*, edited by S. Olzak and J. Nagel. Orlando, Fla.: Academic Press.

See, K. O., and W. J. Wilson. 1988. "Race and Ethnicity." Pp. 223–43 in N. J. Smelser (ed.) *Handbook of Sociology*. Newbury Park, Calif: Sage Publications.

Senechal, Roberta. 1990. *The Sociogenesis of a Race Riot*. Urbana: University of Illinois Press.

Shapiro, H. 1988. *White Violence and Black Response: From Reconstruction to Montgomery*. Amherst: University of Massachusetts Press.

Shorter, E., and C. Tilly. 1974. *Strikes in France, 1830–1968*. New York: Cambridge University Press.

Simmel, G. [1923] 1955. *Conflict and the Web of Group Affiliations*. Glencoe: The Free Press.

Skocpol, T. 1979. *States and Revolutions*. New York: Cambridge University Press.

Skocpol, T., and M. Somers. 1980. "The Uses of Comparative History in Macrosocial Research." *Comparative Studies in Society and History* 22: 174–97.

Smelser, N. J. 1962. *Theory of Collective Behavior*. New York: Free Press.

Smith, A. D. 1981. *The Ethnic Revival*. New York: Cambridge University Press.

Smith, J. E. 1987. "The Transformation of Family and Community Culture, 1900–1940," Pp. 159–83 in *The New England Working Class and the New Labor History*, edited by H. Gutman and D. H. Bell. Urbana, Ill.: University of Illinois Press.

Snow, D. A., E. B. Rochford, Jr., S. K. Worder and R. D. Benford. 1986. "Frame Alignment Processes, Micromobilization, and Movement Participation." *American Sociological Review* 51: 464–81.

Snow, D. A., L. Zurcher, Jr., and S. Ekland-Olson. 1980. "Social Networks and Social Movements: A Microstructural Approach to Differential Recruitment." *American Sociological Review* 45: 787–801.

Snyder, D. 1975. "Institutional Setting and Industrial Conflict: Comparative

Analysis of France, Italy, and the United States." *American Sociological Review* 40: 259–78.

Snyder, D., and W. R. Kelly. 1977. "Conflict Intensity, Media Sensitivity and the Validity of Newspaper Data." *American Sociological Review* 42: 105–23.

Snyder, D., and C. Tilly. 1972. "Hardship and Collective Violence in France, 1830–1960." *American Sociological Review* 37: 312–20.

Sowell, T. 1975. *Race and Economics*. New York: David McKay.

Spero, S., and A. Harris. 1931. *The Black Workers*. New York: Columbia University Press.

Spilerman, S. 1970a. "The Causes of Racial Disturbances: A Comparison of Alternative Explanations." *American Sociological Review* 35: 627–49.

Spilerman, S. 1970b. "Comment on Wanderer's Article on Riot Severity and Its Correlates." *American Journal of Sociology* 75: 556–59.

Spilerman, S. 1971. "The Causes of Racial Disturbances: Test of an Explanation." *American Sociological Review* 35: 427–42.

Spilerman, S. 1976. "Structural Characteristics of Cities and the Severity of Racial Disorders." *American Sociological Review* 41: 771–93.

Stark, M. J. A., W. J. Raine, S. L. Burbeck, and K. K. Davison. 1974. "Some Empirical Patterns in a Riot Process." *American Sociological Review* 39: 865–76.

Stearns, L. B., and J. R. Logan. 1984. "Measuring Trends in Segregation: Three Dimensions, Three Measures." Presented at the annual meetings of the American Sociological Association, San Antonio.

Steedly, H. R., and J. W. Foley. 1979. "The Success of Protest Groups: Multivariate Analysis." *Social Science Research* 8: 1–15.

Stinchcombe, A. L. 1965. "Social Structure and Organizations." Pp. 153–93 in *Handbook of Organizations*, edited by J. G. March. Chicago: Rand McNally.

Suttles, G. 1974. *The Social Construction of Communities*. Chicago: University of Chicago Press.

Taeuber, K. E., and A. F. Taeuber. 1976. "A Practitioner's Perspective on the Index of Dissimilarity." *American Sociological Review* 41: 884–89.

Taeuber, K. E., F. W. Monfort, D. Massey, and A. F. Taeuber. 1984. "The Trend in Metropolitan Racial Residential Segregation." Presented at the annual meetings of the Population Association of America, Minneapolis.

Taft, P. 1964. *Organized Labor in American History*. New York: Harper and Row.

Tarrow, S. 1983. *Struggling to Reform*. Western Societies Program Series, Cornell University, Ithaca, N.Y.

Tarrow, S. 1988a. "National Politics and Collective Action." *Annual Review of Sociology* 14: 421–40.

Tarrow, S. 1988b. *Democracy and Disorder: Politics and Protests in Italy, 1965–1975*. New York: Oxford University Press.

Taylor, C. L., and D. A. Jodice. 1983. *World Handbook of Political and Social Indicators*. New Haven: Yale University Press.

Taylor, D. G. 1986. *Public Opinion and Collective Action.* Chicago: University of Chicago Press.

Thernstrom, S. 1973. *The Other Bostonians: Poverty and Progress in the American Metropolis, 1880–1970.* Cambridge, Mass.: Harvard University Press.

Thorp, W., and W. Mitchell. 1926. *Business Annals.* New York: National Bureau of Economic Research.

Tilly, C. 1978. *From Mobilization to Revolution.* Reading, Mass.: Addison-Wesley.

Tilly, C. 1981. *As Sociology Meets History.* New York: Academic Press.

Tilly, C. 1984. *Big Structures, Large Processes, Huge Comparisons.* New York: Russell Sage.

Tilly, C. 1986. *The Contentious French.* Cambridge, Mass.: Harvard University Press.

Tilly, C. 1990. "Twenty Years of Contention." Chapter 2 in *Mobilization and Contention in Great Britain, 1758–1834* (manuscript).

Tilly, C., L. Tilly, and R. Tilly. 1975. *The Rebellious Century, 1830–1930.* Cambridge, Mass.: Harvard University Press.

Tolnay, S. E., E. M. Beck, and J. L. Massey. 1989. "Black Lynchings: The Power-threat Hypothesis Revisited." *Social Forces* 67: 605–23.

Tuma, N. B., and M. T. Hannan. 1984. *Social Dynamics: Models and Methods.* New York: Academic Press.

Turner, R., and L. M. Killian. 1957. *Collective Behavior.* Englewood Cliffs, N. J.: Prentice Hall.

Tuttle, W. M. 1970. *Race Riot: Chicago in the Red Summer of 1919.* New York: Atheneum.

United States Bureau of the Census. 1975. *Historical Statistics of the United States, Colonial Times to 1970.* Washington, D.C.: Government Printing Office.

United States Bureau of Immigration. 1901. *United States Report on Immigration.* Washington, D.C.: Government Printing Office.

United States National Advisory Commission on Civil Disorders. 1968. *Report of the National Advisory Commission on Civil Disorders.* New York: Bantam Books.

Useem, B. 1980. "Solidarity Model, Breakdown Model, and the Boston Anti-Busing Movement." *American Sociological Review* 45: 357–69.

Useem, B. 1985. "Disorganization and the New Mexico Prison Riot of 1980." *American Sociological Review* 50: 677–88.

Useem, B., and M. Zald. 1982. "From Pressure Group to Social Movement: Efforts to Promote the Use of Nuclear Power." *Social Problems* 30: 144–56.

van den Berghe, P. L. 1965. *Africa: Social Problems of Change and Conflict.* San Francisco: Chandler.

van den Berghe, P. L. 1978. *Race and Racism.* New York: Wiley.

van den Berghe, P. L. 1983. "Class, Race, and Ethnicity in Africa." *Ethnic and Racial Studies* 6: 221–36.

Waldinger, R., H. Aldrich, R. Ward, and Associates. 1990. *Ethnic Entrepreneurs*. Beverly Hills: Sage Publications.

Walkowitz, D. J. 1978. *Worker City, Company Town*. Urbana, Ill.: University of Illinois Press.

Wallace, M., B. A. Rubin, and B. T. Smith. 1987. "The Impact of American Labor Law on Working Class Militancy in the United States, 1902–1978." *Social Science History* 12: 1–29.

Walsh, E. J., and R. H. Warland. 1983. "Social Movement Involvement in the Wake of a Nuclear Accident: Activists and Free-Riders in the TMI Area." *American Sociological Review* 48: 764–80.

Wanderer, J. J. 1969. "An Index of Riot Severity and Some Correlates." *American Journal of Sociology* 74: 500–05.

Weber, M. 1947 (1924). *The Theory of Social and Economic Organization*, edited by A. H. Henderson and T. Parsons. Glencoe, Ill.: The Free Press.

Weede, E. 1987. "Some New Evidence on Correlates of Political Violence: Income Inequality, Regime Repressiveness, and Economic Development." *European Sociological Review* 3: 97–108.

West, E., and S. Olzak 1989. "Organizational Response to Environmental Change: Ethnic Newspapers at the Turn of the Century." Presented at the annual meetings of the American Sociological Association, San Francisco.

White, H. 1980. "A Heteroskedastic-Consistent Covariance Matrix Estimator and a Direct Test for Heteroskedasticity." *Econometrica* 48: 118–138.

White, M. J. 1986. "Segregation and Diversity Measures in Population Distribution." *Population Index* 52: 198–221.

Williams, R. M., Jr. 1964. *Strangers Next Door*. Englewood Cliffs, N. J.: Prentice Hall.

Wilson, K., and W. A. Martin. 1982. "Ethnic Enclaves: A Comparison of the Cuban and Black Economies in Miami." *American Journal of Sociology* 78: 1469–84.

Wilson, K., and A. Portes. 1980. "Immigrant Enclaves: An Analysis of the Labor Market Experience of Cubans in Miami." *American Journal of Sociology* 86: 295–319.

Wilson, W. J. 1978. *The Declining Significance of Race*. Second edition. Chicago: University of Chicago Press.

Wilson, W. J. 1987. *The Truly Disadvantaged: The Inner City, the Underclass, and Public Policy*. Chicago: University of Chicago Press.

Winship, C. 1978. "The Desirability of Using the Index of Dissimilarity or Any Adjustment of It for Measuring Segregation: Reply to Falk, Cortese, and Cohen." *Social Forces* 57: 717–20.

Woodward, C. V. 1938. *Tom Watson: Agrarian Rebel*. New York: Oxford University Press.

Woodward, C. V. 1951. *Origins of the New South*. Baton Rouge: Louisiana State University Press.

Woodward, C. V. 1974. *The Strange Career of Jim Crow*. New York: Oxford University Press.

Wright, G. 1986. *Old South, New South: Revolutions in the Southern Economy Since the Civil War*. New York: Basic Books.

Wynar, L. R. 1972. *Encyclopedic Directory of Ethnic Newspapers and Periodicals in the United States*. Littleton, Ohio: Libraries Unlimited.

Yellen, S. 1936. *American Labor Struggles, 1877–1934*. New York: Monad Press.

Yinger, M. 1985. "Ethnicity." *Annual Review of Sociology* 11: 151–80.

Young, M. C. 1986. "Cultural Pluralism in the Third World," Pp. 113–36 in *Competitive Ethnic Relations*, edited by S. Olzak and J. Nagel. Orlando, Fla.: Academic Press.

Zald, M., and J. D. McCarthy (editors) 1987. *Social Movements in an Organizational Society*. New Brunswick, N.J.: Transaction Books.

Name Index

Aalen, O. O., 73
Alba, R. D., 185, 216
Aldrich, H. E., 38, 39, 141
Allardt, E., 16
Allen, W. R., 185, 216
Amburgey, T. L., 63
Aminzade, R., 48
Appelbaum, M., 7, 23, 41
Archdeacon, T. J., 33, 44, 67, 90, 92, 115, 135, 136, 139, 147, 150
Ayer, N. W., 191

Banton, M., 2, 17, 25
Barth, F., 6, 24–29, 34, 38, 114, 163, 217
Barton, J., 142
Beck, E. M., 4, 21, 61, 110, 112, 113, 117–119, 220
Becker, G. S., 143
Bell, D. H., 38, 67, 92, 93, 117, 139
Bell, W., 137
Bennett, D. H., 1, 28, 33, 34, 36, 44, 45, 109, 114–117, 120, 219
Berk, R. A., 50
Blakeslee, L., 137
Blalock, H. M., 20, 21, 26, 65, 109, 110, 113, 162
Blau, P. M., 137, 144
Blauner, R., 162
Bodnar, J., 34, 35, 37, 38, 67, 82, 90, 92, 94, 113, 135, 138, 139 142, 143, 170, 198, 210

Bonacich, E., 17, 23, 33, 36, 38, 40, 87, 89, 94, 115, 116, 162, 182, 217
Bornschier, V., 18
Boskin, J., 109, 113
Boswell, T., 1, 23, 30, 33, 36, 90, 162
Britt, D. W., 61
Brody, D., 87, 88
Bruce, R. V., 10, 44, 87
Burgess, E. W., 19, 29, 31
Burstein, P., 12, 44, 55, 57, 58

Cafferty, P., 44, 90
Cameron, A. C., 192
Carroll, G. R., 48, 63, 98, 181, 185, 187–190, 194, 200
Carter, D., 64, 137
Chalmers, D. M., 1, 89, 219
Chase-Dunn, C., 18
Chermesh, R., 57
Chirot, D., 61
Coleman, J. S., 63, 137
Commons, J. R., 33, 45, 88, 90, 91, 142, 143
Corzine, J., 21, 109, 110, 113, 117
Coser, L., 182
Cox, D. R., 74, 193
Creech, J., 21, 109, 110, 113

Danzger, M. H., 12, 57
David, P., 71, 119
Davis, M., 87, 91
Delacroix, J., 18, 188, 189
Denton, N., 64, 110, 113, 137, 221

Subject Index

Library of Congress Cataloging-in-Publication Data

Olzak, Susan
    The dynamics of ethnic competition and conflict / Susan Olzak.
        p.   cm.
    Includes bibliographical references and index.
    ISBN 0-8047-2028-2 (cloth: alk. paper)
    1. United States—Ethnic relations.   2. United States—Race relations.
    3. United States—Social conditions—1865–1918.   I. Title.
    E184.A10455   1992
    305.8'00973–dc20   91-38707
                                                                         CIP